*Illustration
and the Novels of
Thomas Hardy*

Illustration
and the Novels of
Thomas Hardy

ARLENE M. JACKSON

ROWMAN AND LITTLEFIELD
Totowa ● New Jersey

Library of Congress Cataloging in Publication Data

Jackson, Arlene M 1938–
　　Illustration and the novels of Thomas Hardy.

　　Bibliography: p.
　　Includes index.
　　1. Hardy, Thomas, 1840–1928—Illustrations.
2. Hardy, Thomas, 1840–1928—Technique.　3. Hardy,
Thomas, 1840–1928—Knowledge—Art.　4. Art and litera-
ture.　I. Title.
PR4751.5.J3　　823′.8　　80-10548
ISBN 0-8476-6275-6

Printed in the U.S.A.

Contents

List of Illustrations

(Plates 1–32 follow p. 48; plates 33–80 follow p. 80)

Preface

Because of Thomas Hardy's pictorial imagination, his novels are remarkably well suited for illustration. His interest in visual art, furthermore, gave him a more serious concern with the graphic, pictorial treatment of his writing, a concern not so evident in other illustrated writers of his time, such as Anthony Trollope, Wilkie Collins, or George Eliot. Hardy corresponded with several of his illustrators, and many of his suggestions, sometimes even his own sketches, found their way into the drawings that accompanied his serial fiction. To some extent, therefore, the illustrations become another medium for Hardy's pictorial imagination. To an even greater extent, the illustrations become the illustrator's interpretation of the text. Illustrations are, in effect, graphic criticism of the text they accompany.

Important though the illustrations to Hardy's novels are, they have either been dismissed as mere curiosities, not worthy of serious critical attention, or they are overlooked altogether. They have never received the sort of attention given to the Dickens illustrations, for instance. The reasons for this neglect are not hard to find. First, the Hardy illustrations do not fall into the supposedly more exciting periods of English illustration; second, the Hardy illustrators did not have the stature of a "Phiz" or Cruikshank, the principal Dickens illustrators; finally, the illustrations themselves seem to lack an aesthetic rationale and appear to be "mere visualization" of the text. Whatever the reason or combinations thereof, the result is manifest: approximately 200 illustrations for Hardy's novels remain an unexplored area of this important author.

The ten Hardy novels that received illustration were published serially in magazines or newspapers after 1870—in one way, at least, a matter of unfortunate timing. In the 1860s, a new school of illustration had replaced the earlier "Phiz" and Cruikshank style of caricature, which had itself derived from the 18th century styles of Gillray and Rowlandson. But by the 1870s, the new school of Millais and Leighton had lost much of its vitality and impressiveness, partially because of changes in reproductive processes, but for a variety of other reasons, as well.

It is important to understand, however, that the primary function of illustration after 1860 was mimetic. The fiction of the time was itself concerned with a realistic presentation of character, setting, and (though sometimes to a considerably lesser extent), events of plot. Thus, illustration for this fiction increased the sense of realism because of its representational style, as opposed to the caricatural style of an earlier period in the history of British illustration. Illustrations that are primarily mimetic, however, are not automatically dispossessed of inspiration, vitality, or even the originality and metaphor aimed at "discovering" the text that are often (but not always) found in the earlier school. Many of the Hardy illustrations, in fact, do discover the text, though in ways that are most often different from the caricature or visual metaphor in the Dickens illustrations.

Assessing the Hardy illustrations involves an examination of the kind of relationship Hardy had with his illustrators, as well as the amount of involvement the novelist had with the final drawings for his stories. While Hardy did not collaborate with his illustrators as closely as Dickens had, he did have contact with most of them—meeting them in person, giving them oral or written suggestions on how a scene should be depicted, even sending them sketches of scenes. Some of the actual, finished illustrations, therefore, are based on Hardy's own ideas and sketches, and can give us an understanding of his pictorial imagination beyond that offered by the text itself. (These several illustrations appear within Chapter III and are separated from the rest of the illustrations where we have no particular evidence for Hardy's personal touch.) The suggestions Hardy gave to his artists, as well as the comments he made about some of the drawings after they had been published with his serialized novels, give insight into Hardy's intentions, particularly in the area of detail and characterization.

The illustrated versions of Hardy's novels must receive critical attention in any truly comprehensive evaluation of Hardy as Victorian novelist, yet no intensive, full-length study of this aspect of Hardy's fiction has been published.[1] The following chapters make no attempt at a comprehensive evaluation of Hardy as novelist, but focus on the "illustrated" Hardy by examining the post-1860 context for the illustrations, tracing the relationship between Hardy and the artists who drew the illustrations, and exploring the very special relationship between picture and text. The unevenness in the quality of the illustrations, the varying degrees of their relationship to the text, a determination of how the Victorian audience would have understood the text because of the illustrations—all this must be taken into any account of the Hardy illustrations. Even though some textual changes did occur between the serial edition and later publication of several of these novels, in most cases that fact does not change the importance of the original, illustrated text.

What many modern readers of Hardy's fiction do not realize is that a very large part of his Victorian audience first read his novels in an illustrated version. At least some of the conditions under which that Victorian audience first became acquainted with Hardy's works need to be clarified if we are to appreciate more fully the illustrations to Hardy's fiction. The illustrations themselves, of course, have been rarely reproduced and difficult to find in their original, serial form of publication. A generous selection of the best of those illustrations cannot help but convey a new understanding of Hardy's novels, as well as give us some additional insight into Hardy's own pictorial imagination and, finally, may enable us to recover and perhaps even to share in that original Victorian response to Hardy's illustrated fiction.

Acknowledgments

The project of examining and evaluating the illustrations to Hardy's novels began in the summer of 1971, when I came across the illustrated serials while working on another project in the Dorset County Museum. My research then took me to the British Library, then back to the University of Michigan and the Detroit Public Library. I wish to thank the people at those libraries who assisted me, especially R. A. Peers, Curator of the Dorset County Museum, and his assistant at the time of my early research, Maureen Samuel.

Many other libraries assisted in the project. My thanks to the New York Public Library (Berg Collection), to Colby College (Waterville, Maine), the Morris Parrish Collection at Yale University, the University of Texas, Bryn Mawr College Library, the Van Pelt Library at the University of Pennsylvania.

My thanks to Eileen Z. Cohen of St. Joseph's University and to Neil Brennan of Villanova University for reading the manuscript in its early stages. A special thanks to my colleagues in the English Department of St. Joseph's University for their constant support and encouragement.

Finally, my appreciation to St. Joseph's University for a summer research grant and a grant-in-aid which enabled me to finish the project.

I

Introduction: Thomas Hardy and the Pictorial Imagination

Literature is more closely related to visual art in the Victorian age than in any other period of English history. From Alfred, Lord Tennyson's poetic "mood paintings" to the medieval portraits in the poetry of William Morris and Dante Gabriel Rossetti, to the sense of picture in many of Robert Browning's dramatic monologues, a deliberate intention of linking literature with clearly defined visual and especially *pictorial* images lies at the heart of much Victorian poetry. In prose fiction, a distinctly visual style adapted to sensation fiction from the earlier Gothic fad marks the works of Harrison Ainsworth, Wilkie Collins, and Charles Reade, as well as of Charlotte and Emily Bronte. The increasing reliance on realism in fiction that becomes evident in the last half of the nineteenth century derives in large part from the Dutch painting of the seventeenth century,[1] thus providing another link with the visual arts. Within many novels, the visual arts become plot device or take on some sort of symbolic significance. The actual painting of pictures, whether as amateur pastime, method of earning money, vehicle of moral theme, or part of the larger art world appears in such varied novels as Charlotte Brontë's *Jane Eyre*, Anne Brontë's *The Tenant of Wildfell Hall*, Oscar Wilde's *The Picture of Dorian Gray*, and George Du Maurier's *Trilby*.

Relationship to the visual arts occurs in ways other than just within the actual verbal text. The distinctive visual imagery within the novels of Dickens and Thackeray, for instance, is complemented either by their own drawings, as in Thackeray's case, or by the drawing of a "Phiz" or George Cruikshank, as in Dickens's case. Later in the century, illustrations accompanied the works of George Meredith, Anthony Trollope, and Thomas Hardy, as well as a host of lesser writers whose fiction appears in issue after issue of illustrated periodicals. At the century's end, finally, the drawings of Aubrey Beardsley and a variety of other art nouveau illustration appeared with the poetry emerging from the "Art for Art's Sake" movement.

But the poets and novelists were not the only artists to work so closely with the literature-visual arts relationship. As the records of the Royal Academy Exhibitions demonstrate, a great many painters of the Victorian period presented works with a narrative basis, either relating a domestic or sentimental theme or interpreting a story from a classical or medieval source. Narrative painting was especially popular among the Pre-Raphaelites, but also formed a substantial part of the works of other artists, as well. In 1863, for instance, the pictures of the year at the Royal Academy exhibitions were all "subject" pictures. Millais's *The Eve of St. Agnes*, Marcus Stone's *Napoleon on the Road from Waterloo to Paris*, Leighton's *Jezebel and Ahab*, and several paintings related to Arthurian materials comprise only part of the list.[2] The evidence tells us that a special distinction of the Victorian artist, whether poet, novelist, or painter, is his predilection for relating picture and story. The relationship becomes an important and consistent part of Victorian aesthetics, and can be most clearly seen in the writings of Ruskin and Pater.

A less formal kind of art than the "show pieces" of the Royal Academy, however, had a much greater visibility for the Victorian audience and, furthermore, has a vital bearing on the development of the English novel. This middle class art form is serial illustration, made possible in the Victorian age by the happy coincidence of Thomas Bewick's earlier revival and perfection of wood engraving, the rise of a middle class reading public which caused the phenomenal growth of the weekly and monthly publication, and a large number of writers and graphic artists eager to be published. The highly popular publication of Dickens's novels, beginning in 1836 with *Pickwick Papers*, and illustrated by artists such as Cruikshank and "Phiz," helped prepare the way for other such ventures. When the commercial advantages became clear to the publishing industry, the Victorian tradition of illustrated serial fiction was firmly established and continued to the century's end.

The novels of Thomas Hardy clearly belong to this tradition, even though they appear more than thirty years after the publication of *Pickwick Papers*. Between 1872 and 1895, quality periodicals such as *The Cornhill Magazine* and *The Graphic*, as well as lesser periodicals such as *Good Words* and *Belgravia*, published ten of Hardy's novels as illustrated serials, including the early *A Pair of Blue Eyes, Far from the Madding Crowd*, and *The Return of the Native*, through the major novels *The Mayor of Casterbridge, Tess of the D'Urbervilles*, and *Jude the Obscure*.

Before these novels were written, however, Hardy spent his early years working in a field rather far removed from that of novelist. Yet these were years during which he trained his eye in the appreciation and formation of pleasing visual structures. As a young man working in a London architectural firm, Hardy not only diligently applied himself to reading and observation in his field of architecture, but spent much of his leisure time visiting art galleries and museums, and attending lectures on art.[3] Throughout his lifetime, in fact, he was to record his observations and judgments on artistic matters in his journals.[4] His own unsophisticated paintings, primarily landscapes in watercolor, and the curious drawings he published in 1898 with his first book of poems demonstrate a continued interest in visual art that he was also able to express in a variety of ways through his novels and poems.

Relatively well into his career as novelist, he commented on this relationship between literature and the visual arts. He believed, in fact, that not enough attention had been paid to the influence that a study of painting and sculpture had in the development of the aesthetic sense: "Probably few of the general body denominated the reading public consider, in their hurried perusal of novel after novel, that, to a masterpiece in story there appertains a beauty of shape, no less than to a masterpiece in pictorial or plastic art, capable of giving to the trained mind an equal pleasure."[5]

Hardy's interest in the visual arts becomes valuable for the special insights it provides into his artistic development, and into the shaping as well as functioning of image and structure in his fiction. Together with the illustration his ten serialized novels received, this interest in the visual arts created a very special experience for Hardy's original audience: the Victorian readers of his serialized, illustrated novels.

Artistic vision is a combination, essentially, of philosophic position and of technique applied to the materials of reality. Yet Hardy's artistic vision has often been tied only to his philosophic position, or what has been interpreted as that position. In the last ten years or so, however, a significant shift in our approach and therefore understanding of Hardy's fiction has occurred. His technique now receives considerable attention: in addition to the more traditional view of Hardy as realist, he has now been called anti-realist and illusionist,[6] among other, less clearly differentiated labels.[7] Hardy's use of the grotesque has been increasingly emphasized and carefully related to his ironic stance toward life as it is conveyed through his fiction. The most important, most distinctive part of Hardy's technique, related to his philosophic position, including but extending beyond his use of the grotesque, is his sense of the pictorial.

Thus Hardy joins not only his fellow Victorians but also that long line of writers who form a special strain running throughout English literature.

From Spenser and Milton to Dryden and Pope, from Blake and Keats to Dickens, D. H. Lawrence, and Virginia Woolf, a long line of great English authors demonstrate their liking for the static scene, a juxtaposition of character and objects caught in a moment of time, yet ready to break into the climax of movement. For these writers, creativity expresses itself primarily through the pictorial. Picture predominates, rather than sound, or dialogue, or even the creation of mood, though this last is closely associated with picture. This pictorial quality does not mean that these other expressions of the creative mind are not present in the author's works, or are not valuable in their own right. But whenever the creation of picture becomes the primary expression of the verbal artist, then he truly possesses the pictorial imagination. The fact that several of these writers have had their works illustrated usually not once but several times, is no accident, but is at least partially due to the pictorial elements already present within the text, as well as to the appropriateness of general subject matter. Illustration for the works of any of these authors is thus neither perfunctory nor accessory, as it may be for other writers, but is intrinsically associated with the text itself.

A distinctive visual impact always results from a precision of form based on composition, perspective, and lighting effects. All writers must in some way and to some considerable extent create visual images in their attempts to make concepts apprehensible to an audience, but *image* is not as complete and formed as *picture*. Picture is the fully formed design, static because it has been caught in time and space, composed of images which are logically related to each other. Lighting, color, and texture are also an important part of picture, but they are more properly a part of the fundamental image or images comprising the pictorial. The visual image, therefore, is to be distinguished from the pictorial; it may or may not be pictorial, but the pictorial always contains the visual image. The verbal artist, furthermore, can present picture in such a way that motion is created, but the motion is really the result of a series of successive, shifting pictures. Motion can also be impending; that is, through juxtaposition of character or body positioning, the static scene may seem to be ready to break into movement. In itself, however, picture should be understood as *tableau*, for however long or short the duration of its capture in time and space, the total design is seen in a static harmony of its parts. The pictorialist is as aware of the *whole* of the design as he is of the individual parts or images within the design.

In *The Sister Arts*, Jean Hagstrum formulates additional qualifications in defining the pictorial. Leading details in the scene must be imaginable as picture or sculpture, but the ordered visual detail need not be restricted to the representational school and may express other styles, such as the impressionistic, the abstract, the symbolic. Stasis must dominate, though as explained earlier, motion may be implied or, according to Hagstrum, may even be already present, as long as it remains subordinate to the static quality. Finally, concludes Hagstrum, the visual presentation must dominate concept.[8] This specified definition thus makes clear that a scene with notable visual detail does not automatically qualify as pictorial—a distinction that often becomes blurred in some studies of the pictorial technique.

Though Hardy's chief fictional techniques are often defined as his use of coincidence, symmetrical positioning of characterization, archaic (and sometimes awkward), vocabulary or syntax, his most distinctive stylistic signature is his use of the pictorial. A considerable part of Hardy's language, in fact, is devoted to creating a sense of the pictorial—so much so, claims Lloyd Fernando, that an actual *pictorial rhetoric* exists within the body of Hardy's novels.[9]

Hardy's pictorial imagination did not go unnoticed in his own day, though what comments were made seem unsophisticated. Contemporary reviews, however, did show considerable perception by praising his pictorial description of landscape as well as his characterization of the rustics who give such a special flavor to his Wessex world. In a *Saturday Review* article on *A Pair of Blue Eyes*, for instance, the reviewer notes: "The rustic circle makes a little gallery of portraiture as distinct as it is lifelike." Hardy includes "many of those sketches of genuine country life in drawing which he has already shown a master's hand."[10] Though the metaphoric, visual arts imagery was often used by Victorian reviewers of fiction, the Hardy reviews are particularly filled with such terminology, from early to late novels. Significantly, the metaphoric terms occur most often in the reviews of earlier novels—when Hardy's own pictorial techniques were more frequently used or at least were more obvious than in his later novels.

These reviews recognize Hardy's peculiar strength: the ability to create pictures which "can later epitomize a whole work in a single memory," as Penelope Vigar explains in her valuable study, *The Novels of Thomas Hardy: Illusion and Reality*. "It is the *impression* of the book which remains," she explains, "a vision of moments which remain distinctly in the mind, a string of outstanding incidents." Yet, as Vigar warns us in a particularly valuable insight into Hardy's method, "often the 'picture' of the whole novel is strangely intense and at the same time strangely incomplete." The unevenness often found in Hardy's works is "not, however, entirely due to the fact that he is an 'intermittent genius.' Rather, the gaps and vivid patches form a fairly consistent pattern showing the strength and weakness of his artistic approach to fiction."[11]

Several earlier studies have noted how his novels so often refer to artists and even particular paintings.[12] Hardy's first novel, *Under the Greenwood Tree*, is an obvious example of his own deliberate attempts to use the visual arts as an approach in the creation of story. Subtitled "A Rural Painting of the Dutch School," the novel makes a very conscious attempt to transfer Dutch realism into fictional form.

Titian and Moroni are referred to by name in the text, and thus begins one of Hardy's chief and most obvious techniques. As Carl J. Weber notes, an examination of only five or six of his novels reveals references to at least thirty-four artists, covering some six centuries of art history.[13] From Giotto to Van Beers, the list also includes Holbein, Durer, Raphael, and Rembrandt, as well as more obscure figures such as Gozzoli, Sallaert, Lely, and Van Alsloot. Contemporary painters besides Van Beers include Wiertz and Danby, as well as near-contemporaries Greuze, Romney, Nollekens, Flaxman, and Turner.

Many of these references seem forced. Certainly Hardy made a conscious attempt to learn about various painters, to take notes that might become useful later. Thus we find the following journal entries:

M. Angelo's frescoes in the Sistine Chapel, wh. Sir J. Reynolds says are the finest paintings in the world, & wh. the unlearned call great rude daubs.[14]

Royal Academy. No. 118. "Death of Ney," by Gerome. The presence of Death makes the picture great. No. 985 "Jerusalem," by the same. The *shadows only* of the three crucified ones are seen. A fine conception.[15]

Self-conscious though some of the journal references and their translations into the novels may sometimes be, the several studies focussing on the use of painting in Hardy's works find these images to have considerable visual and sometimes thematic significance.

Due to the obscurity of some of these references, however, the Victorian audience would hardly have been able to "see" all that Hardy seems to have intended. The problem of obscurity was sometimes compounded when Hardy referred to specific paintings—Greuze's *Head of a Young Girl*, mentioned in *Desperate Remedies*, for instance. Yet, even though his audience might have missed specific scenes or relationships depicted or suggested through the painting references, they would be well aware of the general sense of picture. This would be particularly true of the Old Master references, the Dutch Realist school of painting which finds its way into *Under the Greenwood Tree*. Warm colors and soft tones created by candle or lantern light, silhouettes and shadows, figures framed in windows, designs created by sunlight casting itself through window panes, selected groupings of figures—all are techniques present in this very early work, and combine to create specific responses in the reading audience. The pictorial images in this novel, in fact, serve to "carry" the pastoral idyll; its plot is thin, characters uncomplicated though idiosyncratic, but setting and descriptions rich in texture, form, and perspective.

Here, too, we find the narrator's point of view linked with the pictorial, a linking often present in Hardy's later novels. In describing the chinks of light seeping through the crevices of cottage or shed, for instance, Hardy creates an understanding between author and reader: a narrator within the text observes scene and action with detachment but also with acute powers of observation. Thus Hardy creates a very subtle "doubling" effect with his pictorial images: we as audience view the scene but also include in our vision the "sense," but most often not the specified reality, of another viewer. The technique is a variation of the "frame within a frame" device, and it is provocative in what it suggests of the relationships between voyeur, reality, and emotional distance. It is, in fact, more subtle than other narrator-observer perspectives, such as the famous opening of George Eliot's *The Mill on the Floss*.

The pictorial technique thus has some significant ramifications for our responses to Hardy's novels. We should be aware, too, that Hardy uses other, more modern "openings" into his fictional materials than just the Old Master's references. The Pre-Raphaelite description of Eustacia Vye in *The Return of the Native*, for instance, contrasts markedly with the Rembrandtesque description of Clym Yeobright. Hardy must not be accused of pat symmetry here: the new spirit of Eustacia is, of course, the old way of the body beautiful; the discovery of Clym in Rembrandt lighting (in the Mummer's scene) suggests the conflict within him as he seeks to return to the past and its values, but is forever marked with the signs of the modern spirit.

Impressionism, too, is very much evident in Hardy's works. His journals show his first responses to Impressionism in 1880 and, as Alistair Smart explains, Impressionism as a technique finds its way into the novels immediately afterwards, in *The Woodlanders* (1887). Hardy demonstrates the extent of his understanding of this new school, not accepted or understood by many of his contemporaries, in the way he makes use of "one of the principal canons of Impressionist theory—that all forms lying outside the immediate focus of the gaze are inevitably blurred and indistinct, and that it is therefore legitimate for the painter, having selected his focal point, to treat them as such. . . ."[16] As part of his evidence, Smart selects this view of Marty South, as seen by the barber, Mr. Percomb, who has come to buy her hair. The view is through her cottage window:

In her present beholder's mind the scene formed by the girlish spar-maker composed itself into an impression-picture of extremest type, wherein the girl's hair alone, at the focus of observation, was depicted with intensity and distinctness, while her face, shoulders, hands, and figure in general, were a blurred mass of unimportant detail, lost in haze and obscurity.[17]

Once again, it should be noted, the reader experiences the "doubling" effect, as he sees both the viewer and the scene he beholds.

An additional part of Hardy's pictorial technique is his use of iconography *within* the scene (which, of course, can itself be iconographic). I refer particularly to the use of objects within a scene, because it is an extraordinarily effective, condensed way of conveying meaning. While we are used to understanding Hardy's use of the larger, scenic design of the picture as iconographic (when it relates to a set of ideas located elsewhere than within the picture itself), we are not so aware of how Hardy condenses this technique through the use of carefully constructed images. Icons may be "likenesses" such as pictures or mirrors, but may also be other, less obvious objects. Always, however, these objects are complete in themselves. Thus, photographs in *Jude the Obscure, Desperate Remedies*, and *A Laodicean* become icons, but the amount of their iconographic meaning can vary considerably, and is most evident in *Jude the Obscure*. (In the earlier novels, the photographs relate to a truth-falsehood concept; in *Jude*, photographs relate in one way or another to idealism, just as the Christminster image does.). A variety of other iconographic images appear in Hardy's novels: Christminster cookies baked by Jude and Sue are ironic, reductive comment on the model of Cardinal College that they had made earlier, which is itself ironic comment on Christminster as reality. Statuary in *The Well-Beloved* serves as comment on Pierston's avoidance of and blindness to the very real beauty that lies before him in the real world. Eustacia, Bathsheba, and Arabella gaze into mirrors and ponder the reflections before them. Tess views the D'Urberville portraits with trepidation and with a part consciousness of their relationship to her. Portraits in *A Laodicean* have prime significance in the development of plot and theme.

As these examples indicate, iconography appears most often in Hardy's later novels and demonstrates, I believe, a shift in his use of visual arts techniques, as there is a correspondent decline in his use of the larger, pictorial scene.[18] In addition, this gradual shift in technique relates in a very curious way to his poetry. What is not surprising is that a number of poems do make an effective use of icons: mirrors, miniatures, oil paintings (usually portraits), photographs. These iconographic images become the thematic and visual centers of the poems, as in "I Look into My Glass," "The Photograph," "A Forgotten Miniature," "In Church."

The strange drawings Hardy published as illustration to his first book of poetry (*Wessex Poems*, 1898) ought to be seen in relation to this increasing use of the iconographic. Thirty-two drawings, from sundials to vases of wilting flowers, from spectacles to landscapes, indicate the extreme variety of subject matter, and many of the drawings relate in an iconographic manner to the poems they accompany. Paul Zietlow in his critical study of Hardy's poetry pointedly asks: "The pictures raise the same question as the poems: Are they the naïve gropings of an amateur, or does Hardy exploit amateurish primitivism for deliberate effect?"[19] Seen in context with the iconographic developments in fiction and poetry, they are another sign of experiment toward the dominant, single image, though here another kind of relationship—between text and picture—exists. Though Hardy often disparaged his attempts at illustrating *Wessex Poems*, the several times he did make references to the drawings seem to contradict his "official" diffidence and suggests he was indeed experimenting with iconographic techniques.

All these references to paintings, particular painters or schools of art, the use of iconographic images, as well as the general references to light, framing, composition, design and other ingredients of the pictorial technique create the special Hardy signature. As Lloyd Fernando argues: "Close examination shows that individual phrases, structure of sentences, the trend of whole paragraphs and, in extreme instances, the greater portion of chapters, are all so closely affected by this interest of his as to constitute a rhetoric unique in the art of the novel."[20]

This pictorial rhetoric in Hardy's novels becomes extraordinary in the size of its presence, as well as in its particular visual and thematic impact. Yet Fernando argues that this rhetoric gives a flat, wooden quality to Hardy's style and is a considerable danger to the life of his novels. In creating a series of static scenes, Hardy "eliminates the realistic, everyday vitality of his figures. . . ." Pictures of reality, explains Fernando, are actually pictures of pictures. *The Return of the Native* has more of this static quality than any other of the novels, and that "may account in part for the novel's capacity both to attract and vex."[21] Thus the pictorial becomes partial but important cause for that curious unevenness in Hardy's novels, that sense of incompleteness the reader experiences in both the major and minor works.

Regardless of the dangers of pictorialism, the very use of the technique marks Hardy as a conscious artist, a label he himself dismissed with diffidence, but which modern readers have come to realize is an accurate description of Hardy's approach to his materials. Pictorialism is a technique, but it does not exist in isolation. For Hardy, technique is not just some idiosyncratic expression, but his approach has traditionally been described in just such terms. For Hardy, however, as for all great authors, technique is a way of presenting reality and is intimately associated with *how* he views and interprets reality. As a particular kind of technique, pictorialism shapes, confines materials in an artificial frame (as art itself does) and thus becomes an anti-realistic technique. Staticism, furthermore, can be extraordinarily grotesque. Hardy's pictorialism, in fact, emphasizes the grotesque effects of his plotting techniques and thus increases the sense of tragedy as cosmic forces seem to overwhelm the familiar. As the pastoral quality in *Under the Greenwood Tree* demonstrates, however, it is not just pictorialism itself but the *kind* of pictorial description that determines the grotesque effect.

There are other ways of understanding pictorialism as anti-realistic than the obvious grotesque effect. With the staticism of picture, human action becomes carved in the manner of a woodcut: flesh and blood human warmth becomes either sculptured, or framed, or set into position for display. Hardy's pictorial technique makes us more aware that we are viewers rather than participants, a rather obvious effect of pictorialism but one which seems to have been overlooked, or too much taken for granted. Due to the double viewer or "doubling" effect that Hardy so often uses,[22] the concept of audience as voyeur becomes a significant effect in Hardy's works. Again, this is an effect that theoretically occurs in all audience-art relationships, but Hardy deliberately exploits it. In this sense, Hardy anticipates the "estrangement effect" used by Berthold Brecht in 20th century theater where, through a variety of techniques, the audience is deliberately kept at a distance from the stage world before them.

Pictorialism is thus a way of "making strange." Mirrors and pools of water acting as mirrors of nature, pictures and silhouettes of people or hay ricks set against the sky, rays of sun illuminating scenes or pointing to other parts of nature, framing devices such as doorways and windows—all these are realistic on one level since the physical properties are recognized as real, but their handling in the pictorial scene makes them for the moment seem artificial. Such emphasis as Hardy gives them is not the normal, ordinary emphasis given by the human eye as it scans the visible world. Light and darkness motifs alternating in *The Return of the Native*, lush or barren landscapes alternating in *Tess of the D'Urbervilles*, architectural motifs in *Jude the Obscure*, as well as a variety of other pictorial qualities, shape our responses to the text. Pictorialism conveys a sense of solidity as we recognize objects or scenes, but life itself pauses for a moment as the picture, often emblematic, stops before our eyes, as we make connections within pictures, as we connect pictures with each other. In so much of Hardy's pictorialism, we are aware of our position as observers; we are detached from his world and thus able to measure not only the descrepancy between man's aspirations and the presence or absence of cosmic response, but also the sense of the life that inevitably provides the rationale behind the pictures. Pictorialism in Hardy's hands is a significant way of achieving irony, and is thus integral to his vision of life.

It is important for our purposes here to realize that a very significant part of Hardy's work is based on the pictorial, that an ironic stance toward life, an understanding of man's tenuous position in the universe, is often conveyed by means of the pictorial, often anti-realistic technique. The realism *within* Hardy's pictures, however, the fact that he made use of images the Victorian audience would have recognized from their own visual experience of the external world, as well as from their understandings of paintings and book illustrations, serves as a counter to the anti-realistic effects of his pictorial technique.

The audience of the original publication of most of Hardy's novels—the serial issue that we might call the "first edition"—had an additional experience: illustrations published with the novels. Hardy's own use of picture within his texts was to make his novels particularly appropriate for serial illustration. The recovery of the illustrations themselves, an understanding of their contribution to Hardy's texts which were themselves visual and even pictorial, provides an enriched experience and, it is to be hoped, will enable the modern reader to share in some sense with that visual experience of Hardy's original audience.

II

English Magazine Illustration: The Historic Context

Three periods of English illustration history have importance for an understanding and evaluation of the Hardy illustrations. The Cruikshank-Phiz era (1830–55) refers to the caricatural style marking the Dickens illustrations; the Millais era (1855–70) refers to the representational style of illustration given to Trollope's works. The third period (1870–1895) has no particular artist to identify with, a fact in itself significant, but is a continuation, with some differences, of the representational school of the 1860s. The two earlier periods, with their opposing styles of caricature and representationalism, have had their proponents among art and literary historians: Joan Stevens, Michael Steig, John Harvey, and Q. D. Leavis[1] have in various ways added to our understanding of the visual and moral metaphor found in the caricatural school. Much less in recent years has been done in the Millais school: the exuberance of earlier critics such as Gleeson White and Forrest Reid[2] has possibly forestalled later examination[3] of the representational school. For the period after 1870, however, extraordinarily little criticism exists, unless we move into the specific biographic studies for such artists as George Du Maurier, or into the histories of the 1890 period. The dearth of attention given to the years between 1870 and 1895, between the *Punch* cartoons and the Beardsley drawings, means that illustration in those years is considered undistinguished.

Yet in the field of serial illustration, at least, the post-1870 period was not such an abrupt shift or decline from the 1860s and certainly not as dull as the historians' neglect of the period would lead us to believe. Many of the same writers and illustrators continued to contribute to the magazines as they had in earlier years, and faced many of the same problems that extended back even to the 1830s. The basic style of the later illustration is not altogether different from that of the Millais period, either, though changes in intention and in the degree of freedom in interpretation did occur.

Separating the 1860s from the later period is often difficult. Certainly by the end of the century great changes had occurred, but in those earlier years the changes were slow but gradual. Developments such as the influence of photography, the emphasis on realism in art and literature, a changing audience demand since the days of the early Dickens, and the impact of new developments in reproductive processes do mark a very real shift in English magazine illustration after 1870, and the differences become ever more severe as the century progressed. The history of English magazine illustration thus has a complex but important background, since it provides an explanation not only for the sort of relationship Hardy was to have with his artists and editors, but also for audience expectation and, even more so, for the quality and style of illustration his stories were to receive.

When *The Cornhill Magazine* began publishing in 1860, it made its reputation through quality fiction, published with illustration. Yet before it even had time to build its own reputation, circulation for its first number shot up to 120,000 copies, before it settled down to average some 20,000 for the years thereafter. Success was assured, but its "overnight" aspect was only apparent. As Robert Mayo points out, a hundred years preceded that success, "a hundred years of reaction, compromise, and timid experimentation."[4] These years had seen the publication of novels written by Fielding, Smollett, and Sterne, complete with engraved illustrations, and had witnessed the part-issue publication of Dickens's works, beginning with *Pickwick Papers* in 1836. The hundred years were needed, as Mayo explains, because a "gradual shift in reader sensibility" and a "radical revision of serious critical opinion concerning the English novel" had to occur before "important works of new fiction, commissioned for the magazines and illustrated by leading contemporary artists, were to be granted equal status with the best poetry, criticism, and painting of the day."[5] Thus, the earlier experimentation with part-issue fiction and changes in attitude toward the respectability and artistic value of fiction itself, as well as toward part-issue and magazine fiction, were in large part responsible for the "overnight" success of *Cornhill* and its serialized, illustrated novels.

But it is also true that the quality of illustrations published with the serial fiction was a significant contribution to the magazine's success. Again, background becomes important: *Cornhill* did not wholly depend on its own illustrations, splendid though they were, but on a tradition and audience that had already been established. By the late 1850s there had already developed a large audience whose tastes were ready to move beyond the sensational crime illustrations of the early years in nineteenth century publishing history.[6] Another segment of the reading audience was already quite familiar with illustration through the fiction issued in monthly parts, as in Dickens's novels. This preparation, together with the general Victorian tendency to relate the pictorial with the narrative, helps to explain why illustrated magazine fiction in the 1860s had such a wide appeal and found commercial success.

The 1860s saw the establishment of many other fine illustrated magazines which were to publish in that decade the work of first-rate authors and illustrators. *Once a Week* had been founded in 1859, *Cornhill* and *Good Words* in 1860, *The Graphic* in 1869. Lesser known but still important illustrated magazines such as *The Argosy, London Society, The Sunday Magazine, The Shilling Magazine*, and *The Quiver* were all established in the glory days of the 60s. Important novels such as Trollope's *Framley Parsonage* and *The Small House at Allington*, George Eliot's *Romola*, Meredith's *Evan Harrington*, and Dickens's *Our Mutual Friend* made their first appearance as serial fiction in the 1860s, and were illustrated by such talented artists as John Everett Millais, Frederick Leighton, George Du Maurier, and Marcus Stone. A great surge of fine illustration also appeared with the non-fiction of that decade, for the poetry of Christina Rosetti, for instance, and of course in the related field of book illustration.

The end of the decade, however, did not signal the end of this "golden age" of illustration. Magazine illustration continued to flourish into the 1870s, and in sheer numerical output, to the end of the century. In the 1870s and 1880s, however, all the earlier magazines, joined by the European edition of *Harper's New Monthly* and lesser publications such as *Tinsley's Magazine* and *Belgravia*, continued to produce fiction illustrated by important artists from the 1860s. In the 1870s, for instance, Meredith's *The Adventures of Harry Richmond*, illustrated by George Du Maurier, appeared in *Cornhill;* Trollope's novels, illustrated by Millais, continued to appear in *Good Words;* Wilkie Collins's works appeared in *Belgravia* and *Cornhill;* Henry James's *Washington Square* appeared with illustrations in *Cornhill* in 1880.

Hardy's novels were published in several of these same magazines between 1873 and 1895, and while most of the nine Hardy illustrators were not as well known as George Du Maurier (illustrator of two Hardy novels), they were all quite well known in the tightly knit circle of magazine illustrators. Helen Paterson (afterwards Allingham), Sir Hubert Herkomer, Robert Barnes, William Hatherell each had a fine reputation in the field. Several were staff artists at the finest of illustrated magazines, or were free-lance artists in much demand. Among other popular writers and artists published during this post-1870 period were Walter Besant, James Payn, Dinah M. Mulock (Mrs. Craik), Justin McCarthy, Mrs. Oliphant and (as illustrators), R. Caldecott, Fred Barnard, H. Furniss.

Thus, there was a definite continuity present in the actual writers and illustrators who spanned the 1860 and post-1870 period. There was not a wholesale exodus into the field of book publication—either the writing or illustrating side of that field. Many writers and artists, of course, preferred the more slowly paced field of book publication as opposed to the frenetic pace of magazine work, as will be explained later, but many of the best names among authors and illustrators stayed in the field after 1870. There was also a continuity present in the style of illustration in these two periods of magazine fiction illustration, though there were also some significant changes, and here an understanding of the earlier style of illustration becomes useful.

From the 1830s to the mid-1850s, artists Richard Doyle, John Leech, George Cruikshank, and "Phiz" (H. K. Browne) had continued the tradition of Gillray and Hogarth in graphic satire. The predominant style of literary illustration was caricature, a style that through economy and distortion became metaphorically significant. As John Harvey has demonstrated in his *Victorian Novelists and Their Illustrators*, these early artists were consciously concerned with extending the life of the novel by creating engravings distinctly in tune with the spirit of each individual story.[7] As a general rule, the artist worked in close collaboration with the novelist, and the result was that *picture* became an integral part of the work, marked with the individual style of the artist and emphasizing the basic peculiarities of character, setting, and theme already conveyed through the text. And, most importantly, the illustrations conveyed the spirit of the novel. As Harvey explains, "The illustrations in the monthly parts had faults of melodrama and cramped technique . . . , but they embody an economy of standards . . . worth preserving because it shows how illustrations, while retaining their integrity as visual art, can extend the preoccupations of a novelist." The illustrations of Phiz and Cruikshank, continues Harvey, "were not confined to the vivid suggestion of character and mood; they could develop a novel's themes subtly, delicately, and powerfully, and in essentially visual terms."[8] Some of the finest of these illustrations developed the thematic concerns of the novel in highly individualistic ways. The illustrator was acutely aware of audience delight in macabre scenes and caricature, and while he was exceedingly faithful to the spirit of the text, he was suggestive enough to add significant detail in setting and in character mannerisms.

In addition to the caricature in a scene, for example, the illustrator would add important details of his own conception to the scene's background—mirrors, cobwebs, *objets d'art* (especially portraits), and other items possessing allegoric meaning. Corners become especially important for the details an artist could include. A dead or even live mouse, an empty basket, a crack in the wainscoting, were details that seemed to be afterthoughts, perhaps, but actually served as the finishing, allegorical touch for a given scene. Even vignette initials, such as those which open the chapters of Thackeray's *Vanity Fair*, extended the life of the novel through the inclusion of certain details.[9] The visual, metaphoric meaning present in many of these illustrations is in addition to the situational material drawn from the text itself, and thus gives the illustration considerable independence, or integrity, as a work of art. This is not necessarily true of all the illustrations in a series, but is true of a significant proportion of them, as in *Dombey and Son*, for instance, for the generalization to remain valid.

With the publication of the Moxon edition of Tennyson's poetry in 1857 following the appearance of William Allingham's 1855 collection of poetry, *The Music Master*, another style of illustration became dominant. Among the Moxon illustrators were the Pre-Raphaelite painters Millais, Rossetti, and Holman Hunt, and their illustrations showed the styles of their Pre-Raphaelite painting. They interpreted their material in a highly subjective manner, particularly dependent on blocks of shading to create "mood" pictures. In terms of subjectivity, for instance, the artists would often turn to medieval designs. Sometimes, of course, Tennyson's poems called for such a period illustration because of the subject matter and it was the ornateness of the design that showed the freedom of the artist. Other poems, such as "Locksley Hall," were done in a contemporary, Victorian motif, as indicated by the text. In this poem, however, the situation itself revealed the freedom these artists felt in interpreting the text. In the illustration for this poem, the artist presents two lovers embracing, with the sea as background—but neither the embracing figures nor the sea were part of the actual poem. The artist had felt free to add his own background and, in this case, even the foreground material. The illustration for "The Palace of Art" was still more of a departure from the specifics of the text. Even Tennyson himself, so the story goes, was puzzled over the relationship between his poem and the artist's illustration, but the Pre-Raphaelite belief in the validity of personal interpretation and in the independence of the illustration from the text lay behind the lack of graphic fidelity. The illustrators still believed they operated within the parameters of the text; they believed they were being faithful to the *spirit* of the material they were illustrating.

The art critics of the day (and later) responded enthusiastically to the new school, and found values in the work of a Rossetti or Holman Hunt or Millais that were absent from the earlier styles of Leech or Doyle. Critics

Gleeson White and Malcolm Salaman, for instance, praised the new school to the detriment of the earlier style. As Salaman explains: "Imaginative independence" and "expressive freedom" mark the 1860s when the artists "with the author's subject in mind, and memories well stored with the great traditions of design, would go direct to experience and find in its suggestions fresh creative impulse to vitalise their illustrations, so that these would make their own appeal as works of art while they revealed new significance in the subjects."[10]

As might be expected, the new school soon made its influence felt in the illustration of magazine fiction, though here imaginative freedom was not so much present as it was in the illustration for poetry. Millais's work for Trollope's *Framley Parsonage*, Frederick Leighton's illustrations for George Eliot's *Romola*, and Du Maurier's for the early Meredith are prime examples of the new school's effort in the field of fiction illustration. The illustrations were naturalistic; they aimed at a basic fidelity to the text, paying close attention to realistic detail within a full-frame engraving. Their emphasis on blocks of shading tended to create illustrations with considerable atmosphere and visual drama. The photographic detail of Realism was not yet a dominant characteristic in the 1860 school—but design and composition were crucial. The full frame engraving demanded that every bit of space be used, and the artists obliged with their blocks of shading, with draperies, costuming, trellises all contributing to a larger sense of carefully plotted design, but each having its own intricate, delicate system of lines spelling out design in miniature.

The 1860s were also the years when *Punch* was establishing its reputation for the incisive social and political satire of its cartoons. Whether it be through its cartoons or its plates published with its serial fiction, magazine illustration in the 1860s and afterwards was as much a part of popular art as the illustration in the era of Hablot Browne or Cruikshank had been, even though the new school did not use the kind of caricature or graphic satire of that earlier age of English illustration. One major difference between the two eras is that the tastes of the audience had changed. As Geoffrey Fletcher in *Popular Art in England* explains, "Popular art is produced for the pleasure of the masses. . . . It is, therefore, very general in its appeal, usually to persons of more or less unsophisticated taste. Tastes of this kind nearly always run to the showy. . . ."[11] Victorian gentility, however, had tempered the extravagance of an earlier day. The taste for the "showy" in caricature was now looked down upon by the Victorian middle class and many of the century's art critics. That taste had now changed into a desire for realism—on the part of novelist, illustrator, and audience.

In explaining a basic appeal of the representational illustration from 1860 to the end of the century, artist George Du Maurier somewhat unconsciously revealed a narcissistic aspect in the audience desire for realism: "We like to see ourselves now—at this very moment—as in a looking glass—that we may know 'how it strikes a contemporary.' We also like to see what our sires and grandsires were like, and our granddams when they were young. Our descendents will probably like to see us—just as we are."[12] The many Victorian magazines and newspapers with the term "illustrated" in their titles suggests how much the audience was interested in the pictorial, whatever their reasons.

Influenced by the general movement of literary realism, where the author himself provided a significant amount of concrete detail in his fiction, as well as by a growing interest in photography, because of the camera's ability to capture detail in its exactness, and audience desire for photographic realism, serial illustration from the 1860s to the century's end increasingly emphasized the concrete detail of the illustrated scene. The Pre-Raphaelite illustrators customarily used models to aid them in creating realistic drawings, and some (Rossetti, for instance) even used photographs as an aid. The result was exceptionally fine detail, corresponding to the realities of anatomy, lighting, or design—as in tapestry or other rich fabrics.

In the prominent illustrators of the 1860s, the effect of light and shadow, and the sweeping, evocative lines of the human figure, as well as design, are dominant marks. In the illustrations by Millais, these qualities, and not the realistic details that correspond to the world outside the novel, create the power of the scene. Yet the drawings are certainly representational, both in terms of the text itself and the world outside the text. The Millais drawings, however, actually combine two significant qualities: graphic fidelity to the text and the artist's subjective interpretation of that text. As Millais demonstrates in his illustrations for Trollope's novels, the two qualities need not contradict each other.

Representationalism in magazine illustration becomes more dominant after 1870, sometimes painstakingly so. Instead of the suggestion of mood and character that marks the illustrations of the 1860s, the later illustration was concerned with accuracy of detail as described in the text and as it corresponded to the world outside the text. And as artists found themselves increasingly faced with the competition of the concrete detail of the photograph, they became even more concerned with the realism in their own drawings.

This concern for realism is clearly defined in one contemporary school of thought, as expressed by Victorian Henry Blackburn's *The Art of Illustration:* "The first object of an illustration, the practical part, is obviously to illustrate and elucidate the text—a matter often lost sight of. The second is to be artistic, and includes works of the imagination, decoration, ornament, style."[13] In its fundamental sense, according to this definition, illustration is a picture which clarifies the work of others. The illustrator is thus subordinate to the novelist, and graphic fidelity to the text is of prime importance.

The concept of illustration as clarification applies particularly to a situation where "words fail to express a meaning easily," as in a passage where topography, architecture, or any sort of positioning occurs. In this sense, however, the illustration seems *not* to be subordinated to the text, but only because it may more clearly describe what an author has failed to convey imaginatively. As Blackburn explains:

A curious experiment was made lately with some students in an Art school, to prove the fallacy of the accepted system of describing landscapes, buildings, and the like in words. A page or two from one of the Waverley novels (a description of a castle and the heights of mountainous land, with a river winding in the valley towards the sea, and clusters of houses and trees on the right hand) was read slowly and repeated before a number of students, three of whom, standing apart from each other by pre-arrangement, proceeded to indicate on blackboards before an audience, the leading lines of the picture as the words had presented it to their minds. It is needless to say that the results, highly skilful in one case, were all different, and *all wrong*, and that in particular the horizon line of the sea (so easy to indicate with any clue, and so important to the composition) was hopelessly out of place. Thus we describe day by day, and the pictures formed in the mind are erroneous, for the imagination of the reader is at work at once, and requires simple guidance.[14]

In one sense, Blackburn's comments criticize the writer for not being able to describe scenery in a manner which would satisfy one trained in perspective and composition. The criticism "all wrong," too, is considerably and unnecessarily restrictive to the reader's imaginative response to the textual material. Yet Blackburn is right when he points out that illustration serves a valuable function, since it can present to the reader a physical situation which might be difficult to grasp from the textual description alone. Three illustrations for *The Haven on the Hill* by Mary Linskill, drawn by G. Morton (*Good Words*, 1886) are a case in point. The scenes presented are a set of stairs in a church, the ruins of an abbey, and a set of very narrow stairs between houses in the village. The positioning of walls and other objects was particularly useful for the reader's understanding, and the dark atmosphere surrounding the central interest in each scene would have also heightened the mood as described in the text. This second effect, however, relates more to *interpretation* than clarification, but demonstrates how closely associated these two aspects of illustration could be.

Graphic fidelity to the text, with its increased emphasis on realistic detail after 1870, was not a reflection on the inadequacy of the novelist in his attempt to describe the physical elements of his story, although it was true that second and third-rate magazine writers may well have had this problem. In this case, the illustrations would become vital to an understanding of the story's physical terms. But for the more gifted writers such as Hardy, Besant, Trollope, and Collins, the representational illustration served to clarify the text, not because of the writer's inadequacy, but because of the reader's inability to visualize what he had read. As Thomas Balston points out, "The artists of the later Victorian period rendered the *mise en scène* of a passage, its clothes and weapons, its architecture and furniture, its manners and deportment, with minute exactness, so that they helped the reader to visualize the scene far more clearly than he could have done from the text alone."[15] Though clarification does seem an important aim of illustration, it was surely not the only aim, as will become clear. Another part of the Victorian audience was quite used to the visual experience of picture, and looked to illustration for something other than clarification, or a clarification much more sophisticated than the pointed, visual arrangement of a novel's setting, characterization, or plot. Yet the fact that artist and sometimes novelist talked about re-creation and accuracy of detail does give rise to the prevailing view that illustration after the 1860s became primarily a visual recording of a novel's scenes, with little else to recommend it.

Not all serial fiction was accompanied by illustration. *Macmillan's Magazine* and *The Fortnightly Review*, for instance, did not include engravings with the text of their fiction. That simple fact explains the superficially puzzling problem of why Hardy's *Woodlanders*, so eminently suitable for illustrations, was published without them. It appeared in *Macmillan's Magazine*—and if *Tess of the D'Urbervilles* had been accepted by that magazine, as Hardy had originally hoped, it too would have met the same fate.

Both these magazines, particularly *The Fortnightly Review*, catered to a more specialized, intellectual audience. But the majority of the English weekly and monthly magazines was aimed at a middle-class audience who wanted to be entertained, and who may or may not have needed aid in "seeing" the terms of the text. The range of the reading audience differed slightly, according to the aims of the magazine. *Belgravia* (which published *The Return of the Native*) aimed primarily at "the genteel, middle-class, lady public, of low to fair educational standards."[16] *Cornhill*, on the other hand, had an audience that ranged from the middle to the upper class, politically liberal. *Harper's New Monthly* (an American magazine, but with a European edition beginning in the 1880s) seems to have had an audience similar to *Cornhill's*. Both these magazines issued more than one of Hardy's novels: *Cornhill* published *Far From the Madding Crowd* and *The Hand of Ethelberta*:

Harper's issued *A Laodicean* in its inaugural European edition, and later published *Jude the Obscure*. *Tinsley's Magazine* (the first magazine to publish an illustrated Hardy work with its 1872–73 issue of *A Pair of Blue Eyes*) was aimed at "middle to upper class readers of low to fair education." *Good Words*, which published Hardy's *The Trumpet Major*, was a "decidedly religious magazine, of some intellectual pretensions, and . . . it appealed to the lower to upper middle classes of fair educational standards."[17] Because of its status as a newsmagazine, *The Graphic* (which issued *The Mayor of Casterbridge* and *Tess of the D'Urbervilles*) would have an extremely diversified audience. The audience for *The Illustrated London News* (which published *The Well-Beloved*) would have been even more wide-ranging.

While the works of Hardy, Trollope, and Meredith are now considered as serious, "literary" works of art, it is important to remember that, in their own day, because of the manner of their first publication, these authors shared popularity with such magazine writers as James Payn, Margaret Oliphant, Walter Besant—and Grant Allen, George Mac-Donald, David Christie Murray, Charles Gibbon, Helen Shipton, and William Gilbert. *The Graphic*, for instance, published *The Mayor of Casterbridge* and *Tess of the D'Urbervilles* between 1888 and 1891; it also presented, however, such lesser works as *Matt: A Novel*, by Robert Buchanan (1885), *Cousin Isodore*, by Frances Eleanor Trollope (1885), and *The Scallywag*, by Grant Allen (1893). Earlier, *Belgravia* had published *The Return of the Native* (1878), and in the same volume, Wilkie Collins's *The Haunted Hotel*, a decidedly inferior work. Between 1878 and 1881 the magazine also published *Joseph's Coat* by David Christie Murray; *Queen of the Meadows* by Charles Gibbon; *A Confidential Agent* by James Payn; and Justin McCarthy's *Donna Quixote*. These other magazine serials do not measure up to the quality of most of Hardy's works, but the fact that Hardy's fiction appeared in their midst means that their audience was also his.

Speaking with the voice of authority, since he had illustrated many novels for the magazines, including two of Thomas Hardy's, George Du Maurier explained the relationship between audiences and illustration: "The majority likes to have its book (even its newspaper!) full of little pictures." There are two classes of readers, theorizes Du Maurier, the first containing the reader "who visualizes what he reads (at the moment of reading) with the mind's eye . . . in a manner so satisfactory to himself that he wants the help of no picture; indeed, to him a picture would be a hindrance." Du Maurier believed, however, that a majority of readers did not have that gift of visualizing what they were reading. For this class of reader, "to have the author's conceptions adequately embodied in a concrete form is a boon, an enhancement of their pleasure." Actors on a stage may leave nothing for the imagination to create, but "the little figures in the picture are a mild substitute for the actors at the footlights. They are voiceless and cannot move, it is true. But the arrested gesture, the expression of face, the character and costume, may be as true to nature and life as the best actor can make them. Within the limits assigned," concluded Du Maurier, "these dumb motionless puppets may be as graceful, or grotesque, or humorous, or terrible as people in real life— indeed, more so; they may continue to haunt the memory when the letterpress they illustrate is forgotten."[18] For Du Maurier, clarification and entertainment were the simultaneous result of good illustration.

Illustration after 1870 emphasized the reality of the novelist's verbal world and the correspondence between that world and the world of the reader-viewer. Audience identification is thus a primary result of post-1870 illustration for magazine fiction. Yet it is important to remember that the marks of older styles of illustration could still appear. The allegorical, the use of illustration as visual metaphor, was still possible, even though it was not the prevailing style. The heightened visual drama and suggestiveness present in the earlier, 1860 representationalism could also appear. But the shift to photographic realism that dominates the later period means that this later style must be judged by still other terms. As will be noted later, the complexity and fascination of the Hardy illustrations is that all three styles are present, though certainly photographic realism is a dominant quality. A more specific examination of the aesthetic basis of representational illustration occurs later, but for now, it is enough to realize that such a basis does exist, and certainly extends beyond the more obvious issues of clarification-entertainment.

Though a significant amount of illustration after 1870 did not stop at textual clarification and sought to expand the text in a variety of ways, much of the illustration of the time was purely descriptive— representationalism in its blandest form. At times, this kind of illustration was perfectly respectable, but ran the risk of being redundant, even perfunctory. Such illustration brought very little to the text. But even here, the fully detailed scene meant that the audience who viewed these illustrations would have their responses more controlled, more clearly shaped toward specific understandings of a situation or character than would the audience for the non-illustrated work.

A significant amount of illustration in the 1870s and 1880s is fine work, though it has not had a particular artist to rally around for purposes of identification. Again, this style of illustration has not been understood very well because it has been measured by the aims, methods, and results of the two earlier schools. And when representational illustration is measured by the Cruikshank school, its differences become exaggerated, its positive qualities obscured.

Yet it is also true that much of the illustration for this era is undistinguished. Such a statement is not meant to be disparaging: much of the

fiction is also undistinguished. The heavy volume of fiction and illustration, whether they accompanied each other or not, meant that much of it,
by the simple law of averages, had to be second, even third rate. Sheer
increase in numbers, therefore, was one cause of mediocre work. The
inadequacy of writer and illustrator, as well as the press of publication
deadlines for a myriad of magazines publishing large numbers of serials
written and illustrated by novelists and artists who could not all be of first
rate quality—these are reasons for much spiritless, even shoddy work of
the time. The conditions under which both author and illustrator worked
were often responsible for the quality of illustration. Some of the conditions, however, had advantages as well as disadvantages, and some were
common to all three periods of English illustration.

Before the 1870s, the serial form of publication was a distinct advantage
to the author who saw himself as a storyteller, since it enabled him to be
immediately responsive to audience reaction. The fact that an author
would sometimes radically change his plots indicated his versatility and
responsiveness. Dickens often introduced new characters into his fiction
when he felt circulation was sagging: the appearance of Sam Weller in the
fourth installment of *Pickwick Papers* is a famous case in point.

Possibly the most famous case of such responsiveness was Trollope's
action during the writing of *The Last Chronicle of Barset* (1866–67). After
overhearing two men venting their dislike of the character Mrs. Proudie,
Trollope announced: "I will go home and kill her before the week is over."
This kind of impulsive responsiveness brought its own problems, as
Trollope later discovered: "I have sometimes regretted the deed, so great
was my delight in writing about Mrs. Proudie, so thorough was my
knowledge of all the little shades of her character."[19]

The ability of the author to change direction while he was actually
publishing the novel put the illustrator at a disadvantage, since he did not
have the completed manuscript, with all the character disposition, at
hand. Later in the century, when it became more the practice to submit
the completed manuscript to an editor (and illustrator), the advantage in
author responsiveness was lost, but the illustrator or editor had the
advantage of knowing the complete story, and could select a well balanced
set of scenes for illustration. Still, even after the 1870s, many illustrators
worked from unfinished manuscripts, as some of the Hardy illustrators
did. In this situation, both novelist and illustrator suffered from the
pressure of meeting publication deadlines.

In the earlier years of part-issue illustration, and often in the early years
of magazine serialization, artist and novelist often worked in close collaboration, most notably in the case of Dickens and his illustrators. Later, the
illustrator did not work directly with the author but took his guidance
from the editor who often selected the scenes to receive illustration. The

lack of collaboration between novelist and illustrator in the post-1870 period (and the correspondingly increased role played by the editor) is a distinctive mark of the era.

Punch illustrator George Du Maurier more than once expressed the advantages that would occur if author and illustrator could have consulted on the pictorial treatment that was to be given the particular novel. Ideally, each separate design should have been discussed. Conceding that this would have been impractical, Du Maurier suggested the next best way to handle the collaboration:

> If authors would learn a little how to draw themselves they would not put such difficulties in the artist's way, and expect the impossible from him, such as that he should draw three sides of a house in one picture, or show the heroine's full face, tearstained, as she gazes on the lover vanishing in the middle of the background. It would be a great boon if they could, however roughly, illustrate their own work, that the artist might have some idea of the characters and scenes as these present themselves to him who imagined them first.[20]

Du Maurier's unfulfilled wish to have had Thackeray's own designs for a guide as he illustrated *Henry Esmond*, as Thackeray had supplied for the publication of *Vanity Fair*, lay behind this statement. Du Maurier explained, furthermore, that for authors such as Thackeray and Dickens, who did not "very minutely describe the outer aspect" of characters, sketches of them from the author's own hand would be of immeasurable value.[21]

Collaboration between author and illustrator appears to have been a mixed blessing, because occasionally it became interference. Yet even a very slight contact between author and illustrator could affect the terms of the story, and make the illustrations more integrated with the text. When a story was written with the knowledge that it was to be illustrated, an author could create scenes especially for the illustrator—a visually dramatic scene could begin one of the monthly parts, for instance, or a scene which presented a confrontation between characters would be included in a particular issue. When the author knew not only that his novel was to be illustrated but even the name of the artist, he was able to know the style of illustration, the particular idiosyncracies of the artist, the sort of scene he excelled in drawing. Thus the author could create or revise his text to accomodate the artist.

Collaboration was still possible after 1870, particularly when a manuscript was being completed as its first numbers were being published (so that the author could change his text to fit the needs of the illustrator), but this practice of accepting an incomplete manuscript became much less common in the 1870s and later. A close working relationship between artist and author became an exception in this period, though there was often some kind of contact between the two. The editor came to have an increasingly dominant role, and his decisions seem to have replaced—or interfered with—the collaboration that might have taken place between author and illustrator. Certainly this role of the editor was useful to the author who did not wish to concern himself with illustration.

Very often, the editor would inform the illustrator that one scene, or one scene plus vignette initial, was required for each installment. Sometimes the editor chose the scene to be illustrated, and kept the artist's needs or preferences in mind. More likely, he selected the scenes because of their relation to the over-all arrangement of the serial. One illustration per issue, or an opening or closing illustration (the latter being rare, since the audience was already "captured"), or an illustration carefully placed in the middle of the installment, revealed the editor's understanding that his audience was to be held through the appeal of picture. This was most apparent in magazines such as *The Graphic*, where the illustration served as frontispiece for the monthly segment. Such prominent positioning of the illustration was obviously meant as a direct appeal to the audience.

Another reason for scene selection, other than placement in the text, is explained by James Thorpe in *English Illustration: The Nineties:* "Many editors, when sending a story or article for illustration, are very careful to indicate the passages to be translated into drawings. These generally include a large crowd of people with an extensive background, so that the directors may be assured that they are getting full value for their money. It would be useless and unthinkably improper," continues Thorpe, "for the artist to suggest that he is a better judge of what will make an effective illustration." The successful editor, however, was one who could give the artist free rein, "relying on his discretion and pride in his work to produce the best of which he was capable."[22] Editorial decisions need not be final. For the Harper publications, for instance, the editor would suggest to the artist certain "striking" incidents for illustration, and the artist could then make a final decision.[23] But in magazines where such contact and consideration did not take place (and even where it did exist), the editor would ask that twenty illustrations were to be provided for the twenty-part serial, or twelve illustrations for the twelve-part story, and so on—no matter what the visual demands or possibilities of the text were.

When a story was written without any consideration that it was to be illustrated, and then turned over to the artist, his problems increased. If the particular plot segment for an issue had no scenes with dramatic, visual impact, or with psychological potential, for instance, then the illustrator was limited to a drawing which was perfunctory. Emphasis on detail, often unimportant detail, became the aim of the artist in this difficult situation because he had little else to work with. The inability of the writer to visualize his material for himself, or his lack of concern or understanding of the artist's plight must, in large measure, account for the many illustrations after 1870 which are flat, uninteresting, and deficient in imaginative dimension. The fault was not always the illustrator's.

Other problems existed for the serial illustrator besides the difficulty of sometimes working with segments, and not the whole, of the author's material, or having to illustrate a story with little visual material, having little or no contact with the author, or having to fulfill the demands of an editor. If the artist did not do his own engraving, he was then at the mercy of the wood engraver, and this was often the case after 1870. The houses of Swain and Dalziel could be depended on for fine engravings, but even these excellent firms could not keep up with the demand to produce engravings for an increased number of serial publications with economy and dispatch. Often the engraving work was farmed out to workers of less skill. It was then that the artist's concept ran the risk of crude engraving which would spoil the delicacy or even the tone of his original drawing. In America, however, and especially *after* 1870, the situation was much better. There, the engraver and artist often worked together in the same studio, but "in England the artist, as a rule, did not have any direct communication with the wood engraver."[24] It may not be coincidental that American magazines were known for the excellent quality of their engravings.

On the other hand, the engraver could often improve the artist's work by interpreting the wash of the drawing into strong, clear lines, and by giving more care to small details than the artist had done. As the outstanding nineteenth century engraver Edmund Evans has observed: "The skill of the wood-engraver was often much greater than that of the artists whose work they were responsible for reproducing; their profession was at the very heart of the Victorian book and magazine world."[25]

Sometimes as much as five or six hundred pounds was spent on the illustrations for a single number of a monthly magazine. The result of this amount of money spent on engraving almost ensured superior illustration. But in the last two decades of the nineteenth century, the search for ever cheaper processes, the hurry necessitated by serial publication, meant that less care was given to the engraving of illustrations. Before even this stage was reached in reproducing graphic work, of course, the artist himself had been pressed into producing the finished sketch in record time.

But already, between the years 1875 and 1885, the wood-engraver began to be replaced by the process-block. By 1890, the great age of commercial wood-engraving was almost over. With the elimination of the human hand in engraving, the artist was free of the crude engraver—but he was also bereft of the aid the talented engraver could give to uncertain drawing and to those illustrators new to the field. Thus, each advance in the reproduction of illustration brought with it a loss of some sort: the cheapness of the woodblock make illustration available to the mass reading public, but also meant, in many cases, a decline in quality compared to work done on the steel plate. The search for economy, as well as the pressure of constantly encroaching deadlines of magazine publication, led eventually and inevitably, it seems, to a situation where shoddy work was the norm, instead of the exception. Speaking of the decline in the quality of magazine illustration in the 1890s, Joseph Pennell lamented: "The illustrations many of [the magazines] contain are more primitive in their depth of ignorance than the work of the cave-dwellers. . . . At the present moment we find ourselves in a critical situation, good work crowded out by mediocrity—because mediocrity is cheaper—real artists lost sight of amid the crowd of squirming, struggling, advertising hacks."[26] And, in the 1890s, whether due to commercial, economic, or artistic problems, many magazines no longer published illustrations with their serialized fiction. *Cornhill* and *Belgravia* were among the casualties.

In spite of all these difficulties, the good graphic artist was eager to illustrate for the magazines. It meant a wide audience, and in magazines noted for their fine reproduction of illustrations, such as *Harper's* and *Cornhill*, as well as *The Graphic*, it meant a tremendous advance in reputation. Good artists were attracted by the excitement of the world of journalism and enjoyed the hazards of commission work which enabled them to work for a wide variety of publications. The attraction was particularly strong for those artists who were little known and were anxious to establish their own reputations, but such famous names in the field of magazine illustration as Du Maurier, Millais, Small, and Keene, for instance, contributed regularly to the magazines even after the "golden" 60s. After 1870, *The Graphic* still had on its staff most of the important graphic artists of the day: Fildes, Hall, Gregory, Houghton, Linton, Herkomer, Pinwell, Green, Woods, Barnes. The list is an impressive one.

Some magazines treated the illustrator's work with great respect, and presented the illustrations themselves as works of art. For those magazines which were issued monthly, more time could be spent on preparing illustrations and their engravings onto the wood block. The quality of the illustrations in some cases was superb. According to Pennell, the quality of work in *Good Words* was so excellent that he contended the magazine was one of the "most important art journals England has ever seen. . . ."[27] In addition to *Good Words*, *Cornhill*, *The Illustrated London News*, *The Graphic*, and *Once a Week* were also noted for the excellence of their art work. *Argosy*, *London Society*, *Sunday Magazine*, *Shilling Magazine*, and *Quiver* also paid special attention to illustrations, but their reputations were not as fine as those magazines and newspapers first mentioned. Though *Harper's New Monthly* was published in New York and was essentially an American magazine, its London edition made it a part of the Victorian England assembly of illustrated periodicals. *Harper's* treatment of its engravings as works of art made it an exceptional publication. The young, inexperienced artist was often advised to study the pages of these magazines to learn what good engraving was like.

In *Good Words, Once a Week*, and *Belgravia*, the artist was accorded special recognition through the inclusion of his name in the magazine's index or table of contents. In *Good Words*, the artist was mentioned in a listing of illustrators appearing on the title page, but no authors were mentioned. *Cornhill*, which clearly recognized the illustrations as works of art from the care lavished on their appearance, curiously enough kept the names of the artists from the index and did not give noticeable acknowledgment to its artists. It was not until 1885 that *Cornhill* began to list the names of the illustrators in the table of contents. Certain magazines, such as *The Graphic*, as if to make up for a lack of recognition of its artists, as well as to show off the quality of its art work, would occasionally issue separate publications, such as *Graphic Portfolio*, which contained what the magazine considered its best illustrations over a year or somewhat longer period. In addition, *The Graphic* regularly ran a special column discussing the illustrations and artists appearing in the current issue. Magazines such as these, in addition to their desire to entertain, hold, and increase audience, were conscious of their own reputations as purveyors of good art. They were able to pay for it, and there were many fine artists anxious to work for them.

During the 1870s, however, many fine illustrators, having already established their reputations through the magazines and illustrated newspapers, turned to book illustration. The fact that the artist had the whole, instead of a segment of text to work with, the greater care given to book production because of the time element, the attention paid to harmony, scale, balance and design, and the relation of illustration to type, the ability to see the total set of illustrations as they related to one another, caused this shift on the part of the artist who, naturally enough, was concerned with the best possible display of his abilities.

While greater care could be given to book illustrations, there were certain aesthetic advantages in magazine illustration. One of the disadvantages of book illustration was the separation of the engraving from the text when it was printed on a separate page, particularly when it was printed on a different and better grade of paper than that used for the text. Often a blank page or a sheet of facing tissue separated the book illustration from the text. Sometimes the format called for the book to be turned sideways in order to view the illustration.

In the magazines, and especially newspapers such as *The Illustrated London News*, the engraving often appeared on the same page as the text, and was thus well integrated with the story it accompanied. Occasionally a magazine such as *Belgravia* would print illustrations separate from the text, on a different type of paper, and seemed through this practice to be imitating the practice of book illustration. The result was to destroy, at least to some extent, the visual-verbal synthesis that occurred in other magazines because of the physical integration of illustration and text.

Some magazines, such as *Cornhill*, seemed to have given as much consideration to harmony and design as book illustration did. The quality of paper, use of the vignette initial, the practice of harmonizing illustration with text through the vignette initial, the general layout of illustration and text—all these demonstrated concern for illustration as art. Audience appeal was evident through the use of the double-page spread to open the first number of a story, in some instances. It served as frontispiece to the serial, in effect, and could not be overlooked, as would sometimes happen in books.

Serial illustration, therefore, did have a system behind its presentation, even though it was inevitably affected by the pressures of publication deadlines. As these successful magazines and newspapers demonstrated, illustration could be integrated with the text, could be visually pleasing, and could enhance the text. An effective narrative-pictorial synthesis—in both a physical and imaginative sense—was the result.

This synthesis was still quite possible in the illustrated serial published after 1870, even though much originality had disappeared from magazine illustration as artists subordinated their own imagination to the details of the text, and to the needs and desires of an audience who mixed gentility with their interest in realism. An effective narrative-pictorial synthesis, in fact, does occur in several of Hardy's novels, in spite of the many difficulties affecting post-1870 magazine illustration. The story of the Hardy illustrations becomes important, not only for what it reveals about this neglected period of English magazine illustration but, more specifically, what it reveals about Hardy's actual involvement with the visual interpretation of his own texts.

III

Hardy and His Illustrators

I

"The best illustrator I ever had."
(1872–1876)

The 1860s saw the establishment of an increasing number of illustrated magazines aimed at capturing a middle class audience, and *Tinsley's Magazine* was one of these. William Tinsley himself explained the birth of his 1867 publishing venture: "About this time I started it there was a rage amongst publishers for shilling magazines, and I was one of the foolish sheep who rushed through the gap. . . ."[1] The gap seems to have been much too narrow, as Tinsley lost £3000 on the first twelve numbers of his magazine. Nevertheless, the audience grew to 10,000 in 1868, comparing favorably to *Cornhill* with its circulation of 18,000 in the same year. Like all publishers in those shaky financial years of establishing a magazine, Tinsley was on the lookout for promising young writers, and he was successful in obtaining the work of Justin McCarthy and B. L. Farjeon, as well as the fiction of an even more popular writer, James Grant. It is in this context that Thomas Hardy's first illustrated novel was published.

The publishing house of Tinsley Brothers had earlier committed itself to this unknown writer by issuing *Desperate Remedies* in three volumes in 1872. When Tinsley asked Hardy in July of that same year if he had any manuscript available for serial publication in the firm's monthly magazine, he agreed to send what he had written of *A Pair of Blue Eyes*, though he also explained that he was not quite ready to submit the manuscript. Nevertheless, Tinsley had the first installment of five chapters in hand by August. Upon finishing that first installment, Hardy had quickly sent it off, "though he had shaped nothing of what the later chapters were to be like."[2] After sending off what he had written, Hardy left for a visit to Cornwall, where he was courting Emma Gifford, and which also happened to be the setting for his story. Returning to London, Hardy discovered he could not write there, and so he went back to Dorset in late September. A diary entry on September 30 noted that the manuscript up to page 163 was sent to Tinsley.

Hardy's correspondence with Tinsley reveals that he was hard pressed to fulfill his promise to send future installments by the first of each month. While he was in Cornwall, he had received an urgent letter from the editor asking for more of the manuscript. His ability to finish the first installment "in an incredibly quick time,"[3] had possibly given him a mistaken view of what it was like to write for serial publication. Unused to literary deadlines, Hardy began to feel the pressures of magazine writing. An additional result of the pressures of installment writing, believes Carl J. Weber, was that it "had led him into inartistic prolixity;"[4] he had padded his manuscript to fill the spatial demands of his editor. Later, Hardy realized what demands serial publication had made on his writing as he revised and cut this text for subsequent editions.

In addition to his own problems in producing a manuscript, Hardy became aware that others also had their deadlines. He had been informed by Tinsley that he had to be "ready with the first monthly part of his story for the magazine soon enough to give an artist time to prepare an illustration for it, and enable it to be printed in the September number, which in the case of this periodical came out on August 15."[5] There is no evidence that Hardy knew who this artist would be.

Most certainly an editor's choice, artist J. A. Pasquier had considerable experience in the world of magazine illustration. He had already illustrated fiction for *Tinsley's Magazine* before he had accepted the commission for Hardy's novel, and he had also published his work in *London Society*, *The Sunday Magazine*, *The Quiver*, and *The Illustrated London News*. In addition Pasquier had contributed drawings to an edition of *Foxe's Book of Martyrs* and, in 1863, had provided the drawings for an illustrated edition of Richardson's *Clarissa*. His technical expertise became clear in his *Picturesque Groups*, a collection of drawings of the human form, to be used as instruction for students of the graphic arts. Tinsley's had thus selected an artist who was not only technically proficient but also very versatile in his ability to capture a wide range of subject matter. Pasquier was more than capable of illustrating the work of this unknown Dorset author.

Hardy was interested enough in the relationship between the artist's illustration and his own concepts that he sent at least two sketches, and possibly more, to be used as guides for the engravings (Plates 1 and 2) that would accompany the September and October installments. Hardy would have sent no more sketches at that particular time, of course, because the rest of the manuscript was as yet unwritten. It may well have been, however, that Hardy sent no more sketches beyond these two.[6] It was never his practice to send sketches for all the projected illustrations of his serialized novels, not even when he was more familiar with the practices and policies of magazine publication, and not even when he had a completed or nearly completed manuscript before the publication of the first installment.

Hardy's interest in the Cornwall setting and the similarity between his fictional heroine Elfride Swancourt and the woman he was courting (Emma Gifford) would have made him initially concerned with the illustrations that would be published with his text. These were the years, too, when he was making many visits to London museums and galleries, and the pictorial aspect of his own art must have been reinforced by these visits. Though it is not certain how much the first two plates rely on the sketches Hardy submitted to *Tinsley's Magazine*, a remarkable resemblance exists between these two views of Elfride Swancourt and the available pictures of the young Miss Gifford. It is highly likely, therefore, that the artist did use Hardy's sketches as the basis for his finished drawings.

Certainly Hardy did not receive the finished illustrations for his approval before they were published with the text, as there was no time for such amenities. Hardy was concerned enough to send sketches so that the illustrator would know how the novelist had visualized his own material, yet he was content to leave the matter of the finished illustrations in the hands of *Tinsley's Magazine* and Pasquier. The pressure of serial writing, the fact that he was not accustomed to the way things were done in the world of magazine publication, and that he did not at this time fully realize the potential impact of illustration may explain why Hardy took no further interest in these illustrations.

In November of 1872, Leslie Stephen, editor of *The Cornhill Magazine*, had written to ask if Hardy had a story available for publication. Hardy replied that, although *A Pair of Blue Eyes* was already spoken for, his next work would be a pastoral tale, and he would be agreeable to submitting it for publication in *Cornhill*. In June and again in September, Hardy sent what he had completed of his new story to Stephen. Contrary to the magazine's general policy of accepting only completed manuscripts, Stephen agreed to publish *Far from the Madding Crowd* when he had read as little as one quarter of what eventually comprised the completed manuscript, "some of it only in rough outline."[7]

Hardy thought he had time in hand to work at his novel, and was therefore surprised to find, in October of 1873, that Stephen intended to publish the first installment in the January number of *Cornhill*. Stephen wrote to ask if Hardy could change his plans to allow for an earlier publication date than the Spring, as had been originally intended. The time was indeed short: "The ms. has to be in our hands some time before in order to allow for illustration. The January number [which would be out in the third week of December] should be in to us for this purpose by the beginning of December."[8] Hardy agreed, believing he could send in the installments as required.

Caught in the pressure of time, as he had been with *A Pair of Blue Eyes*,

Hardy this time showed more interest in the quality of the illustrations—not in terms of the artist's technical proficiency, but in the way the unknown artist would interpret some of the characters and the pastoral details of his story. In an October letter, Hardy expressed "a hope that the rustics, although *quaint*, may be made to appear *intelligent, and not boorish* at all. . . ."[9] Later, Hardy wrote, "in reference to the illustrations, I have sketched in my note-book during the past summer a few correct outlines of smockfrocks, gaiters, sheep-crooks, rick-'straddles', a sheep-washing pool, one of the old-fashioned malt-houses, and some other out-of-the-way things that might have to be shown. These I could send you if they would be of any use to the artist, but if he is a sensitive man and you think he would rather not be interfered with, I would not do so."[10]

Hardy received no reply from Stephen about the sketches and illustrations, and so he thought plans had been changed again, and that his story would not appear as early as January. In late December, when he opened a recently purchased copy of the *Cornhill*, he was surprised to see his story in print, surprised to find that it was the first item to appear in that issue, and was just as surprised to see that it was illustrated. "He had only expected, from the undistinguished rank of the characters in the tale, that it would be put at the end, and possibly without a picture."[11] *Far from the Madding Crowd*, in fact, was to have first place in *Cornhill* in nine out of twelve installments, a lead position which was considered quite complimentary in the world of magazine serialization.

The illustrator was unknown to Hardy until that day when he saw the first installment in print, and was pleased to note that the story had first place with "a striking illustration."[12] (Plate 3) A further surprise to Hardy was the discovery that the illustrator was a woman, Helen Paterson, afterwards Mrs. Helen Allingham.

Helen Paterson was the only female illustrator for the contemporary, serial publication of Hardy's novels, although twentieth century illustrated editions are dominated by noted women artists such as Vivien Gribble, Agnes Miller Parker, and Clare Leighton. In her own day, Miss Paterson was well known as an illustrator to children's books, excelling in poignant facial expressions, but she remained in the shadow of the immensely talented and renowned Kate Greenaway. She had illustrated for the widely circulated *Cassell's Magazine*, as well as *London Society*, and was for many years on the staff of *The Graphic*. In 1876, when *The Graphic* selected notable engravings from their magazine for separate publication, two of her drawings were published in *Graphic Portfolio*.

Miss Paterson had studied at the Birmingham School of Design, and also at Academy schools in 1867 under John Everett Millais. Other teachers included noted illustrators Fred Walker and Frederick Leighton. Shortly after completing her formal training, she found work in the newly launched *Graphic*. Her marriage in 1847 to William Allingham, poet and member of the Rossetti circle, points up the close relationship between the worlds of visual and verbal art in the Victorian era. Allingham's poems (*The Music Master*, 1855), for instance, had been illustrated by Rossetti and Millais; Miss Paterson's teachers had, with Holman Hunt and Rossetti, illustrated the Moxon edition of Tennyson's poems in 1857; Tennyson himself, in later years, was a friend and walking companion of William Allingham.

After her marriage, which occurred near the end of her commission for *Far from the Madding Crowd* (thus accounting for a change of initials on the engravings), Mrs. Allingham did very infrequent book or magazine illustration and turned, instead, to the medium of water-colour. In this field she became noted for the simplicity and charm of her rural scenes until, finally, she received formal recognition by becoming the first woman to achieve full membership in the Royal Watercolor Society in 1890. She then chose the English cottage as her special field, and her several illustrated books on the subject became of some importance in the history of English art. Besides the charm and peace of her rural scenes, she also brought to her treatment of the English cottage a fine accuracy of detail. As one critic commented, "all the little eccentricities of form which give character . . . are faithfully delineated" in her cottage scenes.[13] These details, in her later watercolors as well as in earlier magazine engravings, captured and conveyed a way of life through the medium of graphic art much the same way that Hardy caught and presented a special (and vanishing) way of life through his fiction.

Mrs. Allingham's work received the public notice of two eminent literary figures of her day. Thomas Carlyle remarked that she was the only person who had ever made a successful portrait of him, and in 1875, John Ruskin called her "an accomplished designer of wood-cuts." Though Ruskin believed that serial illustration had only a temporary purpose and thus could not be seriously treated as art, he considered that Mrs. Allignham was successful in making the serial illustration "forever lovely."[14] Later, Ruskin praised her abilities in illustrating English country life.[15]

Hardy had no contact with Helen Allingham for the first few months that *Far from the Madding Crowd* ran in *Cornhill*, and did not have the chance to voice an opinion on the first few illustrations, at least. On January 8, 1874, Leslie Stephen finally wrote, "I hope you approved of the illustration."[16] Hardy's reply in print has not survived, but his unqualified approval of the way Mrs. Allingham handled the pictorial side of his novel is clear enough. At a London dinner in May, Hardy finally met "his skillful illustrator . . . and gave her a few points," as he recounts.[17] By this time, he had completed the manuscript and could have given her information on the remainder of the plot, as well as particulars about the characters. It seems likely that she had used and benefited from the sketches Hardy had mentioned to Stephen, since "smock-frocks, gaiters" and "sheep-crooks" appear either in the vignette initials (Plate 4) or the full-format illustrations (Plate 5), many of them published just previous to the May meeting. It may well be that Hardy had earlier given some explicit directions for the third illustration, the Bible and Key scene (Plate 6), since the situation depicted is based on a local custom that Helen Allingham might not have known.[18] At this point in her career, too, Mrs. Allingham might not have been familiar with the details of country costuming (Dorset-style), and Hardy's early sketches for Leslie Stephen and the details given during the May visit would have been important aids to the artist. For Hardy himself, these small details of local color were central to the way he visualized his own material. Atmosphere, for Hardy, depended on accurate detail.

Hardy's concern with detail was even more evident in a series of sketches he had submitted to Leslie Stephen with his manuscript. Gabriel Oak and one of the rustics, Jan Coggan, were in one chapter described as pursuing what they thought were horse thieves. Oak and Coggan find tracks made by horses, and identify the progress of the "thieves" by the tracks, which indicate "a stiff gallop," "a canter," "a trot," and so forth. Hardy included drawings of the hoofprints with his manuscript to illustrate these different paces—ostensibly to demonstrate visually for the reading audience that such detective work was quite possible. Stephen did not think such an aid was important enough to include with the manuscript in *Cornhill*, and so the sketches were not printed.[19] Though Hardy's inclusion of the hoofprints has a humorous side, his action does reveal that he thought of illustration as a means of clarifying the unfamiliar for its middle-class, genteel reading audience.

Most of the novel's reviewers did not mention the illustrations, but they immediately recognized the pictorial quality within the text itself. These early reviews reveal an interesting choice of metaphor which was to repeat itself, though in lesser degree, in reviews of Hardy's later novels. Whether it be from Hardy's own creation of picture, or from the illustrations that were published with the novel, the language in these reviews reveals the influence of the pictorial. References to "graphic," "sketches," "portraits," often appear, and while this is no surprise, since Victorian criticism of fiction often used this kind of metaphoric language, there is too much of it in the *Far from the Madding Crowd* reviews to be satisfactorily dismissed as mere coincidence. Whatever the cause, the reviews demonstrated that Hardy's contemporaries were acutely aware of his pictorial talents for creating scene and character.

The Times, for instance, noted that in Hardy's characterization of

Bathsheba, "Every stroke tells in the portrait, nor is there one too many or too few."[20] *Scribner's Monthly* simply noted that Hardy's chief distinction was his "peculiarly pictorial way of looking at things. . . ."[21] *Harper's New Monthly* referred to the "pictures" in this story of English rural life, then noted: "But the artist is rather a skillful copyist than an original student of nature. . . . There is a minute attention to detail, too, which is possibly commendable, but which accompanies a singular ignorance of or indifference to the relative importance of the objects in the scenes, which are painted, so to speak, without perspective."[22] The criticism is harsh and unjust, but strikes at an aspect of Hardy the artist that will emerge more clearly in later works. An interest in detail is one of the most notable qualities that marks Hardy's relationship with his illustrators, and reveals his concern with transferring at least one aspect of the pictorial quality of his text to the illustrated scenes published with the story.

Saturday Review gave a more penetrating insight into Hardy's method as pictorialist, not just for individual scenes, but in the novel as a whole. The reviewer first questioned the authenticity of the language which, in turn, led him to question the credibility behind some of the story's events. Yet the reviewer praised the individual scenes as "set-pieces," and admitted they were handled with "unusual skill and care." "Each scene is a study in itself, and, within its own limits, effective. And they all fit into the story like pieces of an elaborate puzzle, making, when they are so fitted in, an effective whole. Mr. Hardy's art consists principally in the way in which he pieces his scenes one with the other."[23] Whether the presence of the Allingham illustrations with the novel's first publication in book form or the inherent pictorial nature of the text itself influenced the reviewer, *Far from the Madding Crowd* established Hardy early in his career as a writer whose stories had much pictorial content.

Hardy was so pleased with Mrs. Allingham's handling of the illustrations for *Far from the Madding Crowd* that he later asked her to illustrate *A Laodicean*, but she had by that time given up illustrating for the magazines. Many years later, Hardy continued his praise in a letter to his friend Edmund Gosse:

The illustrator of *Far from the Madding Crowd* began as a charming young lady, Miss Helen Paterson, and ended as a married woman—charms unknown—wife of Allingham the poet. I have never set eyes on her since she was the former and I met her and corresponded with her about the pictures of the story. She was the best illustrator I ever had. She and I were married about the same time in the progress of our mutual work but not to each other, which I fear rather spoils the information. Though I have never thought of her for the last 20 years your inquiry makes me feel 'quite romantical' about her (as they say here), and as she is a London artist, well known as Mrs. A., you might hunt her up, and tell me what she looks like as an elderly woman. If you do, please give her my kind regards, but you must not add that those two almost simultaneous weddings would have been one but for a stupid blunder of God Almighty.[24]

No doubt Hardy's marital troubles and the passage of time gave him this nostalgic and "romantical" view of Mrs. Allingham by the letter's 1906 date, but he had always been consistent in his praise of her as an illustrator of his work. Certainly he was personally involved with the illustrations for *Far from the Madding Crowd*, not as much as he would be with later novels, but much more so than with the earlier *A Pair of Blue Eyes*. His own contribution was primarily limited to advice on details relating to local color, rather than to a psychological reading of character or to a dramatic handling of events. Yet Hardy's suggestions and offers of his own sketches demonstrate a conscientiousness towards his material and an awareness of audience needs, as well as an understanding of the role detail played in illustration. Hardy's concern for accuracy of detail is also a concern for the realism and credibility of his pastoral tale.

Arrangements for serializing another novel in *Cornhill Magazine* had begun almost immediately after publishing *Far from the Madding Crowd*. Hardy's third illustrated novel, *The Hand of Ethelberta*, is a radical departure from his earlier as well as later works, since it deals with characters and a life style drawn from London society. He had felt almost obligated to try his hand at a society novel because he thought he could not hold his growing audience with rural novels alone, yet he did not feel sure about his own abilities to write such a novel.[25] Certainly he had good reason to doubt his ability to create a society novel, since he was by temperament, background, and his present environment cut off from the very subject matter he wished to present. In spite of these doubts, Hardy went ahead with the novel, desiring to prove he was not limited to the rural novel but could expand his materials into the society world of a Thackeray or Trollope.

The Hand of Ethelberta appeared in *Cornhill Magazine* from July, 1875 through May, 1876, with Hardy struggling to complete the work while the first numbers were being published. *Cornhill* selected George Du Maurier as illustrator, and he contributed a full page illustration and a vignette initial for each of the novel's eleven installments.

Du Maurier has incorrectly been described by Carroll A. Wilson, in his commentary for the Grolier Club Exhibition of Hardy materials, as relatively unknown at the time of the *Ethelberta* illustrations.[26] As a matter of fact, Du Maurier had a considerable reputation by this time, due to his many contributions to serial fiction illustration, as well as his caricatures for *Punch*. He had contributed to *Punch* as early as 1860, and was a member of the regular staff by 1865. He had illustrated Mrs. Gaskell's *Wives and Daughters* for *Cornhill* in 1864–66, and had also illustrated a re-issue of Thackerary's *Henry Esmond* in 1868. During the 1860s, Du Maurier illustrated Mrs. Gaskell's *Cranford* and, at the end of this decade of artistic achievement, he contributed the engravings for Meredith's *The Adventures of Harry Richmond.* By the time he accepted the commission to illustrate Hardy's novel, therefore, he was no unknown artist in the field of fiction illustration. His chief fame, however, rests upon his *Punch* illustrations dealing with the foibles of the upper middle-class drawing room.

Very little communication took place between Hardy and Du Maurier on the strategy of the *Ethelberta* illustrations. Although Hardy was by now familiar with the advantages of effective illustration, he was still content with leaving the matter of dealing with the artist in the hands of his editor. While he had sent sketches to his earlier artists, and had communicated details in person with Helen Paterson Allingham, there is no evidence of Hardy sending rough drawings to Du Maurier, nor, it seems did he discuss the illustrations with his artist in person.[27]

That Hardy and Du Maurier did not, for whatever reason, collaborate closely on the engravings for *The Hand of Ethelberta*, is indicated in a letter from Du Maurier, written several years later, in 1880:

I am very much obliged to you for your kind and flattering letter, and truly glad you are pleased with my illustrations to "The Hand of Ethelberta."

If we were neighbors and I could have consulted you easily, I should have been better able to realize your conceptions, and in many cases I should have asked you by some trifling alteration in the text to help me to a better picture or to a different choice of subject. Such an ideal state of things however as illustrator and illustratee working together is not often to be met with—and I am only too happy to have pleased you.[28]

Though Hardy did praise the Du Maurier illustrations, as the artist himself indicates, *The Hand of Ethelberta* was not a literary success, and Victorian reviewers found fault with the illustrations as well as with the story.

Hardy had shown concern for the graphic depiction of his novels by sending sketches to guide the artists in their work for *A Pair of Blue Eyes* and *Far from the Madding Crowd*, but probably not for *The Hand of Ethelberta*, judging from Du Maurier's remarks. Still, Hardy soon after this wrote to one of his publishers, "I have occasionally supplied . . . sketches to the artists who illustrated my previous stories, with good results."[29] And he was so taken with the value of picture in this early period of his career that, when it came time to publish *A Pair of Blue Eyes* in book format, he suggested that he could supply a photograph of Cornwall that would make a good frontispiece. This, he thought, would gain more interest for his novel.[30] Thus was Hardy aware of the contribution that picture could make to his text.

II
"It is rather ungenerous to criticize; but. . . ."
(1877–1886)

Hardy's involvement with the illustration of his novels changed significantly after *The Hand of Ethelberta* experience, and the change may have been due to the reviewers' criticism of Du Maurier's drawings. Leslie Stephen's guidance in the matter of illustration had proved helpful in the *Far from the Madding Crowd* drawings; it had not proved so in the *Ethelberta* illustrations. With a greater understanding of how to handle deadline pressures in serial publication, Hardy had more time in hand to consider the illustrations that would accompany his work. As a recognized and established author, furthermore, Hardy was in a more confident position to deal with his editors and illustrators.

In 1877, Hardy was at work on the manuscript of *The Return of the Native*, apparently expecting that his story would be accepted by Stephen for publication in *The Cornhill Magazine*. To his surprise, Stephen rejected the unfinished manuscript because, in Hardy's words, "though he liked the opening, he feared that the relations between Eustacia, Wildeve, and Thomasin might develop into something 'dangerous' for a family magazine, and he refused to have anything to do with it unless he could see the whole. This I never sent him, and the matter fell through."[31] Hardy then sent what he had completed of the manuscript to the monthly magazine, *Belgravia*, a Chatto and Windus publication. Hardy himself seems to have been aware that *Belgravia* was distinctly inferior in literary quality to *Cornhill*, as explained in *The Life of Thomas Hardy:* "On November 8, parts 3, 4, and 5 of the story were posted to Messrs. Chatto and Windus for publication in (of all places) *Belgravia*—a monthly magazine then running."[32]

Subtitled "A Magazine of Fashion and Amusement," *Belgravia* was not known for the high quality of its fiction, but was trying to make a reputation for its art work. Editors Mary Elizabeth Braddon and her husband John Maxwell aimed at presenting good art for their middle class reading public. Speaking many years later of the magazine's aims and problems, William Tinsley explained: "Maxwell was fond of drawings in magazines, and if pictures had been as cheap when he and Miss Braddon started 'Belgravia' as they are now it would have been quite an art production." By the turn of the century, magazine illustration did not cost a shilling per inch due to the cost-cutting, new processes of reproduction.

The illustrations for *Belgravia* and other magazines of that period thirty years earlier, however, often cost £2-3 per square inch for drawing and engraving.[33]

Belgravia shared such popular authors as Justin McCarthy, James Payn, Charles Gibbon, and David Christie Murray with other magazines of the day, but also had the distinction of publishing Wilkie Collins, though his *Haunted Hotel*, which ran simultaneously with *The Return of the Native*, is only a mediocre novel. (*Cornhill*, on the other hand, was publishing Thackeray, Trollope, Meredith, and Henry James—ample evidence of its consistently better literary material.) *Belgravia's* interest in quality art, rather than literature, is revealed by its table of contents—there, in contrast to so many other magazines of the day which did *not* list illustrators by name, *Belgravia* not only named its artists but did *not* name its writers. The magazine was proud to announce to its audience that artists such as Fred Barnard, Arthur Hopkins, and R. Caldecott were among the contributors. In order to discover who had written the fiction, however, the reader had to turn to the beginning of the story itself for the author's name. The actual engraved plates of *Belgravia* also show the magazine's concern for art, since each plate has a protective facing page, in the manner of book illustration.

The Return of the Native was published in *Belgravia* from January to December of 1878, with twelve illustrations by Arthur Hopkins. The artist, younger brother of Gerard Manley Hopkins,[34] was a regular illustrator for the magazine and, as Reid in *Illustrators of the Sixties* points out, was "one of the mainstays of Miss Braddon's magazine."[35] Hopkins had studied at Academy schools and at Heatherley's, and was later to become a member of the Royal Watercolour Society. Though he later called magazine illustration "fearful work," even "artistic hack work,"[36] he often contributed to *Punch* and *The Graphic*. In these "society" illustrations, he shows a strong influence of Du Maurier. (George Du Maurier later recommended Hopkins to Hardy as a possible illustrator for *A Laodicean*, but then agreed to illustrate the novel himself.) A staunch admirer of John Everett Millais's work, Hopkins in his own drawing demonstrates a "strong dramatic sense, to which is added a sense of character," as his illustrations for *The Prescotts of Pamphillon* (*Good Words*, 1873) and *Whiteladies* (*Good Words*, 1875) reveal.[37] On the surface of things, Hopkins appeared to be an excellent choice as illustrator for *The Return of the Native*, even though he was not personally selected by Hardy but received the commission by virtue of his position as staff illustrator for *Belgravia*.

When Hardy submitted the story to *Belgravia*, the text was changed considerably from its Ur-version, and there were additional changes for the definitive text of the 1912 Wessex Edition. These changes reveal how much of the conscious artist Hardy had become, and his increasing interest and conscious shaping of his text parallel a concern with how the text was to be illustrated. In some measure, too, these changes help explain Hardy's attitude toward several of the completed drawings.

As John Paterson in *The Making of The Return of the Native*[38] has clarified, the text underwent some remarkable changes, not only in the story's structure, but also in the presentation of character, especially that of Eustacia Vye. The Ur-version reveals the story was to be pastoral, with many of the qualities of the romance ballad, including a demonic figure in the person of Avice (later Eustacia) Vye. The pastoral concept soon gave way to a classical motif, which in turn was somewhat damaged because of magazine publication in *Belgravia*.[39] Both Leslie Stephen and the editors of *Belgravia*, according to Paterson, shared responsibility for changes in plot and structure.[40] The analogy between his story and Greek tragedy, however, appears to have been Hardy's own concept.

Between the Ur-version and the 1912 edition, Eustacia changed from Satanic antagonist to Promethean protagonist, a change that would not have been required by the bowdlerization of the novel's plot and structure. "The truth seems rather to be," according to Paterson, "that in the course of revising the Ur-chapters, Hardy discovered and indulged an unconscious and even reluctant sympathy with the demoniacal creature he had initially conceived."[41] Thus, the change in setting and atmosphere from a narrow, pastoral world to a widened world, filled with classical analogies, also included Eustacia's change from demon to Promethean rebel, in the manner of a Shelleyan or Keatsian romantic hero. In the process, Hardy's sympathies had shifted.

Eustacia's change, however, had still another step—this time, in the kind of romantic rebel Hardy conceived her to be. In the serial version, for instance, her features suggest those of Marie Antoinette and Lord Byron; in later editions, her appearance is compared with Sappho and Mrs. Siddons. In the serial version, her dignity "was the gift of heaven—it was a happy convergence of Natural Laws." In later editions, Hardy qualified the heritage by adding "Perhaps it was the gift of heaven . . . ." Her father's dignity, and a possible link with "Phaeacia's isle" are also added in later editions, but are not present in the serial version. (Her dignity came "from no side passage from Fitzalan and DeVere," states the *Belgravia* passage.) Omitted from the 1912 Wessex Edition is the statement "her chief priest was Byron; her anti-Christ a polemical preacher at Budmouth, of the name of Slatters." The serial version presents Eustacia more in the light of helpless, introspective victim—one who comes close to enjoying her suffering. Later editions, however, present Eustacia as willful rebel, with a cool defiance of circumstances, and much more in control of her emotions. Thus, there is a more adolescent quality in the *Belgravia* Eustacia; she has a more mature, even royal dignity in later editions. The changes are important, of course, because it is the Eustacia of the *Belgravia* edition that Arthur Hopkins illustrated, and not the Eustacia that later readers of the novel were familiar with through the Wessex edition. To a considerable extent, the misunderstanding between Hopkins and Hardy and Hardy's dissatisfaction with some of Hopkins drawings, are due to these changes in the conception of Eustacia. Hardy seems to have the later Eustacia in mind, while Hopkins labored to depict an earlier version.

The Return of the Native marks a clear change in Hardy's relationships with his illustrators. For the first time, he was in frequent correspondence with his artists, and the letters between Hardy and Hopkins reveal that Hardy paid close attention to how the artist interpreted his concepts.

Following his earlier procedure, Hardy sent sketches to the illustrator as a guide for the finished drawing. This very act, however, caused some difficulty between the two men on the matter of Eustacia's presentation. When Hardy saw the first view of Eustacia (Plate 7), he wrote to Hopkins and indicated his disappointment. Hopkins replied:

I am sorry about Eustacia; the more so because the story has been giving me the greatest pleasure, and I had hoped to make something better than usual of the drawings.[42]

Hopkins admitted that the second picture (the plate of Eustacia referred to by Hardy) was not as successful as the illustrations for the first and third installments. This deficiency he blamed himself for, but noted the engraving work itself for Eustacia's drawing was not as well done as for the other two illustrations, then added that otherwise Swain the engraver was doing "capital work" for him lately. The illustrator's difficulties in controlling the quality of his work from original sketch to finished engraving became apparent to Hardy when Hopkins explained:

I have not yet seen the drawing as it appears in the current number, but I feared that it would suffer in the printing, when I saw the proof.

Will you kindly point out the particular points in which I have failed most. Your little sketch does not differ very much from the face I drew, except in the chin.

What it looks like in the number I hardly dare guess.[43]

Hopkins's attitude toward Hardy was deferential, yet he was also strong in his own defense. The novelist, it seems, was being critical of the artist's work when it did not differ so much from Hardy's own drawing and, while Hopkins may have been trying to excuse his work, his comment on the finished engraving served also as a gentle reminder to Hardy that there was another step to the process of illustrating—one where the illustrator, unless he did his own engraving, exercised no control.

In the same letter, Hopkins also commented that he was at work on the April drawing, which was to depict Thomasin Yeobright. Here, he thought, this character would have the benefit, since he admitted his sympathies at this point in the story were with Thomasin. (Hopkins, of course, did not have the whole of the manuscript to work from, though it seems Hardy might have finished it in late Spring of 1878.)[44] Hopkins found that he was not attracted to the character of Eustacia Vye, and this lack of sympathy must surely have hampered his illustration.

In his reply, Hardy expanded his criticism of the Eustacia drawing, and then explained his concept of the plot, together with the disposition of the characters:

It is rather ungenerous to criticise; but since you invite me to do so I will say that I think Eustacia should have been represented as more youthful in face, supple in figure, and, in general, with a little more roundness and softness than have been given her. . . . Perhaps it is well for me to give you the following ideas of the story as a guide—Thomasin, as you have divined, is the good heroine, and she ultimately marries the reddleman, and lives happily. Eustacia is the wayward and erring heroine—She marries Yeobright, the son of Mrs. Yeobright, is unhappy, and dies. The order of importance of the characters is as follows—1 Clym Yeobright 2 Eustacia 3 Thomasin and the reddleman 4 Wildeve and 5 Mrs. Yeobright.

Hardy also explained, possibly to sooth Hopkins's feelings, that he had liked the first illustration, thought the third plate (which he had not yet seen) sounded good, and "I myself thought Thomasin in the apple-loft would be the best illustration for the fourth number."[45] Hopkins thanked Hardy for his reply and his "kind offer to help me on the sketches" and then promised "to improve on Eustacia next time she makes her appearance."[46] Later, Hardy complimented Hopkins on the illustration of Eustacia (Plate 8) which appeared in the August number of *Belgravia:* "I think Eustacia is charming—she is certainly just what I imagined her to be, and the rebelliousness of her nature is precisely caught in your drawing."[47] The arrangement of the three figures also struck Hardy as very effective.

Hardy had also expected to see Eustacia included in a scene with the other of the Heath's Mummers (Plate 9), and had sent a sketch to Hopkins depicting the sort of costume she would wear. Hopkins, however, exercised his perogative as illustrator and decided not to include Eustacia in the scene, presumably because of the difficulty of identification. The magazine audience, for instance, would have to be able to identify her, but since the Egdon natives do not perceive her femininity, let alone her specific identity, the situation for the artist would be most difficult.

The kind of detail Hardy gave Hopkins as a guide in the illustration becomes evident in Hopkins's letter:

> I am now at work on the May drawing. I have chosen the incident in the party scene where Grandfer Cantle asks to be looked over with the view of finding an improvement in his personal appearance.
>
> I avoided introducing Eustacia as in consequence of her disguise I believe it would be unwise.
>
> But there is room on one side to introduce a Mummer or two among the group. The Mumming costume you sketched I presume was Eustacia's. Would not some of the less important of these have a less complete costume. I thought one might have no more than his best smock adorned with many ribbons, a plume and a sword.
>
> But I will wait to finish the drawing til I hear from you.[48]

Hardy agreed with Hopkins's decision not to include Eustacia, and sent the artist some sketches of a Mummer's smock and ribbons, as well as the staff or spear carried by the player. (These details were included in Hopkins's illustration.) After giving these details, Hardy wrote Hopkins that he ought not to be "at all hampered by my suggestions"[49]

Hardy's willingness to leave final decisions to Hopkins becomes evident in his remarks about the depiction of Clym Yeobright: "I should prefer to leave Clym's face entirely to you. A thoughtful young man of 25 is all that can be shown, as the particulars of his appearance given in the story are too minute to be represented in a small drawing."[50] Hopkins wrote that the May drawing (Plate 9 with Grandfer Cantle and the Mummers) "introduced Clym conspicuously,—I can only hope you will like him."[51]

Thus, although Hardy had outlined the order of importance for his characters, and had placed Clym in first position, he was much more interested in the depiction of Eustacia, content to leave Clym in the hands of the artist. As far as the other characters and scenes of the novel were concerned, Hardy was aware of potential problems in their illustration, but left the difficulties in Hopkins's hands, admitting, however, that "the scenes are somewhat outlandish, and may be unduly troublesome to you."[52] His offer of sketches was made, as he explained, because of the difficulties inherent in some of his scenes. His attitude toward several of these scenes, however, emphasizes his considerable effort to insure that the illustrator would do justice to his own conception of his "Queen of the Night."

In addition to the specifics of the various illustrations for *The Return of the Native*, Hopkins and Hardy also corresponded on the business of serial illustration in general, and on the relationships that ought to exist between artist and novelist. Hardy had briefly expressed a wish for better communication between the two, and Hopkins had replied:

I quite agree with you about the desirability of the artist and author being in constant communication—or still better, personal intercourse. The thing might be well and thoroughly done then, which is not the case in practice.

The novel of the day is, practically, not illustrated but embellished with a dozen drawings having some sort of connection with the story.

However, I do not suppose that I shall improve all this; under the circumstances it is inevitable.

But I do hope in the case of the 'Return of the Native' to supply some drawings of a strength and character in keeping with the strength and character of the story.

Although I believe that nobody but the author himself could really *illustrate* a story (since no two people ever picture a described scene alike) still I think that some drawings certainly form an additional attraction to the public; and I can remember several cases where the story was much more vividly imprinted in my mind and fancy and stamped in my memory, by its illustrations.[53]

In referring to "the desirability of the artist and author being in constant communication," Hopkins had first written *necessity*, but then crossed it out and substituted *desirability*, an indication that he had second thoughts about the limitations he had placed on the artist's freedom of interpretation and basic ability. Though Hopkins was against "embellishment" and firmly believed in graphic fidelity, he also believed in the artist's freedom to make judgments, to illustrate as he saw fit—in terms of what *could* be done in a scene, and also what *ought* to be done, given the elements of the story itself, as demonstrated in his unwillingness to make Eustacia a major figure among the Mummers in the May illustration. Yet Hopkins was astute enough to realize how much of an aid the novelist could be in creating illustrations that would do justice to the story—a matter of illustration being faithful to the details of the text, in contrast to illustration serving to embellish the text with the artist's personal interpretation.

Hardy had already understood the contribution that illustration could make in the clarification of his text; now Hopkins had pointed out that illustration could also *intensify* certain scenes in the story and make them memorable beyond what the text could normally do. An understanding of both these roles seems behind Hardy's later contribution of a Wessex map for the book publication of *The Return of the Native*, even though Hardy characteristically reveals diffidence and understatement as he explains his motives to the publishers, Smith-Elder:

I enclose . . . a sketch of the supposed scene in which "The Return of the Native" is laid copied from the one I used in writing the story and my suggestion is that we place an engraving of it as frontispiece to the first volume. . . . I am of opinion that it would be a desirable novelty, likely to increase a reader's interest. I may add that a critic once remarked to me that nothing could give such reality to a tale as a map of this sort: and I myself have often felt the same thing.[54]

Hardy's suggestion was followed, and thus Hardy's own map of the Wessex locale was included. The Hopkins graphics, however, were not reproduced when the novel was published.

Hardy's interest in authenticity of detail continued into the illustration for his next novel, *The Trumpet Major*. Throughout his life, he had been fascinated by the Napoleonic era, particularly in the threatened French invasion of England's Dorset coastline. As a child he had heard of the Dorset Militia's preparation for the invasion, and he was proud of his own ancestor Thomas Hardy's involvement with the Battle of Trafalgar. Numerous poems, especially *The Dynasts*, as well as several short stories, reflect this interest. *The Trumpet Major* is Hardy's longest fictional excursion into this historical period.

Very little information exists on the background of the novel's composition. There is evidence that it was outlined for *Cornhill's* editor Leslie Stephen in February of 1879, and that *Macmillan's Magazine* was interested, but the serial was finally published in *Good Words* from January through December of 1880. Publisher William Isbister and editor Donald Macleod were quite pleased with the manuscript Hardy submitted, as Macleod wrote to Hardy on August 22, 1879: "Isbister speaks in glowing terms of what he has read. . . . Isbister says that that you have quite hit our target!" The praise proved to be somewhat misleading, as Hardy later had to change a few minor details, including the language of his soldiers and sailors, to conform to the religious tone of *Good Words*. Macleod closed his letter to Hardy by sharing his concern with the art work that would accompany the story. "But what of the illustrations? Have you . . . heard of any artist likely to succeed?" After referring to the ever present problem of "hasty block-cutting," a problem that plagued *Good Words*, Macleod urged Hardy to have his illustrator begin work on the sketches as soon as possible.[55]

Hardy was therefore in full charge of selecting the artist he wanted for illustrating *The Trumpet Major*. John Collier accepted the commission when it was offered by Hardy, explaining, "I should like very much to illustrate a story of yours."[56] Collier was a graduate of Eton and Heidelberg, and had studied art in Munich, Paris, and at the Slade Institute in London. Later, he gained fame as a portrait painter and became a member of the Royal Academy. He worked briefly with Alma-Tadema, though he was not actually a student of the great painter, and learned much from Sir John Everett Millais, "who used to look at and criticize his work as well as admitting the student to his own studio while he was painting."[57]

In addition to his work in portraits, Collier also became a skillful painter of dramatic historical and domestic scenes, as witnessed by a collection of his paintings reproduced in *The Art Annual* of 1914. In both portraits and dramatic scenes, Collier was known for accuracy of detail. This skill was also present in his earlier career as magazine illustrator, and was sufficient reason why Hardy had thought Collier to be the right man for the commission. *The Trumpet Major* was to require great attention to detail; concerned over the kind of illustration required by this period novel, Hardy had apparently expressed the problem to his artist. Collier promised in his reply that he would "certainly spare no pains" to be accurate "in the costumes and accessories—indeed I hate inaccuracy."[58]

As he had for his earlier novels, Hardy sent Collier sketches to aid in the handling of detail. Collier wrote again to thank Hardy for the drawings:

They are just what I want the interior of the old kitchen [Plate 10] being especially serviceable to me—I shall very likely adapt your arrangement with only a little compression. I haven't heard anything from Isbister about making a sketch of the Trumpet Major to serve as an advertisement but I will make one anyway as it will always serve to introduce into the text—

From what source did you get the costume? Pollack's uncle appears to be unable to get us into the U. S. [United Service] Museum. If you like we could try to force an entrance for ourselves.[59]

It is not clear whether Hardy was ever able to gain entrance to the United Service Museum, but he did travel elsewhere to gather information for his novel. His concern for historical accuracy in the illustrations, as well as in his own textual description, is revealed in his British Museum Notebook, entitled "Notes Taken for 'Trumpet Major' and other works of time of Geo III in (1878–79)".[60] Most of the notebook's entries deal with references to George III's several appearances at Weymouth, or are anecdotes, particularly from the years 1804–05, instructions for military parades, and similar jottings that became either events or descriptive details in *The Trumpet Major*. Quite often Hardy made comments on the dress of that day: "Summer dress, 1804—muslin frock—shawls of crimson muslin."[61] His information on incidents and costuming came from such sources as the *Morning Post* and the *Lady's Magazine*, as well as from military sources. The notebook contains sketches for military uniforms, as well as rough drawings of female coiffures, styles of bonnets, references to walking dresses, complete with a sketch of the sort of neckline that type of dress would have. These references to costumes were no more than perfunctory—an example of a methodical man seeking out accurate material for his own textual description and for the illustrations that would accompany the serial. These small details of dress do appear in many of the Collier illustrations, and it is thus clear that Hardy worked closely with his artist on the matter of periodic details of dress—both fashionable and military. Again, Hardy's involvement was limited to the matters of accuracy and clarification—both highly important, however, in the re-creation of the novel's historic setting.

Hardy's next novel, *A Laodicean*, was accepted for publication by *Harper's New Monthly Magazine*, which was just beginning its European edition. Hardy's serial was chosen to appear in its opening number, and he was aware that *Harper's* European success "depended largely upon the serial tale."[62] For the last five months of the novel's composition, however, Hardy had to dictate from his bed, where he had been confined because of internal bleeding. The pressure on Hardy in this situation was intense, since he felt obligated to complete the novel. In spite of pressure and illness, Hardy was able to finish the novel according to contract. *A Laodicean* appeared from December 1880 to December 1881, with George Du Maurier supplying an illustration for each of the thirteen installments.

In his preliminary arrangements with *Harper's*, however, Hardy had not yet decided on his illustrator, nor if the story was even to have illustrations. This last question was to be decided by the editors, and Hardy was ready to assist. As he wrote to Harper's, "I may add that should you choose to illustrate the story I would furnish the artist with hints, rough sketches, etc., precisely as I should do for an English magazine."[63] In May of 1880, *Harper's* wrote to Hardy and explained the procedures and requirements of the magazine:

We should like a large and a small illustration for each part. Can you have them made for us (at our expense, of course) by a first class artist and engravers? We are anxious that the engravings should be better than the usual work of this kind in the English Magazines, and as good as those in W. Black's "White Wings." They ought to be done in England, so as to be under your eye, and so that the literary and artistic features may thoroughly correspond.

In addition, *Harper's* stipulated "that we shall receive here the copy and electrotypes of the woodcuts of the first part by Oct. 1, 1880, and that the same priority at least be maintained during the progress of the story."[64]

With *Harper's* requirements in hand, Hardy then set about to find an illustrator for *A Laodicean*. On June 5, Helen Peterson Allingham wrote to decline Hardy's "flattering invitation" to illustrate his new book because she had "entirely given up book illustration."[65] On June 7 of 1880, artist Frank Dicksen also declined because his commitment to other work did not permit him to take on the pressures of magazine illustration.[66] On June 9, Du Maurier tentatively agreed to illustrate his second Hardy novel, subject to some qualification:

I have received your note and in reply would say first that I should be very glad to illustrate your tale myself if it is of a kind my style of drawing is likely to suit, and the first instalments could be got ready for illustration soon, so that I might not have to do the drawings for them during the autumn holiday—my price would be 20 guineas for each drawing.

A perplexing sight.

PLATE 1. *A Pair of Blue Eyes*. J. A. Pasquier. *Tinsley's Magazine*. September, 1872.

On the cliffs.

PLATE 2. *A Pair of Blue Eyes.* J. A. Pasquier. *Tinsley's Magazine.* October, 1872.

Hands were loosening his neckerchief.

PLATE 3. *Far from the Madding Crowd.* Helen Paterson Allingham. *The Cornhill Magazine.* January, 1874.

THE
CORNHILL MAGAZINE.

MAY, 1874.

Far from the Madding Crowd.

CHAPTER XXI.

TROUBLES IN THE FOLD: A MESSAGE.

ABRIEL OAK had ceased to feed the Weatherbury flock for about four-and-twenty hours, when on Sunday afternoon the elderly gentlemen, Joseph Poorgrass, Matthew Moon, Fray, and half-a-dozen others came running up to the house of the mistress of the Upper Farm.

"Whatever *is* the matter, men?" she said, meeting them at the door just as she was on the point of coming out on her way to church, and ceasing in a moment from the close compression of her two red lips, with which she had accompanied the exertion of pulling on a tight glove.

"Sixty!" said Joseph Poorgrass.

Vignette initial.

PLATE 4. *Far from the Madding Crowd.* Helen Paterson Allingham. *The Cornhill Magazine.* May, 1874.

"*Do you happen to want a shepherd, Ma'am?*"

PLATE 5. *Far from the Madding Crowd.* Helen Paterson Allingham. *The Cornhill Magazine.* February, 1874.

"Get the front door key." Liddy fetched it.

PLATE 6. *Far from the Madding Crowd.* Helen Paterson Allingham. *The Cornhill Magazine.* March, 1874.

She lifted her left hand.

PLATE 7. *The Return of the Native.* Arthur Hopkins. *Belgravia.* February, 1878.

Unconscious of her presence, he still went on singing.

PLATE 8. *The Return of the Native.* Arthur Hopkins. *Belgravia.* August, 1878.

"If there's any difference, grandfer is younger."

PLATE 9. *The Return of the Native.* Arthur Hopkins. *Belgravia.* May, 1878.

"Welcome, Master Derriman."

PLATE 10. *The Trumpet-Major*. John Collier. *Good Words*. February, 1880.

"But, my dear lady, you promised."

PLATE 11. *A Laodicean.* George Du Maurier. *Harper's New Monthly Magazine.* December, 1880.

"Fine old screen, sir!"

PLATE 12. *A Laodicean*. George Du Maurier. *Harper's New Monthly Magazine*. January, 1881.

"What an escape," he said.

PLATE 13. *A Laodicean.* George Du Maurier. *Harper's New Monthly Magazine.*
February, 1881.

There stood her mother, amid the group of children, hanging over the washing tub.

PLATE 14. *Tess of the D'Urbervilles.* Hubert Herkomer. *The Graphic.* July 4, 1891.

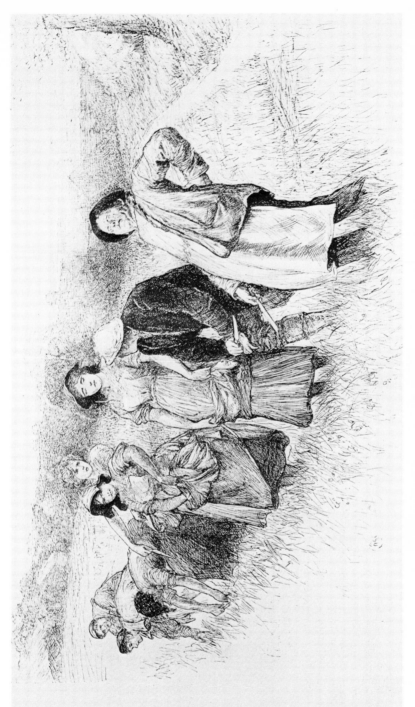

"This here stooping do fairly make my back open and shut," exclaimed the dairyman.

PLATE 15. *Tess of the D'Urbervilles.* Hubert Herkomer. *The Graphic.* August 29, 1891.

Jude at the milestone.

PLATE 16. *Jude the Obscure.* William Hatherell. *Harper's New Monthly Magazine.* November, 1895.

Elfride's freak on Endelstow Tower.

PLATE 17. *A Pair of Blue Eyes.* J. A. Pasquier. *Tinsley's Magazine.* January, 1873.

A scene in the Belvedere.

PLATE 18. *A Pair of Blue Eyes*. J. A. Pasquier. *Tinsley's Magazine*. March, 1873.

Elfride's attempt to help Knight.

PLATE 19. *A Pair of Blue Eyes.* J. A. Pasquier. *Tinsley's Magazine.* February, 1873.

She stood up in the window-opening, facing the men.

PLATE 20. *Far from the Madding Crowd.* Helen Paterson Allingham. *The Cornhill Magazine.*
May, 1874.

Her tears fell fast beside the unconscious pair.

PLATE 21. *Far from the Madding Crowd.* Helen Paterson Allingham. *The Cornhill Magazine.*
October, 1874.

She opened a gate within which was a haystack, under this she sat down.

PLATE 22. *Far from the Madding Crowd.* Helen Paterson Allingham. *The Cornhill Magazine.* September, 1874.

Bathsheba flung her hands to her face.

PLATE 23. *Far from the Madding Crowd.* Helen Paterson Allingham. *The Cornhill Magazine.* July, 1874.

"I feel—almost too much—to think," he said.

PLATE 24. *Far from the Madding Crowd.* Helen Paterson Allingham. *The Cornhill Magazine.* April, 1874.

"There's not a soul in my house but me to-night."

PLATE 25. *Far from the Madding Crowd.* Helen Paterson Allingham. *The Cornhill Magazine.* August, 1874.

She took up her position as directed.

PLATE 26. *Far from the Madding Crowd.* Helen Paterson Allingham. *The Cornhill Magazine.* June, 1874.

THE
CORNHILL MAGAZINE.

APRIL, 1874.

Far from the Madding Crowd.

CHAPTER XV.

A MORNING MEETING: THE LETTER AGAIN.

THE scarlet and orange light outside the malthouse did not penetrate to its interior, which was, as usual, lighted by a rival glow of similar hue, radiating from the hearth.

The maltster, after having lain down in his clothes for a few hours, was now sitting beside a three-legged table, breakfasting off bread and bacon. This was eaten on the plateless system, which is performed by placing a slice of bread upon the table, the meat flat upon the bread, a mustard plaster upon the meat, and a pinch of salt upon the whole, then cutting them vertically downwards with a large pocket-knife till wood is reached, when the severed lump is impaled on the knife, elevated, and sent the proper way of food. The maltster's lack of teeth appeared not to sensibly diminish his powers as a mill. He had

19.

Vignette initial.

PLATE 27. *Far from the Madding Crowd.* Helen Paterson Allingham. *The Cornhill Magazine.* April, 1874.

He brought the tray to the front of the couch.

PLATE 28. *The Return of the Native*. Arthur Hopkins. *Belgravia*. October, 1878.

Something was wrong with her foot.

PLATE 29. *The Return of the Native.* Arthur Hopkins. *Belgravia.* September, 1878.

All that remained of the desperate and unfortunate Eustacia.

PLATE 30. *The Return of the Native.* Arthur Hopkins. *Belgravia.* December, 1878.

The stakes were won by Wildeve.

PLATE 31. *The Return of the Native.* Arthur Hopkins. *Belgravia.* July, 1878.

"Did'st ever know a man that no woman would marry?"

PLATE 32. *The Return of the Native.* Arthur Hopkins. *Belgravia.* January, 1878.

Du Maurier then suggested other artists who might be available for the commission in case he himself would not be able to accept. "If on the other hand you would like *me* to illustrate it, it would be I think wise that we should meet and talk at once; in which case will you come and lunch with me here?"[67]

It is clear from the dates of the correspondence that Hardy was losing no time in arranging for the illustration of his novel. On June 11, he wrote again to *Harper's:*

I have been making inquiries on the subject of illustrating the story, to learn if I could undertake the supervision of the same, and be ready at the time you fix. I find it will be possible to do so, and I therefore agree to the arrangements detailed in your letter of May 24, though perhaps you will allow your agent to assist me a little in keeping the engravers and electrotypers up to time should you wish this part of the illustrating done in England after what I have to say.

As I felt, with you, that it would be important that the English edition should start with every possible advantage in the way of an artist, I applied to Mr. George Du Maurier (who has often told me he would like to illustrate another story of mine) and who, as you are aware, is by far the most popular illustrator here— especially since he has achieved such wide celebrity by his "English Society at home" sketches reprinted from *Punch.* He agrees to do the drawings, provided I can instruct him soon for the early ones, so as not to interfere with the holidays: in which I see no difficulty. His price would be twenty guineas for each larger drawing, and ten guineas for each small one half the size.

There are of course men who would execute them on lower terms. But it would I think be desirable to engage him, even if we have only one drawing a month instead of two—since apart from the merit of his drawing, his name would carry a great deal of weight in placards or advertisements of the new edition of the magazine and would help greatly to attract attention here.

Hardy's handling of the business arrangment, as well as his comment on the weight of Du Maurier's name, indicates his coming of age in the business of magazine publication. His full understanding of the procedure followed by the illustrator is indicated in the letter's continuation, as he discussed Du Maurier's perferences:

His plan of working is not by drawing on the wood, but by finishing his drawing in ink on cartridge paper, to a larger size than is required for the engraving: this is afterwards photographed on the wood (a matter of a few shilling's cost) and cut in the ordinary way. All his *Cornhill* and *Punch* drawings are done in this way. In discussing the subject with him yesterday he says that in the event of his doing the work he should much prefer to send you his original drawings on the paper and let you photograph and engrave them. He adds that your engravers work so much more carefully than ours that he could finish the drawings in better style if he knew they were to be cut in America and thinks it would be a pity to lose the advantage.

In this case it would I suppose be necessary to deliver up the drawings to your agent here a fortnight or three weeks sooner each month than will be necessary for the ms.

If however you still wish the engraving to be done here I will see to it, and put your agent into communication with the engravers.[68]

All these matters concerning Du Maurier were spelled out before the artist officially agreed to become the illustrator. The engravings, however, were eventually done in England by the House of Swain, and not in America as Du Maurier had asked. (No vignette initials or small engravings were used; instead, Du Maurier contributed thirteen full size engravings.)

On June 23, Du Maurier wrote to Hardy, this time to express his pleasure at becoming the illustrator for *A Laodicean*, and to invite Hardy again to lunch. Thus began a close collaboration between novelist and illustrator. The amount of surviving correspondence suggests it was the closest collaboration Hardy was to have with any of his illustrators. The very fact of this collaboration, however, was to lead to some problems, at least from Du Maurier's point of view. Writing to thank Hardy for his compliments on the earlier *Hand of Ethelberta* drawings, Du Maurier had expressed a wish for the "ideal state' of things—that there could be a close collaboration between novelist and illustrator. When such a relationship actually occurred in the work on *A Laodicean's* drawings, however Du Maurier complained to Harper's London Agent, R. R. Bowker.

Bowker seemed pleased with Du Maurier's work, at first. Writing in his journal on July 30, 1880, Bowker explained what he had learned of Du Maurier's techniques:

Saw some drawings of Du Maurier's at the engraver's. Hardy had told us he knew nothing of dress, but left that to his wife, who drapes all his models. This would surprise those who see his strength at toilettes. The children of his pictures are his own children. He *does* notice faces and is fond of bric-a-brac. I find he draws altogether in pen and ink, having the sight of but one eye, his engraver tells me, so that he cannot use a brush, scarcely seeing accurately where its point touches the paper.[69]

On December 10, Bowker again visited Du Maurier:

I finally told him out and out that we were disappointed in his drawings for the Hardy story . . . whereupon he rather owned up that he was better at working his own will in social satire than under the limitations of other people's stories—though his Thackeray illustrations are among his best work. He said Hardy came up and gave him the points minutely and of course he felt constrained within these limits.[70]

A few weeks later, as E. McClung Fleming recounts in his biography of

Bowker, the agent for Harper's again criticized the artist's work. "Du Maurier admitted the justice of these and agreed to make the corrections, on another occasion charging Bowker with having a 'microscopic eye.' English artists were not accustomed to the American magazine art editor who often made critical suggestions which artists were glad to accept."[71]

The Du Maurier-Hardy relationship, however, does not appear to be as Du Maurier himself described it—one where Hardy "gave him the points minutely." The implication from Du Maurier here is that Hardy pressured him. The correspondence between the two men reveals that Du Maurier asked for aid on the illustrations, received considerable advice from Hardy, some of which was undoubtedly unsolicited, but had almost complete freedom with the drawings during the period of Hardy's illness—a period of time extending from October 23, 1880 to April, 1881. The manuscript of *A Laodicean* was finished on May 1, 1881. As a rough estimate, Du Maurier was without Hardy's "minute points" for half the drawings for *A Laodicean*.

The sequence of events clarifies the amount and kind of collaboration between novelist and illustrator. Hardy sent Du Maurier two sketches, to be used as a guide for the first two installments, together with the suggestion that he should call on Du Maurier "with the MS in my hand, read it over to you, & finish our talk about the first picture."[72] By July 12 (only one month since Du Maurier had accepted the commission), he had all but finished the illustrations (Plates 11 and 12) for the first two installments, and wrote to inform Hardy of this:

I should like to meet Mr. Harper—at the same time I am very anxious that you should see the two first drawings before they are finished—would it be possible for Mr. Harper and yourself to lunch *here*, either Wednesday, Thursday, or Friday? instead of my dining with you?—I leave here on Monday next and am very anxious to get the two drawings into the engraver's hands before I go. I have adopted your composition of figures for #2 and should like you much to see it before the faces are put in; your sketch of furniture etc. is most useful to me—I should prefer Wednesday to Thursday and Thursday to Friday, on account of these same drawings—the sooner you see them the better.

. . . .

I have made two compositions (for No. II) of the luncheon party, from opposite points of view, still keeping to your distribution of the figures. I am particularly anxious that you should see them before selecting one for illustration—Tomorrow would suit me equally, if you can bring Mr. Harper to lunch here—.[73]

Du Maurier's anxiety stems from a desire to clear things with Hardy as well as an eagerness to finish the first two drawings so that he could go on vacation—though his plans to leave seem to have been changed.

Hardy, Du Maurier, and Harper met for lunch at New Grove House,

Du Maurier's home, on July 21, 1880, in order to discuss the illustrations for *A Laodicean*. On July 28, Du Maurier again wrote to Hardy, asking him to look at the illustrations (Plates 35 and 36) for the first two installments before they were sent to the engraver. Thus, it seems that Hardy had criticized them on his first viewing, and Du Maurier had to change the drawings—not so much for the faces, but for the composition of the figures.

A short time later, Du Maurier again asked Hardy to lunch for the purpose of conferring over the illustrations, and then explained his problem:

No. 3, so rich in other ways, is poor in subjects for your poor artist. There are only 3—Somerset putting Paula's finger into the moulding—only two figures— Somerset and Paula hand in hand after their escape from the train—two figures again! and finally, the carriage near the tunnel, with the three ladies, and Somerset standing by—a drawing to fill a page, but not a dramatic incident.
    If I had your photo, or drawing of a ruined chapel, or knew where to get one, the first would be I think the best subject.[74]

A photo was sent, but if it were that of a ruined chapel, it must not have served, since this was not the subject of illustration for the third install- ment. (Du Maurier's second choice was the scene actually illustrated. Plate 13) Du Maurier again wrote to Hardy, reminding him of the problems of the illustrator:

Many thanks for the photograph—but I have done, as well as I could, the scene by the [tunnel] . . . Think of the poor artist, please, and give me a scene in every number if you can. When you have a notion for a picture, & feel inclined to move, come & lunch with me—we will talk of the next illustrations & after luncheon I will paint your portrait.[75]

Leonée Ormond's biography *George Du Maurier* describes Hardy as being overly concerned with the business of illustration, and that he had sent the artist a photograph as a guide to the landscape because he felt that "Du Maurier's illustrations were too vague and generalized for his precise topographical descriptions."[76] Yet it was Du Maurier who several times asked for aid in his drawings. His uncertainty about these first illustrations may have been caused by Hardy's comments, but the correspondence reveals Du Maurier was uncertain before Hardy had seen the illustrations. When Hardy had to take to his bed in October, Du Maurier had very much of a free hand with the illustrations. Since the last six or seven drawings in the series are much more in Du Maurier's usual style, and are considerably more lively than the first illustrations, it appears that the artist was indeed bothered by Hardy's directives—or even potential criticism. Hardy had become a stickler for detail, as his concern for the illustrations to his earlier novels reveals. Yet Du Maurier's request for aid in the illustrations indicates that the collaboration was not so restrictive as the artist later claimed.

Du Maurier's comments on Hardy's interference did not damage the relationship between novelist and illustrator, however, since Du Maurier later spoke of Mr. Hardy as his close friend, and seemed to have fond memories of his time as Hardy's illustrator.[77] And, at least for the first few illustrations, Du Maurier's wish for a close working relationship between artist and writer had come true. His belief that close collaboration could be an "ideal state," however, was not to become true, at least not in the illustrating of *A Laodicean*. What the close collaboration between Hardy and Du Maurier does show, however, is—at least for the first few illustrations of the series—Hardy's greater understanding of the technical and business side of illustration, as well as a new concern with the composition of some of the early plates. Unfortunately, Hardy's illness interfered with collaboration between writer and illustrator. And it is even more unfortunate because it was just at this point that Hardy seems to have been on the verge of taking a much more active role in the illustrating of his novels.

Hardy's next illustrated novel represents a significant departure from the earlier serials, since he wrote the entire manuscript of *The Mayor of Casterbridge* before the first installment was ever published, and thus avoided the pressures that deadlines had placed on his earlier works. Hardy was working on the novel as early as the Spring of 1884, and had finished most of the story before the end of that year. *The Mayor of Casterbridge* was not published in *The Graphic* until January of 1886, so Hardy had sufficient time to improve the text.

Even though Hardy was not bothered by deadlines with this novel, he was still disturbed by the business of serial publication. As he wrote on his distress in *Life*:

It was a story which Hardy fancied he had damaged more recklessly as an artistic whole, in the interest of the newspaper in which it appeared serially, than perhaps any other of his novels, his aiming to get an incident into almost every week's part causing him in his own judgment to add events to the narrative somewhat too freely. However, as at this time he called his novelwriting 'mere journeywork' he cared little about it as art, though it must be said in favour of the plot, as he admitted later, that it was quite coherent and organic, in spite of its complication.[78]

The text underwent significant revision when it was published in novel form and, as will be noted later, these revisions affected some of the illustrated material.

Hardy had the advantage of earlier dealings with *The Graphic*, one of the finest illustrated magazines in the later Victorian period. His first publication in that magazine was "The Romantic Adventures of a Milkmaid," appearing in June of 1883. Owing to his past dealings with *The Graphic*, as well as his growing reputation, there seems to have been little difficulty in placing the manuscript for publication. Hardy had been in early communication with editor Arthur Locker and, as early as October of 1885, the story was in proofs, and instructions had been given to the artist. As Locker wrote to Hardy:

I find that a complete set of proofs have already been sent to Harper by us, and they were also told that there was *an illustration* for *every three slips*—This appears to have been the instruction given to Barnes the artist, and will make twenty illustrations in all. I would have preferred an illustration to every two chapters, but I suppose Mr. Thomas (our manager) arranged it—.[79]

Robert Barnes was a staff illustrator for *The Graphic*, and it was customary for that magazine to have its own men do the illustrations for serialized fiction. Thus, Hardy did not choose his own artist, as he had done for the last two novels. The feeling that neither Collier nor Du Maurier had been satisfactory must have made Hardy somewhat content in letting Locker arrange for the "right" illustrator—particularly since Locker was able to read the entire manuscript and thus knew the spirit of the story, as well as its more immediate visual demands, before choosing an illustrator.

Unfortunately, Barnes seems to have become one of the forgotten illustrators of the Victorian era. Extremely little account of him can be had from the standard histories of illustration. When he does receive mention, his drawings for *The Mayor of Casterbridge* are often overlooked. In his *Illustrators of the Sixties*, Forrest Reid concludes that the illustrator lacked imagination and consistently demonstrated a preference for a somewhat bovine type of beauty in his female characters:

If ever human beings sprang straight from English soil they are the men and women, the boys and girls, drawn by Robert Barnes. But these men and women and boys and girls are so limited in type that they might nearly all be members of a single family—a family of the well-to-do farming class, healthy, sturdy, producing no disquieting variations from the sound yeomen stock that has reached back from generation to generation. Barnes would have been the right man to illustrate George Eliot's earlier novels, he would have been the wrong man to illustrate the novels of Mr. Hardy.[80]

Surprisingly enough, Reid thus seems unaware that Barnes had illustrated *The Mayor of Casterbridge*, but then mentions that the artist had supplied excellent drawings for the "semi-bucolic serials in *Good Words* and *The Sunday Magazine*." Barnes did not often have the chance to illustrate novels where strong, dramatic creation was required but, as Reid explains, when he did have the chance, he rose to the occasion. Such was the case in his illustrations for Charles Reade's *Put Yourself in His Place*, published in *Cornhill Magazine* in 1869. Here Barnes's drawings are "bold, strong, and very much alive."[81] In his drawings for *The Mayor of Casterbridge*, Barnes delineated character with considerable skill, and he was also able to come to grips with the dramatic situation, though his achievement seems largely unrecognized.

Though the illustrations for *The Mayor of Casterbridge* are among the finest of the drawings for Hardy's novels, the author himself had little to do with them—certainly far less than he had to do with the making of the plates for *The Return of the Native*, *The Trumpet Major*, and *A Laodicean*. There is no evidence that Hardy recognized the exceptional quality of the *Casterbridge* illustrations, but if he had contrasted their excellence with the generally mediocre quality of some of the earlier illustrations, where he had more actively participated, the contrast must have given him pause for thought.

III
"Allow me to express my sincere admiration"
(1887–1896)

After *The Mayor of Casterbridge* and for the remaining three serialized novels, Hardy demonstrated no active interest in the business of illustration. He remained interested in what his artists had to say in their visual interpretations of his works, but other concerns now usurped the position that illustration had previously held for him. The lack of direct participation might have been due to the after effects of his illness during the writing of *A Laodicean*, or to disappointment with the Du Maurier illustrations, or to the tedious details of working so closely with the artist, as he had done with the early drawings for *A Laodicean*.

At the same time, Hardy had become interested in other matters, most notably the expression of his view of "the universal scheme of things." The novels themselves show some signs of this change. After the mid-1880s, and though the novels still have a marked visual quality, they show a shift in emphasis from precision of physical detail, which had characterized the earlier works, to a more panoramic and even symbolic view of nature, and to the substitution of ideas for image in the conceptualization of his vision. One final and quite practical reason for his declining involvement in the preparation of the later novels' illustrations was that both *The Mayor of Casterbridge* and *Tess of the D'Urbervilles* were published in *The Graphic*. Artists who were on the staff on *The Graphic* were accustomed to a considerable independence from the novelists whose works they were commissioned to illustrate. Whatever the specific reason, there is no record of Hardy working directly with the artists in the illustrations for *The Mayor of Casterbridge* and later novels *Tess of the D'Urbervilles*, *The Well-Beloved*, and *Jude the Obscure*. While there is no evidence of direct collaboration, his response to the illustrations for at least one of these later novels does give insight into how he imaginatively visualized his own characters.

Even though Hardy believed that serial publication had caused him to insert too many plot complications into *The Mayor of Casterbridge*, he must have felt relief from the pressures of magazine serialization by having the entire manuscript completed before the first issue of *The Graphic* made its appearance. A large factor in Barnes's success in the Casterbridge illustrations, certainly, was due to the artist's being able to read the entire story before having to depict characters and scenes from the early installments. The publishing history for *Tess of the D'Urbervilles*, however, marks an even greater departure from anything Hardy had previously experienced. He discovered he would have to make changes in his manuscript because of the formidable "Mrs. Grundy," that prominent figure in Victorian publishing, especially where family magazines were concerned.

Hardy had originally planned *Tess* to be published by the fiction bureau run by Tillotson and Son, in the form of newspaper syndication. At this point, the manuscript was not quite completed, but contained the seduction and midnight baptism scenes. It was while reading the printer's proofs that Tillotson's editor William Brimelow realized the kind of story they were about to publish. With amicable relations between publisher and author undisturbed, the manuscript was returned, together with three illustrations that had been already prepared.[82] (Neither the Tillotson manuscript nor the illustrations are known to have survived.)

Hardy immediately sent the manuscript to *Murray's Magazine*, and then to *Macmillan's Magazine*, but both rejected it on the grounds that it was not suited to their middle class reading audience. As *Life* recounts the story, Hardy "adopted a plan till then, it is believed, unprecedented in the annals of fiction." He decided to send out the manuscript with chapters and parts of chapters cut from the text, these last to be published "elsewhere, if practicable, as episodic adventures of anonymous personages." Hardy was upset because of this mutilation of the text, however, and he "resolved to get away from the supply of family fiction to magazines as soon as he conveniently could do so."[83]

The bowdlerized version (the original manuscript minus the seduction and baptism scenes) was accepted by Arthur Locker, editor of *The Graphic*, though he was soon to ask for changes in the text. In the definitive, 1912 edition, Hardy subsequently restored the text, and the result is that there are several significant changes between the 1891 serial and the later text. (These changes will be noted in Part III of this study, since they do affect the subject matter of the illustrations.)

Editor Arthur Locker, "sensing that he had a really important work in hand,"[84] commissioned Hubert Herkomer, a regular staff contributor to *The Graphic*, to do the illustrations. With the Herkomer appointment began one of the most interesting and confusing collaborations in the history of the Hardy illustrated serials.

Herkomer shared the commission with three of his students. Out of the twenty-five illustrations, Herkomer himself contributed six, E. Borough Johnson six, Daniel A. Wehrschmidt eight, and J. Syddall five. Johnson and Wehrschmidt later became fairly well known in their own right. Wehrschmidt, in fact, became the art master at the Bushey school and achieved considerable reputation as a portrait painter, mezzotint engraver, and lithographer.

At the time of his commission to illustrate *Tess of the D'Urbervilles*, Sir Hubert Herkomer had already established himself as a noted painter in oils. He had received much acclaim for his exhibit of "The Pensioners" in 1875 and "The Last Muster" in 1878, among several other paintings, and in 1890 became a member of the Royal Academy. Earlier in his career, he had established his art school in Bushey, Herfordshire. Herkomer believed that training and practical experience in the line drawing used in magazine illustration was excellent preparation for the painter in oils, and so he urged his students to get experience, as well as financial assistance, through magazine work. As Herkomer explained, he made it a practice to get commissions for promising students,[85] and soon many people asked him to recommend his students for various commissions. The use of four artists to produce work for one novel would have given his students valuable experience, under his own direction. Since *The Graphic* often used four different engravers working on the large plates for news stories (a quarter block assigned to each engraver, to be pieced together afterwards), Sir Hubert Herkomer's sharing his commission with three of his students would not be considered too unusual.

In the words of Carroll A. Wilson, the result of this collaboration was a "curious diversity of interpretation" in the various drawings for the novel, particularly in the presentation of Tess Durbeyfield herself. Wilson explains further: "There was not much liaison between Herkomer and the pupils, so that the different Tess-es and Angel Clare are strangely unlike; but some of the drawings, notably those by Herkomer, are of unusual power."[86]

Certainly, Herkomer's considerable artistic talent emerges through the illustrations he contributed. His paintings were noted for his ability to convey intense feelings—"The Last Muster" and "The Pensioners" are powerful precisely because of this intensity. The suffering human figure is his forte, and, as J. Comyns Carr has noted, his paintings reveal his own clear sympathy "with the pathetic aspect of modern life."[87] Herkomer was more at home with the human figure than with landscapes, as his illustrations for *Tess* indicate, and the intensity he captured in oils also emerges from his drawings for Hardy's novels. Most graphic historians, however, ignore Herkomer's work for *Tess of the D'Urbervilles*, yet such an uneasily satisfied and outspoken critic as Joseph Pennell has commented that Herkomer, "in his illustrations to Hardy's *Tess of the D'Urbervilles*, has, within the last few years, done some of his most striking work."[88]

There is no indication of Hardy's specific response to the *Tess* drawings as a series, and no available information on his involvement with the business of illustration for this novel. From the practices of *The Graphic*, and the fact that Herkomer was guiding three of his students through the *Tess* drawings, however, it is hard to imagine how Hardy would have been able to have the sort of involvement he had, for instance, with Arthur Hopkins or George Du Maurier. Herkomer did give Hardy two of the original drawings—the May Day scene (Plate 14) and the Mead scene (Plate 15)—which Hardy then placed in his Max Gate home. (These two, together with several Borough Johnson drawings now hang in the Dorset County Museum, but these latter were not presented to Hardy in his lifetime.)

One year after the beginning of *Tess's* serial publication, Hardy's ninth illustrated novel made its appearance in *The Illustrated London News*. In serial format, *The Pursuit of the Well-Beloved* ran from October 1 to December 17, 1892, and each weekly installment contained a single headpiece and two illustrations. The decorative headpiece was the same for each installment, and depicted a blindfolded male figure reaching out toward three beautiful but elusive women, all four figures draped in the costuming of Ancient Greece. The headpiece thus reflects the pursuit of an ideal, the frustration of that quest, and possibly even the ironic possibilities of Hardy's serial text.

The serial issue was a reworking of a story Hardy had written much earlier, but then had put aside when he became interested in developing his other ideas into fiction. Finally, he agreed to write a story for the Tillotson firm, reworking his early materials into *The Pursuit of the Well-Beloved*. He revised once again for the story's publication as a novel under the shortened title *The Well-Beloved* (1897). The opening and particularly the ending of the serial version were the most revised portions of the story when it appeared in novel format.[89]

Hardy's practice since *The Mayor of Casterbridge* had been to leave the choice of artist in the hands of the editor, and such was the case with the commissioning of an illustrator for *The Pursuit of the Well-Beloved*. Clement Shorter, editor of the *Illustrated London News*, selected Walter Paget to illustrate Hardy's latest work, though Wal Paget, as he was sometimes referred to professionally, was really no stranger to the Hardy material. Only a year earlier, in December of 1891, Paget had illustrated Hardy's "On the Western Circuit," a short story published in the *English Illustrated Magazine*. Paget was a familiar name among the coterie of magazine and newspaper illustrators, but he also had considerable experience as a book illustrator, with several novels of Scott, Defoe's *Robinson Crusoe*, and many boy's adventure stories to his credit.

Typical for these last novels, there is no evidence that Hardy took any interest in overseeing the illustrations. What did occupy his energies, however, was the adverse criticism he was now receiving for the subject matter and "values" expressed in his fiction. Hardy's theme of the evanescence of the Ideal in *The Pursuit of the Well-Beloved* seemed innocuous enough, but when the story was published (particularly later, in its format as novel) it received some scathing criticism for its "immorality." 1892 was not a good year for Hardy, since he further discovered that Mrs. Grundy lived on both sides of the Atlantic. In that year, *Harper's* had published *Tess of the D'Urbervilles*, first in serial version, then in revised, or restored, manuscript as a novel. As J. Henry Harper recalls, *Harper's* had received many complaints from "anxious mothers" who "were solicitous of the reading matter entering their homes which might find its way into the hands of their daughters."[90]

In 1894, Hardy entered into arrangements with *Harper's* to serialize his next story, and Hardy assured the editor, H. M. Alden, that the new novel would be suitable for the *Harper's* audience. J. Henry Harper comments, however, that Hardy later said the characters had taken things into their own hands, and it was not the story he had originally intended. Because he realized the novel would not be suitable for *Harper's*, Hardy tried to cancel the agreement. The agreement held, but Hardy was asked to alter the manuscript, and thus the serial version of *Jude the Obscure* differs considerably from the later version,[91] where Hardy restored the manuscript to its original state, and where he also made new changes in the text.

Jude the Obscure was published in *Harper's New Monthly Magazine*, from December, 1894 to November, 1895, under the title *The Simpletons* for the first issue, and then as *Hearts Insurgent* for the remainder of the serialization. The story was published with twelve illustrations by William Hatherell, who was a regular contributor to *The Graphic*, eventually spending twenty-five years with that magazine. In addition to illustrating current events for *The Graphic*, Hatherell was frequently commissioned by *Century*, *Scribner's*, as well as *Harper's*, three publications which were among the finest American magazines and which, according to Percy Bradshaw, for years had held unchallenged supremacy as the best illustrated monthly magazines in the world. As Bradshaw further notes, Hatherell was one of a very few British illustrators who had received such frequent commissions from these magazines.[92]

Hatherell became noted for his refusal to be pressured into hasty work. For illustrating current events, for instance, he used models, often carefully posed in his backyard garden (carefully cultivated in Georgian style), or in his modern studio. This familiarity with models and backdrops may be the reason for the kind of illustration Hatherell customarily created: "He always tried to make a *picture* instead of a mere photographic illustration. He would never be led into the production of a diagrammatic drawing of unnecessary detail—a kind of jig-saw puzzle of 'little bits.' He always had the painter's appreciation of colour, the sense of the values of broad masses, and a feeling for atmosphere."[93]

Again, as he had done with *Tess of the D'Urbervilles* and other late novels, Hardy was content to let his editor select the artist, but this time Hardy had already had experience with work of the illustrator. William Hatherell had illustrated Hardy's short story "The Fiddler of the Reels" for *Scribner's* in 1893, and later, in 1900, he was to illustrate another story, "Enter a Dragoon," for *Harper's*. Hardy must have been satisfied with the 1893 work of the artist; certainly he was more than pleased with the quality of Hatherell's work for *Jude the Obscure*, for he wrote to the illustrator when the work was completed:

> Allow me to express my sincere admiration for the illustration of "Jude at the milestone." The picture is a tragedy in itself; and I do not remember ever before having an artist who grasped a situation so thoroughly.[94]

Hardy suggested that Hatherell should exhibit the original and expressed the wish that he possessed a copy or a photograph of it himself. Hatherell presented Hardy with a complete set of the illustrations, and Hardy eventually had the entire set framed and hung in his own study.

The publication of *Jude the Obscure* marks the last time Hardy was engaged in serial publication and, for that matter, marks the end of his career as novelist. In the course of that career, Hardy had shown varying degrees of interest and involvement with the illustration of his works. As he became more familiar with the business of magazine publication, he began to take a more active role in the illustration of his fiction. Though later he was to move away from this involvement, he still showed appreciation for the work of the illustrator.

In a letter to Frederick Macmillan in which Hardy discussed arrangements for publishing an edition of his novels, he commented: "I hope, by the way, you have acquired the plates of the illustrations."[95] Hardy's comment suggests his interest in the illustrations almost thirty years after the first of them had appeared, and also suggests that he wanted them to be (at some time, if not with the edition at hand) published with his novels. There is no record of Macmillan's reply, however, and the 1902 re-issue as well as the later, 1912 Wessex Edition, also by Macmillan, were published without illustration.

The kind of involvement Hardy had—his care in the details of the pastoral setting of *Far from the Madding Crowd,* for Dorset customs in that work and in *The Return of the Native,* for period costume in *The Trumpet Major,* for characterization (possibly) in *A Pair of Blue Eyes* and (certainly) in *The Return of the Native,* for composition in *A Laodicean*—demonstrates his understanding of the primary, clarifying role of illustration. But Hardy was also quick to praise the work of his artists, especially when they seemed to him to capture the atmosphere or spirit of his works. Thus, he praised Helen Paterson Allingham, George Du Maurier, and William Hatherell, and praised individual engravings contributed by Arthur Hopkins and Hubert Herkomer, as well as by Hatherell. Whether his praise was verbalized, or demonstrated by his acceptance and display of several of the original drawings in his home, Hardy's pride in the artist's interpretation of his work is clear.

Hardy's own care in the details for several of the drawings, his praise for the detail and spirit of others, reveals the precision of his pictorial imagination. More than being just "a good hand at a serial," as he characteristically understated his accomplishments and aims, Hardy was a conscientious worker—an artist who became aware of the visual pleasures offered by the well-executed illustration, as well as the support such drawing could give to the detail, character, and atmosphere of his text.

IV

Illustration and the Novel

An Aesthetic Rationale

"The history of taste," writes Ernest Gombrich, "is a history of preference." To understand the choice, we must reconstruct the situation.[1] Critics have certainly disparaged the middle-class "taste" of the Victorians in furniture, architecture, even clothing. But in the matter of illustration at least, that genteel taste was based on a preference for a visual experience they could recognize and even identify with, as George Du Maurier explained.[2] The growth of periodical publications, the tremendous need and economic opportunity for writers, illustrators, engravers and, later, those who could handle photographic processes, define just how popular was the illustrated serial—no matter that the style of illustration had changed quite radically from the etchings of Cruikshank. This change in style from the Cruikshank to the Millais drawings of the 1860s reveals a changing preference—on the part of audience, writer, and illustrator—for a mimetic experience, both literary and visual. The change in taste is thus inextricably linked with the style of serial illustrations, and is particularly important for understanding the aesthetics of representational illustration.

In the history of nineteenth century fiction, we are accustomed to broad differentials in style, in intellectual orientation, in the atmosphere of the "world" of writers from Dickens to George Eliot, from Thackeray to George Gissing. But we can also find, of course, considerable differential within the works of an individual author. This is true of the Dickens canon, as the tremendous shift in vision from *Pickwick Papers* to *The Mystery of Edwin Drood* indicates. Paralleling the change, but not entirely dependent on it, is the shift in the style of illustration the Dickens novels received. Only the early Dickens novels received the much praised, caricatural style of Cruikshank and Phiz; later works illustrated by Phiz or Marcus Stone received a representational treatment.

In her stimulating study of Dickens, Q. D. Leavis offers explanations for the value of the early illustrations and the changes found in the later works. The illustrations for the novels written before *Bleak House,* for instance, "are a unique addition to the text, not only visualizing a scene for us in its historical social detail, and giving a visual embodiment to the characters which expresses their inner selves for us. . . . The illustrations are frequently indispensable even to us, the highly-trained modern reader, in interpreting the novels correctly because they encapsule the themes and give us the means of knowing with certainty where Dickens meant the stress to fall."[3] But, Leavis contends, novels from *Bleak House* onwards no longer needed illustration. When caricature was no longer needed, as in *Our Mutual Friend,* there was nothing for Dickens's later illustrators to fall back on but academic art and photographic naturalism.[4] As this particular approach contends, Dickens's increasing move toward realism meant that he had surpassed the need for illustration. And, as this approach strongly implies, illustration and caricature are synonymous, or nearly so. Certainly Leavis has spelled out her belief that realism and illustration do not go well together.

Thus, even Dickens's works do not escape a considerable degree of disparagement because of their relation to the new school of representational illustration. The onus falls much harder on general English magazine illustration for fiction after 1860,[5] and particularly after 1870. The major criticisms of the later style of illustration are clear: representational illustration does not provide the audience with visual metaphor and does not "discover" the themes of a novel the way that earlier illustration had done. Representational illustration is "mere visualization," considered a redundancy because it is only a faithful recording for several of a novel's scenes. Since illustrators did not work closely with novelists, the choice of scene was not particularly important: one scene might just have well have been chosen over another, or so the criticism implies. Photographic realism was seen as a reduction in quality (possibly related to the increase in quantity of illustration), and caused the new school to be dismissed not only as "mere visualization," not only as redundancy, but sometimes even as "hack work."

Thus, the conflicts here are between metaphor and realism; between caricature and representationalism; between the imaginative visual comment upon a work that becomes an expansion of the text, and the faithful re-creation that *mirrors* the text. These conflicts, however, are only apparent: the terms cannot be, and ought not to be, so surely and easily dichotomized.

Representational illustration has an aesthetic of its own. It ought not to be judged by the standards, aims, or techniques of the earlier school of caricature. In his *Art and Illusion,* Ernest Gombrich notes how representative art develops, and explains how conventions reign supreme until an artist happens along who has the courage to violate conventions and, in fact, begin a new convention.[6] Thus, the old schema of caricature and metaphor, extending back to the graphic satire of Gillray, Rowlandson, and Hogarth, gave way to the new style of the 1860s. Millais and other Pre-Raphaelites become particularly important for this contribution to design, to realistic, intricate detail, as well as to the possibilities of creating mood in the wood engraving.

But there are other causes for change here than the circumstance of a group of painters-illustrators who had a different vision of art. The aesthetics of illustration relate to several circumstances of scientific process and larger movements in art and literature. An increasing interest in photography as process[7] did enable wood engravings to be reproduced with greater accuracy and economy than had been possible earlier in the century. But, more than this, an interest in photographic *style*, as well as a continuing interest in genre painting, joined with the specific, Pre-Raphaelite techniques and themes to create a new schema which was to inform magazine illustration until close to the century's end. A movement that encompasses all these changes is Literary Realism. The gradually growing move toward not only specificity but a *recognizable* concreteness appears in the English novel from the 1840 factory novels onwards, culminating in the great mirrors of Victorian life that are the novels of George Eliot, Anthony Trollope, and Thomas Hardy. Finally, there are structural, thematic, and metaphoric bases for representational illustration, and this internal rationale operates just as much for representational art as it did for the caricatural. But always, what is of crucial importance is the mimetic quality of illustration after 1860, and increasingly so after 1870.

In the process of illustration, whatever its kind or style, the linguistic reality of the author's imaginative world translates into the visual reality of picture. The illustrated text is thus a synthesis of two media, since translation does not replace, but becomes an addition. In a very basic sense, therefore, the illustrated text is always an expanded text. The concept of the expanded text may seem obvious—as of course, it is, on one level. Yet expansion here means a very special relationship between picture and text, as well as a different understanding of the text in itself. Focusing on the *integrity* created by the relationship, J. Hillis Miller explains: "illustrations establish a relation between elements within the work which shortcircuits the apparent reference of the literary text to some real world outside." This is true, contends Miller, even when the illustrations are photographs, such as those of actual Dorchester scenes published with twentieth century editions of Hardy's novels.[8] The relation of illustration and text to the external world drops away until the illustrated text exists as a self-enclosing entity, where picture and text constantly refer to each other.

When we know an author has chosen certain scenes for illustration, or has worked closely with the artist on matters of detail, we do indeed have another entry into the mind that created the verbal text, and we know precisely where the author meant the stresses to fall. Intention and interpretation are closely linked together in this particular situation. But in representational illustration, where authors had much less—sometimes nothing—to do with selection or creation of scene, the illustrated text still has vital importance. It does not matter, on this level of aesthetic interpretation, who chose or created scene, or how much collaboration existed between author and illustrator. What does matter is the existence of the pictorial narrative. The illustrated text is a thing-in-itself, a new entity, and can be examined without much reference to author, or illustrator, though of course an understanding of these other aspects always adds to our appreciation of any literary work.

Thus, an illustrated text always differs from the same text issued without illustration, not just because of the obvious addition of picture, but because of the mutual reference—the interdependence—of illustration and text. The narrative element may be the same in either version, but the imaginative comprehension of the work is different. The narrative-pictorial synthesis is just that: a complementary situation that is complete in itself.

The audience does not have total control over its own imaginative response to the illustrated text, though any audience still conjures up images from its fiction-reading to supplement the relatively few that are possible in the illustrations to a text. The illustrated text has, however, a distinct advantage: it has the power to control, to shape responses that the non-illustrated text has only through its linguistic dimension.

Theoretically, then, the illustrated text has a much greater hold on its audience. When the author is also the illustrator, as in the case of Thackeray, or when he has worked closely with the artist, as in Dickens's case, the control is very much in the hands of the original "conjurer" of the novel's images. An interesting effect occurs when the illustrator has worked independently from the author: we have at least two imaginations working within the novel's world (and three, if we count the editor, or four, if we count the engraver, before photographic process took over the business of reproduction). Potentially, therefore, the "world" of the novel as expressed through narrative-pictorial synthesis offers exciting possibilities for critical interpretation. The illustrated text is thus very much a thing-in-itself, larger than the particular vision of a Trollope, a Collins, a Hardy, though always at bottom the author's vision remains a constant. Particularly after 1870, when artists were not nearly so subjective in their visual readings, the author's vision itself controlled much, though certainly not all, of the graphic interpretation of the novel. Still, the illustrated *Jude the Obscure*, let us say, becomes a thing in itself. The illustrator's involvement in shaping audience understanding of *Jude's* world means we are forced to widen our comprehension of the novel: it is no longer "only" Hardy's *Jude*.

Though Miller's interpretation of textual *integrity* as the self-enclosed world of picture and text seems particularly appropriate for the metaphorical and caricatural style of the earlier school of English illustration, it provides a valid and insightful way of understanding the narrative-pictorial synthesis of the later school as well. Yet representational illustration has another dimension to consider besides this visual-verbal integrity. We must understand that representational illustration expands the text precisely because of its mimetic relationship to the material within the text (which itself relates mimetically to the external world of non-fiction), and the objective world outside the novel. This mimetic relationship between illustration and text, and between illustration and external world, becomes important for understanding the expansive effects of illustration after 1870, when the text conveyed all the business of literary realism. It also becomes particularly important, therefore, for understanding the aims and contributions for the illustrations to Hardy's novels.

The aesthetics of the later illustration depend in very large part on a realistic style modeled on the photograph and the sort of information it could convey. Illustration of the Cruikshank school, as noted earlier, could convey considerable metaphoric information through iconographic materials within the drawing, such as paintings, statuary, mirrors, and particularly in the corners of the illustration, where small objects as cobwebs seem fully afterthoughts but, in effect, convey symbolic comment on the central focus of the scene. Rarely was the fully etched or engraved plate used, however. But in the later school, artists utilized the full engraving. Details in the entire scene became important, not usually for the moral metaphoric style that prevailed earlier, but for the creation of realistic illusion. Most often, those details seemed to be nothing more than what the audience might see in a contemporary world, given the particulars of the novel. The clarity of detail, the amount of information about various life styles conveyed through such details as buckets and brooms, parlor furniture, styles of clothing (and, when the engraving was particularly well done, quality of clothing fabric) reinforce and sometimes considerably expand the novelist's "world." The illustration's details thus could convey the rustle of taffeta, the luxury of fur, the coarseness of a heavy cloth tunic—in fact, a whole semiotic system. The visual signals could be social, economic, psychological, religious. (For us, of course, the semiotics of representational illustration remain all these, with the addition of the historic).

The extraordinary care given to the noun lines of the engraving, and the cross-hatching which created the illusion of shadow or quality of fabric can also be seen in the shaping of furniture, various farm and domestic implements, as well as posture and mannerism found in human figures. All this care was an attempt to duplicate the extraordinary effects of photography, which itself was understood as an accurate recording of the world as it was. Representational illustration was an attempt to re-create reality, in the way the camera had done it, in the way one's own eyes saw the world.

In the process of creating the illustration, artists after 1870 were careful to subordinate their own imaginations to the texts they were commissioned to illustrate. They saw themselves as assisting the novelist by supporting and clarifying the text. But, at the same time, they were aware of their dual responsibility—toward the audience, as well as the text. The Victorian audience could increase its enjoyment of the text by recognizing and identifying with the novel's phyical terms as they were expressed through picture. Within the frame of the illustration was the solid, massive reality that has come to describe so much of Victoriana in general, from its architecture and furniture to the size of its part-issue and three-decker novels. The realism that occurs in the fiction of the century's later years quite naturally found its way into the illustration for that fiction. And, even though illustration was careful to follow a novel's direction and signals, it often went beyond the details of the text to delineate a scene more completely than it had been in its linguistic dimension.

Representative illustration is thus Victorian in a way that caricatural illustration was not, and could never be. Related to the Gillray and Rowlandson style, the Cruikshank school was more closely associated with the 18th century. But with its almost scientific emphasis on realistic detail, representational illustration reassures the Victorian audience of the solidity of their world—indeed, a wonderful stability in light of the technical, economic, and religious changes from the 1860s to the century's end.

The realism that the Victorian writer could actually convey through the details of his fiction was, when we think of it, relatively limited. The best authors, in fact, suggest the completeness of a scene through carefully selected detail, even through impressions of details, counting on the audience's imagination to fill in the scene. (As John Harvey reminds us, no audience ever comes to a text, illustrated or not, with an imaginative vacuum.)[9] Obviously, the reader's previous experiences, visual or otherwise, operate in his comprehension, in his imaginative visualizing of any story. Some carefully selected details could be counted on to jog imaginations into filling in the scene. Illustrators and editors, in their various ways, added to these carefully selected textual details, filling in (or advising on) what might *not* be part of the audience imagination.

We must not overlook the immensely important role played by editors in this process. Dickens might have worked closely with his illustrators, but later writers seem to have been glad to leave the matter of illustration, or at least a large part of it, in editorial hands. (And Dickens worked closely with his illustrators, not always because he had an aesthetic zeal but because he could not bear to let anyone else take control or manage something within his purview.) Editors may well have underestimated the visual abilities of the audience, just as they might have overestimated the numbers (but not powers) of the Mrs. Grundies in the Victorian middle-class, magazine audience. Still, the new middle class, the increasing numbers of "fringe" lower-middle class readers, as well as urban readers of all classes with little or no experience of a rural, provincial world—all these needed visual details to define and clarify the novel's world. The correspondence between Hardy, his illustrators, and editors, in fact, demonstrates how important clarification and definition were to both writer and illustrator. Clearly, representational illustration, and for our purposes the Hardy illustrations, ought to be judged, at least in part, on how well they carry out this intention.

But it is academic art and photography, or more precisely, the schema of *picture* within nineteenth century art and photography that gives us even more valuable ways of understanding representational illustration. First, the new school defined illustration as *picture*, an art form that existed in its own right. In the Millais years, when the Pre-Raphaelite style was more apparent in the drawings for *Framley Parsonage* and *The Small House at Allington*, for instance, it is easier to see picture. This ease seems due primarily to what we now know about the Pre-Raphaelite styles of a number of later painters, as well as of Millais himself. The illustrations' pictorial quality stems from the Pre-Raphaelite themes of naturalism, Beauty (a peculiar combination of the sensuous and the spiritual), foreground emphasis on the human form, and the contributions of design (and the picture within design) found in the patterns of screens, tapestries, carpeting, clothing. The pictorial effects here were so dominant that Victorian William Black spoke of the illustrations of *Framley Parsonage* remaining "vivid to the mind when the characters in the novel have all faded away into shadow or downright oblivion."[10]

While some in the Victorian audience would indeed have the admittedly limited but still very valid response of enjoying the illustration because they recognized the familiar, others were more attuned to the semiotics of academic art and photography, and would certainly have responded to the schema of post-1860 illustration. This schema consists of gestures, posture, and facial type as far as the human form is concerned. In terms of movement or situation, the schema consists of such actions as the opening of letters, the handing of letters or other objects from one person to another, people clasping each other in moments of joy, sorrow, desperation, situations such as death bed or sick bed scenes. Eavesdropping, "waiting," and even moments of ennui are other situations within illustrations that help define its schema. All of these surely are the staples of fiction (for what novel can do without them), but they are particularly present in the Victorian novel, and we are aware of their staged quality, associated with the melodrama of Victorian literature. But these are also the domestic scenes of Victorian genre painting and of photography, which of course modelled its subject matter on genre painting, at least to some extent.

Since these are full frame engravings, the illustrations could contain a plethora of details. A handkerchief, sheet music on a piano, birds in cages, pictures, statuary, tools, domestic furnishings, in addition to the immediate items of clothing or human actions, act as referents for social hierarchies, economic distinctions, occupational categories, moral situations, and emotional states. Holman Hunt's painting "The Awakened Conscience" is a prime example of this genre art, and demonstrates the sort of artistic experience the Victorian audience for magazine illustration would have had. That audience was used to paintings that told a story. Exhibited in 1854, Hunt's painting depicted the theme of The Fallen Woman. The titled sheet music resting on the piano, a mirror reflecting nature, a cat with a captured bird, wallpaper with the design of birds eating corn are details which spell out a moral message and are wonderfully evocative when joined with the expression on the women's face. Photographers such as Oscar Rejlander and Henry Peach Robinson continued this tradition in their work by using posed, costumed figures to tell a story, as did Francis Frith with his heavily symbolic photographs. Each of these men was producing work of this sort in the 1860s; they were joined in the late 1870s by John Thomson's fascinating collection of photographs in *Street Life in London*. The latter photographer had a wide audience, by virtue of this one published work, but that audience would already have had ample opportunity to become familiar with the semiotics of picture,[11] particularly the sort of picture that helps formulate representational illustration.

We are so used to the phrase "One picture is worth a thousand words," that we have forgotten the basic validity of the statement. To the Victorian audience, pictures did tell stories; when those pictures were illustrations for novels, they offered opportunity for the artist to recreate the conditions of the story through carefully detailed images of a recognizable reality. But they also had the capacity to awaken in the reader-viewer's mind the image of similar scenes, or types of scenes, observed elsewhere. Interestingly enough, *Harper's New Monthly* and *The Graphic* were in the habit of publishing not only illustrated fiction, but also reproductions of classic and contemporary paintings. A reader of *Harper's*, for instance, could not help but make a relationship between the social, moral, and psychological signals found in the reproduced painting and whatever signals lay within the illustration accompanying the magazine's fiction.

Examination of some of the serials published in *Cornhill*, *Harper's*, and *The Graphic* in the 1870s and 1880s reveals the presence of many such signals. *The Atonement of Leam Dundas*, (*Cornhill*, 1875) written by Elizabeth Lynn Linton and illustrated by Arthur Hopkins and George Du Maurier, has plates that convey many of the genre painting "messages": wallpaper, flowers, shrubbery controlling intricate designs; a woman lying in the grass, with a child observing her; a man, woman, and dog all having the same determined expressions on their faces. There is the sense here of containment, suffering, endurance. In *My Faithful Johnny* (*Cornhill*, 1880), written by Margaret Oliphant and illustrated by W. Small, one plate depicts a woman reading a letter while another woman lies prostrate on the floor, handkerchief in hand. The illustration is a direct descendant of the genre painting.

Just as not all the illustrations for any one Dickens novel convey moral comment or give uniformly valuable insight into the novel's themes, so not all of the illustrations for a Trollope, Collins, or Hardy novel should be expected to participate in Pre-Raphaelite or genre painting semiotics. Many do, however, and an understanding of these signals can give us a much richer appreciation for representational illustration. The dismissal of this school of illustration as undistinguished and uninteresting because of its fidelity to the text is a mistake because it misses an important point: since the text itself is often related to the sort of scene or situation found in genre painting, the illustration that is faithful to the text is capable of transmitting a whole system of signals. Since we see this as merely a recapitulation of the text, we are prone to miss the richness of both text and picture participating in a system of signals. And surely any text is richer for this participation.

But even when the message of representational illustration is "merely" the well drawn, carefully detailed human figure or any object or setting associated with the business of daily living, representational drawings still have considerable value. The well drawn illustration enhances the visual pleasure of the printed page, to be sure, and provided the joy of the familiar to the Victorian audience. An additional pleasure derives from an increased awareness of the novel's particular atmosphere, as well as of its dramatic and psychological dimensions in themselves, and not as they relate to pictorial signals described earlier. These dimensions of atmosphere, drama, and psychology have the greatest practical significance for representational drawing.

Setting was the first to benefit directly from this detailed treatment of the novel's world, for the illustrator often had to go far beyond the author's words in his need to fill the engraving frame. Realistic though a novelist might be, he cannot risk creating a fully detailed scene, for the reader will not spend the time necessary to translate the verbal into his own visualization, nor would it be worth the effort involved on the part of the author. Photographic realism would not be the author's primary intention; he was creating the scene for purposes of atmosphere, or simple background for plot and character. But the illustrator was almost forced to supply details, to go beyond the novelist's description. And what most illustrators did was to fill the engraving with recognizable Victoriana. Thus, the settings found in this kind of illustration become quite accurate measures of the physical context for Victorian life, as it existed on several different levels.

More significantly, psychological reality emerged from the supposedly limited mimetic illustration. Trollope and Hardy, as a matter of fact, often did not give particulars of facial detail. Hardy would impressionistically mention eyes or brow, but rarely would describe more than one or two features in any case. The artist had to fill in facial detail, and in doing so he created a vital, responsible human being, more particularlized than in the author's original description. Sometimes, however, the Pre-Raphaelite influence could be a detriment. The sometimes moody, often idealized faces that attracted the Pre-Raphaelite illustrators possessed a sameness, an unreal perfection. What could work in the 1860s, because of other, harmonious qualities in the illustration, did not always work so well in later drawing, when design intricacy gave way to photographic detail, or concreteness of object. Many of the faces in post-1870 illustration appear to be the same person, and this is particularly the case with female characters. Idealization of facial feature, however, can be useful in examining the effect of illustration, and in understanding illustration as textual interpretation. Individualized faces become even more interesting when measured against idealized features. Whether individualized or idealized, the artist *had* to go beyond the text when the description was not complete. Sometimes he had the author's guidance, but even if the interpretation was his own reading, his care in creating character, particularly the individualized character, was to emphasize and even in some cases to create, a very intense psychological realism.

Beyond these areas of setting and atmosphere, or character, were other ways of expanding the text. The principle of selectivity operated in post-1860 illustration as it had earlier, and this meant that the actual choice of illustrated scenes emphasized certain aspects of the text. Types of scenes selected for illustration, confrontations between characters, ironic reversals or parallels between the engraved set-pieces are structural aspects of illustration. In certain novels scene selection sets up rhythmic patterns which potentially have an immense influence on the way in which a novel would be understood, or "seen," by its Victorian audience. The use of melodrama, or of scenes stressing the isolated figure (versus crowd or domestic scenes), symbolic motifs, the artist's use of light and dark tones to create atmosphere—these are all in addition to details of setting and characters individualized through dress, facial detail, posture.

Illustration for a given novel, when viewed as a series of drawings, has the capacity to create a pattern of stresses as it visualizes the author's text. Depending on the special insights of this pattern as a whole—insights into atmosphere, drama, and character psychology—representational illustration can make a very special and at times powerful contribution to the spirit of the text.

What is true of representational illustration in general is particularly true of the Hardy illustrations. Though there is considerable unevenness in technical quality in these drawings, and though there is not always judicious scene selection, Hardy's novels do have an additional dimension because of the illustrations. Even while setting forth in recognizable, clarifying and fixed images the details of background, and in using line and shading to create atmosphere, the illustrators found their best subject matter in the human figures of Hardy's Dorset world.

Distinguishing Hardy from other Victorian authors of illustrated texts, however, is that the linguistic, textual reality of his novels includes not just two but three basic areas or types of subject matter: setting, with its local color, concrete detail, and general atmosphere; the human figures who take their origin from the specifics of locale and who work through various plot situations; and the cosmic forces which in one way or another surround and affect their lives. The illustrators' emphasis on two areas of Hardy's imaginative reality counters the three areas conveyed through the text. While setting and character combine to create atmosphere in the illustration, this atmosphere, or tone, is not the same as the sense of cosmic interference, indifference, or merely extra-dimensional existence. The distinction between the cosmic reality in Hardy's text and the human dimension of the illustrations creates a certain kind of tension in the narrative-pictorial synthesis. This tension offers interesting possibilities for interpreting the relationships between illustration and text, though some tension must always exist between the linguistic and graphic "readings" of such areas as character.

A weak novel cannot be saved through illustration, though often it may be strengthened through good drawing simply because of the visual pleasure an audience experiences. For a good novel, however, illustration can significantly enhance the text. Hardy's novels are of uneven quality, and the relative significance of the illustrations bears a striking but not surprising relationship to textual quality. Whether of minor or major significance, however, Hardy's illustrated works demonstrate many of the splendid possibilities and, admittedly, even the limitations of representational illustration for the Victorian novel.

An Early Work: *A Pair of Blue Eyes*

Though a minor novel, *A Pair of Blue Eyes* remained one of Hardy's favorites. The three central characters are involved in the conventional love triangle, but have splendid moments of revelation, as frustration, innocence, good intentions, and missed moments occur. Cornwall's rugged terrain emphasizes the relative helplessness of the three as they work out their destinies. This early work presents several scenes of considerable dramatic force because of their description of imminent physical danger, or for their penetrating character insights, however brief. Plot contrivances and melodrama continually threaten the story, however, and characters are too easily reduced to personality traits, such as Elfride's coquetry, Smith's naiveté, and Knight's ponderous attitude. Nevertheless, it is a fine early novel and gives promise of later accomplishments, particularly in the creation of female character and in the ability to set character against and within landscape.

Tinsley's Magazine published the novel's eleven installments from September, 1872 to July, 1873, each number accompanied by one illustration. (Though Hardy was later to revise the manuscript, no textual variants between the 1872–72 serial and the 1912 Wessex Edition affect the illustrations.) The visual power of the first five, possibly six, of the plates contrasted to the flatness of the later ones lends support to Richard Purdy's suggestion that Hardy sent more than just the two early sketches as a guide to his illustrator.[12]

The illustrations as a series present only a slight view of Cornwall. The text, however, places considerable emphasis on the distinctive landscape, sometimes the source and always the massive background of the novel's human drama. The illustrations, on the other hand, emphasize this human drama, but offer little in the way of supportive details of place or atmosphere. Several of the drawings, however, are nicely executed. Lines are strong, details of costume emerge with clarity, blacks and whites are effective, and characters are individualized, though some differences in the appearance of Smith and Elfride occur between the early and later plates. The difference may be deliberate, as a means of showing suffering and character change.

Pasquier's drawings do have some nice details, but their contribution to Hardy's novel goes beyond the visually pleasurable. Scene selection and arrangement demonstrate what the representational illustration can contribute to a novel in the way of emphasizing important plot events and focusing on particular character traits. The Pasquier illustrations also demonstrate that the post-1870 illustrator did not feel himself particularly bound to reproduce *all* the textual details of a given scene, or that he could not add, delete, or combine, according to the dramatic and compositional needs of his drawing.

Surprisingly enough, in a novel which stresses the youthful naiveté and blunders of its heroine Elfride Swancourt, only two of the drawings really stress this side of her character. Both depart somewhat from the text, since Hardy's own description of each scene does not explicitly convey her coquettish ways. But the illustrations convey the spirit of the text, certainly, in their handling of facial detail and posture as signals of an emotional state. The artist's treatment of her eyes and the toss of her head in the first plate, as Elfride and smith are on the cliffside path (Plate 2), and his placement of her arms in a defiant position in the church parapet scene (Plate 17) are nice touches, giving special insight into this provocative young woman.

Elfride's hair has a curious significance in several of the plates. At times, her coiffure is formal: her hair is swept back from her face, and fixed into place, giving her an older, dignified appearance. But in other plates, her hair hangs loose—particularly when she is in the company of one of her suitors. We are to understand restraint in the one situation, freedom and joy in the other.

Of major importance in understanding the dramatic and psychological significance of these illustrations are those scenes which depict eavesdropping, a type of scene which seems to have been one of the staples in magazine illustration. In one of the issues which carried *A Pair of Blue Eyes*, for instance, *Tinsley's Magazine* also carried a scene for a story called "Poor John," (July, 1873). The scene is remarkably similar to one from Hardy's novel, when Smith comes upon Knight and Elfride walking through the woods (Plate 18), and obviously having a private conversation. Another illustration, for "London's Heart," also in *Tinsley's*, written by B. L. Farjeon, is somewhat similar to Pasquier's view of Elfride looking through Mrs. Jethway's cottage window. Eavesdropping, in fact, provided very good drama for the magazine illustrator: the scene carried its own drama because of the basic situation, and could be visually powerful because of character positioning. In addition, the audience viewing the illustration would be gripped by the suspense of possible discovery. The frequent occurrence of such scenes in serial illustration was due, of course, to the heavy reliance on the eavesdropping situation by masters of the suspense novel. Writers such as Ainsworth, Collins, and Dickens commonly used this type of scene as a device to complicate plot and incite interest, Hardy himself frequently used the eavesdropping situation; it appeared throughout his novels from *Desperate Remedies* to *Jude the Obscure*, although most of the sensationalism was gone from his handling of this type of scene in his later novels.

In addition to their dramatic qualities, the illustrated eavesdropping scenes in *A Pair of Blue Eyes*, at least, also stress the psychological aspect by emphasizing the loneliness of the listener. Elfride's unintentional view of the silhouettes at the window of Endelstow House causes her considerable pain and misunderstanding. And although the confusion is cleared up quickly enough, the pain of misunderstanding forecasts the later and permanent pain of the three central characters. Smith's observation of Elfride and Knight in the Belvedere scene (Plate 18) proves he has been supplanted in Elfride's affections; posture and the expression on Elfride's face as she peers into Mrs. Jethway's cottage emphasize her desperation in trying to discover if the vengeful widow will speak of the journey to London. The stress of pain and loneliness in these various eavesdropping scenes, furthermore, helps to tone down the many plot contrivances in this early novel, even though the eavesdropping situation itself depends on the coincidence of being in the right place at the right time.

The Belvedere scene has other importance, this time in its detail that provides a metaphoric signal. In the serial text, when Smith has his hand on the sapling to support himself, he cannot at that time actually see Knight and Elfride, who are moving into the Endelstow summerhouse. It is only afterwards, when he has moved, that he is able to see the pair. At that time, "Part of the scene reached Stephen's eyes through the horizontal bars of woodwork, which crossed their forms like the ribs of a skeleton." But the drawing sacrifices this grotesque image and, by compressing two scenes, achieves something else. Stephen's hand, now resting on the sapling, conveys his need of support, conveys how much he is disturbed by what he sees. But it also repeats the pattern ahead of him; as Smith's arm is on the tree, so is Knight's arm around Elfride. Smith's emotional state is thus signaled, as is the reason for it, through a metaphoric repetition. Interestingly enough, the grotesque quality in Hardy's image gives way to a human interest in the illustration.

The remaining Pasquier drawings deal with a series of dramatic confrontations. Stephen Smith faces Parson Swancourt's anger when he learns of Smith's humble ancestry and his desire to marry Elfride; Mrs. Jethway accuses Elfride of causing her son's death; Henry Knight asks

Elfride for the truth of her relationship with past suitors. The library scene is particularly well drawn, with positioning of characters signalling the situation. The stolid figure of Parson Swancourt, surrounded by heavy desk and chair (and a curiously large wastebasket in the foreground) is set against a very slender and unsubstantial Smith, with a nervous Elfride in the background. Smith's unsuccessful confrontation with the Establishment could not have been better signalled. In the last scene, Hardy stresses the tomb of Mrs. Jethway's son, since Knight and Elfride first sit on it, then move away, but are still able to see it during their conversation, as the text carefully notes. Pasquier's illustration, however, omits the tomb and emphasizes the living pair.

In each of these confrontation scenes, Elfride is a passive figure, and her positioning in the drawings stresses inexperience and an innocence that Knight too late perceives makes her believe in her own guilt. The confrontation scenes have some dramatic power by their very nature, even though Elfride's position is passive, but their greatest importance is this emphasis they give to a sensitive, suffering Elfride. The illustrations thus shape an understanding of Elfride which is somewhat different from the text. There are simply more illustrations stressing her suffering than her coy, teasing, and sometimes exasperating attitudes and actions.

The Pasquier illustrations thus demonstrate how choice as well as handling of illustration can create certain understandings that are not particularly stressed through the text. Two melodramatic scenes (Plate 17 & 19) also stress an ironic reversal not so apparent from the textual presentation of the same scenes. The melodrama, however, is carefully controlled through irony.

Both scenes present Elfride and Knight against a strong background of either church architecture or cliff. An important contrast between the scenes is in the two views of Elfride—first as teasing female, then as unselfish heroine. Because of the rescue-yearning motif conveyed through the positioning of the two figures, both scenes create imposing drama. In addition to this basic dramatic sense, however, is the ironic reversal created through a juxtaposition of the plates. In the first scene, Knight reaches to secure Elfride from falling; in the second, Elfride reaches forward to save Knight from plunging into the rocks below. The irony in the reversal is in the text, of course, but does not clearly emerge until the illustrations are juxtaposed. Here, too, the reversal of background also works more clearly.

One detail in the first plate may have special iconographic significance. As Elfride poses on the parapet, her figure echoes the position of the cross lying just below and to her left. Of course, the cross is a normal part of the church architecture—but it need not have been included in the illustration, and its presence is precisely the kind of detail that genre painting, or even the Cruikshank school, would include in order to make some kind of comment on the situation. In Elfride's case, the cross, though it is not well drawn, suggests her future suffering.

The selection of Knight's rescue scene also demonstrates the careful planning and thoughtfulness that lay behind representational illustration. Yet this particular scene, or rather its selection, has been misunderstood in the past. Carroll A. Wilson labels the illustration a "curious Victorian depiction . . . of the quite un-Victorian text . . . where the heroine rescues her second hero to safety on Beeny High Cliff by a rope made from all her undergarments.[13] Pasquier's illustration, however, shows Elfride stretching out her *hand* to rescue Knight, and *not* using a rope made of her undergarments. In this case, Pasquier has not departed from the text, but is simply illustrating an earlier scene. Chapter 22, in which Elfride actually rescues Knight with the rope of her clothing, was included in the next installment, the seventh monthly issue. The drawing presented in the criticized scene, however, depicts the earlier, unsuccessful rescue attempt, and appeared with the previous, sixth installment. (Still the artist does depart slightly from the text: Elfride loses her telescope after this attempted rescue, but Pasquier has substituted a walking stick for the telescope.)

The artist's delineation of the attempted rescue, complete with outstretched hands clutching air, is a great deal more dramatic than the later scene would have been, since the later one is successful, and since the hands would lose their position of importance to Elfride's use of the undergarment rope. *Tinsley's Magazine* may have been guilty of Victorian prudery—but not in this instance. The dramatic impact of the drawing, its ironic reversal of the situation in the earlier scene with Elfride on the church parapet, its revelation of Elfride's strength of character, and its emphasis on the two human beings unsuccessfully reaching for each other, make it one of the most powerful of the Pasquier graphics. While in the text the actual rescue scene may be much more powerful than the attempted one, the unsuccessful rescue as presented in the pictorial version has its own significance. The inability of Elfride and Knight to reach each other forecasts their later separation. To have depicted the successful rescue attempt would have missed the prophetic element and, in terms of the story's drama, would have been anti-climactic.

Though there are several high points in the illustrations to *A Pair of Blue Eyes*, there are also some omissions which tend to shape the novel differently from the non-illustrated version. Unfortunately, the Pasquier drawings do not visualize Hardy's rustic characters, thus missing out on one of the more pleasing parts of this early work. Another omission, though not as obvious, is the absence of the isolated, or single figure scene. (Only one such scene appears in the series.) Even in this early novel, several instances do exist in the text where Elfride, Smith, and then Knight become conscious of their loneliness. Elfride gazing into the water, observing her reflection, and Knight's wait upon the cliff are the stuff from which psychologically provocative illustration can emerge, but this is not the style of representational illustration. Group scenes, confrontation-type scenes (with a psychology of their own) between two figures are the most usual kind of scene depicted, as it was in genre painting. With the exception of the eavesdropping scenes, which do stress loneliness, those insights into character which could emerge from the single figure scene are sacrificed in favor of the visually dramatic, or for scenes which stress painful relationships *between* characters.

The illustrations control dramatic emphasis, and the control, in turn, shapes the text. One particular problem Hardy had in this early work was the obvious plot contrivance, such as the lost earring episode, or the two men returning to Cornwall on the same train bearing Elfride's coffin. But with the primary emphasis on human relationships and careful selection of dramatic scenes, the more mechanical part of the novel is de-emphasized through illustration. Melodramatic scenes are not exploited but depend more on their thematic contribution and ironic reversal for their impact.

The illustrations draw upon some of Hardy's own pictorial techniques, though not nearly enough for our satisfaction. The strong composition found in the textual handling of the church parapet and the cliff scene occurs in the illustrations. More particular effects of *picture* appear in the first eavesdropping scene, where the shadows are seen framed in the window. Again, the window device appears in the Jethway cottage drawing. The last few drawings give special attention to lighting effects, thus attempting to duplicate Hardy's references to Turner's lighting effects. Clearly, this is not much in the way of duplication, and we are made aware that, though the illustrations may use some of Hardy's devices, they are intent on creating their own sense of picture, complete with signals suggesting emotional states, or composition, suggesting a variety of relationships and situations.

The inherent pictorial qualities in Hardy's texts make the illustrator's work that much easier, but the illustrations themselves emphasize certain aspects of the text and de-emphasize others. The Victorian audience would have been less conscious of plot manipulation but more aware of emotional and dramatic elements found in human relationships. The fact that the last half of the drawings served as frontispieces for their respective installments means that this human element visually dominates the last half of the novel. Elfride's character change, too, is visually captured, as she moves from coquette to heroine. Such a psychological and structural use of illustration means that the representational drawing can make a powerful, meaningful visual statement, particularly when the illustrations are viewed in relationship to one or more other set-pieces in the series. The series as a whole is not consistently powerful, but it does at times expand the novel in important ways, and demonstrates some of the possibilities of representational illustration.

The Major Novels

Far from the Madding Crowd: A Pastoral Tale

The first of Hardy's major novels, *Far from the Madding Crowd* appeared in *The Cornhill Magazine* from January to December, 1874, with each of its twelve installments presenting a full page engraving and a vignette initial. The illustrations enhance Hardy's text in several ways, not the least being the perfection of the drawings. They are exceptionally strong in the handling of detail, not just in the business of providing pastoral background, but in the entire subject matter. The distinctiveness of the engraved lines, a contribution of artist, engraver, and a mark of *Cornhill's* care in reproducing its art work, enhances the artist's careful and realistic handling of detail. The human figure is as carefully rendered as the details of nature, or of costume and interior setting. Much care is given to Bathsheba's presentation, especially in the drape of her clothing. In several illustrations, the arrangement of branches in the background forces our eyes toward the human figures in the foreground. Folds of clothing repeat the lines found in nature. The Allingham illustrations thus demonstrate an economical and effective use of line drawing.

Composition is another of the artist's strong points, particularly in the many double figure scenes. Her habit of balancing the double figure scenes by shading one figure in dark tones and delineating the other (usually Bathsheba) in white clothing creates dramatic power, metaphoric meaning, and simple visual interest. One noticeable lack in the illustrations, however, is in facial delineation. Mrs. Allingham's faces are not distinctive, and except for Boldwood, are the same even-featured, idealized faces that peer out from so much post-1860 serial illustration. (An exception occurs in the sheep-shearing supper (Plate 20), where the faces of the rustics are highly individualized, though they are not fully delineated.) Mrs. Allingham is at her best in the double figure scene, where she divides her attention between the human figures and the precise rendering of foreground detail. The double figure scene gives her the opportunity to emphasize social or moral distance through the simple technique of juxtaposition: Oak standing before Bathsheba on horseback (Plate 5), or Bathsheba standing to one side of a kneeling Troy, for instance (Plate 21). The physical contrast conveys a pleasing sense of depth and dimension, and has metaphoric meaning as well.

Occasionally the illustrations clarify a situation or custom for an audience unfamiliar with Hardy's Dorset background, as in the Bible and Key scene[14] (Plate 6), but the Allingham illustrations are more important for their handling of character relationships, and for justification of events as they are related to motivation. Scene selection in general reveals a healthy balance between the depiction of Bathsheba and each of the three major male figures in her life, and stresses the reasons why Bathsheba is attracted to first one then others of this supporting cast. The vigorous lines of Mrs. Allingham's drawing (and of the engraver's hand) reflect the strong wills of the four central characters—Bathsheba, Oak, Troy, and Boldwood—and give the reader-viewer significant character insight, particularly in terms of character relationships. The vignette initials, on the other hand, stress psychological states of individual characters, rather than relationships and, in a more obvious way, effectively contribute to the creation of an idyllic, pastoral atmosphere because of their emphasis on the static, rural scene.

The specific scene selection in the Allingham drawings shapes the pictorial version of *Far from the Madding Crowd* in several basic ways. A pastoral, romantic situation is established in the very first installment, which depicts Bathsheba trying to revive Oak (Plate 3), who has collapsed from the smoke filling his shepherd's hut. The drawing's focus on the proximity and handsomeness of these two young people strongly suggests this engraving's purpose: to capture an audience by presenting a highly romantic, physical situation in the very first installment. Selecting the destruction of Gabriel's flock as the opening illustration would have conveyed a panoramic view of nature and a thematically more consistent view of a nature at odds with men's desires. Yet the selected scene establishes the importance of human relationships and forecasts the eventual union of these two figures. There is some drama in this first scene, but it is not as striking nor certainly as effective in establishing the role that Chance is to have on the major figures as other possibilities for illustration. What the drawing does, finally, is to sacrifice insight into a proud Gabriel Oak and a capricious Bathsheba Everdene of the novel's early sections for a romanticized situation, calculated to appeal to *Cornhill's* audience.

Leslie Stephen had cautioned Hardy about his handling of Fanny Robin's story, since *Cornhill* was a "family" magazine, and the "Fallen Woman" theme might bring down severe criticism from the Mrs. Grundies in the audience. The illustrations appear to reflect this caution by devoting only one scene to Fanny (Plate 22). The details of clothing, so evident in other scenes with other characters, are absent here to good effect. Mrs. Allingham fills her engraving frame with haystack, wooden fences, farmyard, and tall trees as background, making the slumped, pathetic figure of Fanny seem like a bundle of discarded clothing. In

"Hay-trussing—?" said the turnip-hoer, who had already begun shaking his head.
"O no."

PLATE 33. *The Mayor of Casterbridge.* Robert Barnes. *The Graphic.* January 2, 1886.

Her mother whispered as she drew near. " 'Tis he."

PLATE 34. *The Mayor of Casterbridge.* Robert Barnes. *The Graphic.* January 16, 1886.

The hag opened a little basket behind the fire, and, looking up slily,
whispered, "Just a thought o' rum in it?"

PLATE 35. *The Mayor of Casterbridge.* Robert Barnes. *The Graphic.* January 9,
1886.

"I don't drink now—I haven't since that night."

PLATE 36. *The Mayor of Casterbridge*. Robert Barnes. *The Graphic*. January 30, 1886.

She knelt down on the hearth, and took her friend's hands excitedly in her own.

PLATE 37. *The Mayor of Casterbridge*. Robert Barnes. *The Graphic*. March 13, 1886.

Henchard, with withering humility of demeanour, touched the brim of his hat to her.

PLATE 38. *The Mayor of Casterbridge*. Robert Barnes. *The Graphic*. April 10, 1886.

"Well, Lucetta, I've a bit of news for ye." he said gaily.

PLATE 39. *The Mayor of Casterbridge.* Robert Barnes. *The Graphic.* April 17, 1886.

Lucetta's eyes were straight upon the spectacle of the uncanny revel.

PLATE 40. *The Mayor of Casterbridge.* Robert Barnes. *The Graphic.* May 1, 1886.

"I have done wrong in coming to 'ee . . . I'll never, never trouble 'ee again,
Elizabeth Jane."

PLATE 41. *The Mayor of Casterbridge.* Robert Barnes. *The Graphic.* May 15,
1886.

"Don't cry—don't cry," said Henchard, with vehement pathos. "I can't bear, I won't bear it."

PLATE 42. *The Mayor of Casterbridge.* Robert Barnes. *The Graphic.* February 20, 1886.

"Now," said Henchard between his gasps, "Your life is in my hands."

PLATE 43. *The Mayor of Casterbridge.* Robert Barnes. *The Graphic.* April 24, 1886.

"Elizabeth, my child, come and hearken to what we are talking about, and not bide staring out o'window as if ye didn't hear."

PLATE 44. *The Mayor of Casterbridge.* Robert Barnes. *The Graphic.* May 8, 1886.

Young Farfrae repeated the last verse. It was plain that nothing so pathetic had been heard at the King of Prussia for a considerable time.

PLATE 45. *The Mayor of Casterbridge.* Robert Barnes. *The Graphic.* January 23, 1886.

In stagnant blackness they waited through an interval which seemed endless.

PLATE 46. *Tess of the D'Urbervilles.* Daniel A. Wehrschmidt. *The Graphic.* July 18, 1891.

On going up to the fire to throw a pitch of dead weeds upon it, she found that he did the same on the other side. The fire flared up, and she beheld the face of D'Urberville. The unexpectedness of his presence, the grotesqueness of his appearance in a gathered smock-frock, such as was now worn only by the most old-fashioned of the labourers, had a ghastly comicality that chilled her as to its bearing. D'Urberville emitted a long, low laugh.

PLATE 47. *Tess of the D'Urbervilles*. Hubert Herkomer. *The Graphic*. December 5, 1891.

He lay on his back as if he had scarcely moved.

PLATE 48. *Tess of the D'Urbervilles.* Hubert Herkomer. *The Graphic.* December 19, 1891.

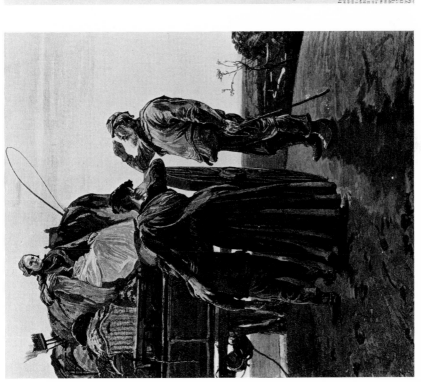

"You be the woman they call Mrs. Durbeyfield, I reckon?" he said to Tess's mother, who had remounted.

PLATE 49. *Tess of the D'Urbervilles.* Daniel A. Wehrschmidt. *The Graphic.* December 12, 1891.

"I don't know about ghosts," she was saying.

PLATE 50. *Tess of the D'Urbervilles.* Daniel A. Wehrschmidt. *The Graphic.* August 15, 1891.

He jumped up from his seat, and went quickly towards the desire of his eyes.

PLATE 51. *Tess of the D'Urbervilles.* J. Syddall. *The Graphic.* September 5, 1891.

Tess flung herself down upon the undergrowth of rustling spear-grass as upon a bed.

PLATE 52. *Tess of the D'Urbervilles*. E. Borough Johnson. *The Graphic*. September 19, 1891.

The plantation wherein she had taken shelter ran down at this spot into a peak, which ended it hitherward, outside the hedge being arable ground. Under the trees scores of pheasants lay about, their rich plumage dabbled with blood.

PLATE 53. *Tess of the D'Urbervilles.* J. Syddall. *The Graphic.* October 31, 1891.

"I would rather take it, sir, in my own hand."

PLATE 54. *Tess of the D'Urbervilles*. E. Borough Johnson. *The Graphic*. July 25, 1891.

"What makes you draw off in that way, Tess?"

PLATE 55. *Tess of the D'Urbervilles*. E. Borough Johnson. *The Graphic*. August 22, 1891.

Clare came down from the landing above in his shirt-sleeves, and put his arm across the stairway.

PLATE 56. *Tess of the D'Urbervilles.* Daniel A. Wehrschmidt. *The Graphic.* September 26, 1891.

She slid down upon her knees beside his foot. . . . "In the name of Heaven, forgive me!" she whispered.

PLATE 57. *Tess of the D'Urbervilles.* E. Borough Johnson. *The Graphic.* October 10, 1891.

They reached the cloister-garth, where were the graves of the monks. Upon one of these graves he carefully laid her down.

PLATE 58. *Tess of the D'Urbervilles.* Hubert Herkomer. *The Graphic.* October 17, 1891.

Something seemed to move on the verge of the dip eastward as a mere dot. It was the head of a man approaching them from the hollow beyond the Sun-stone. Clare wished they had gone onward, but in the circumstances decided to remain quiet. The figure came straight towards the circle of pillars in which they were.

PLATE 59. *Tess of the D'Urbervilles.* Daniel A. Wehrschmidt. *The Graphic.* December 26, 1891.

She looked into his eyes with her own tearful ones.

PLATE 60. *Hearts Insurgent.* William Hatherell. *Harper's New Monthly Magazine.* April, 1895.

On the farther side of the stream three young women were kneeling.

PLATE 61. *The Simpletons.* William Hatherell. *Harper's New Monthly Magazine.* December, 1894.

"See how he's served me!" she cried.

PLATE 62. *Hearts Insurgent.* William Hatherell. *Harper's New Monthly Magazine.*
January, 1895.

There on the gravel lay a white heap.

PLATE 63. *Hearts Insurgent.* William Hatherell. *Harper's New Monthly Magazine.* June, 1895.

Sue excitedly continued to tear the linen into strips.

PLATE 64. *Hearts Insurgent.* William Hatherell. *Harper's New Monthly Magazine.* October, 1895.

A small voice rose from the shade of the fireside.

PLATE 65. *Hearts Insurgent.* William Hatherell. *Harper's New Monthly Magazine.* August, 1895.

"I ought not to be born, ought I?" said the boy.

PLATE 66. *Hearts Insurgent.* William Hatherell. *Harper's New Monthly Magazine.* September, 1895.

All before them was a sheet of whiteness.

PLATE 67. *The Hand of Ethelberta.* George Du Maurier. *The Cornhill Magazine.* April, 1876.

Round her, leaning against branches, or prostrate on the ground, were two or three individuals.

PLATE 68. *The Hand of Ethelberta.* George Du Maurier. *The Cornhill Magazine.* September, 1875.

"In the writing of the composer," observed Lord Mountclere with interest.

PLATE 69. *The Hand of Ethelberta*. George Du Maurier. *The Cornhill Magazine*. March, 1876.

She lessened in his gaze, and was soon out of sight.

PLATE 70. *The Hand of Ethelberta*. George Du Maurier. *The Cornhill Magazine*. May, 1876.

She was standing before the looking-glass, apparently lost in thought.

PLATE 71. *The Trumpet-Major.* John Collier. *Good Words.* June, 1880.

Anne swept with her eyes the tremulous expanse of waters around her.

PLATE 72. *The Trumpet-Major.* John Collier. *Good Words.* November, 1880.

The candle shed its waving light upon John's face and uniform.

PLATE 73. *The Trumpet-Major.* John Collier. *Good Words.* December, 1880.

At Étretât: Somerset now made them known to one another.

PLATE 74. *A Laodicean.* George Du Maurier. *Harper's New Monthly Magazine.* December, 1881.

"Is the resemblance strong?"

PLATE 75. *A Laodicean.* George Du Maurier. *Harper's New Monthly Magazine.* May, 1881.

The young man was at her side before she had crossed the pavement.

PLATE 76. *A Laodicean.* George Du Maurier. *Harper's New Monthly Magazine.* June, 1881.

Pearston stooped and examined the cause of discomfiture.

PLATE 77. *The Pursuit of the Well-Beloved.* Walter Paget. *Illustrated London News.* November 26, 1892.

He moved back to the church wall, warm from the afternoon sun, and sat down upon a window-sill facing the grave.

PLATE 78. *The Pursuit of the Well-Beloved.* Walter Paget. *Illustrated London News.* October 22, 1892.

Jocelyn sprang up to leave the room.

PLATE 79. *The Pursuit of the Well-Beloved.* Walter Paget. *Illustrated London News.* October 15, 1892.

"I suppose you'll marry some day, Avice," remarked Pearston, regarding her thoughtfully.

PLATE 80. *The Pursuit of the Well-Beloved.* Walter Paget. *Illustrated London News.* November 12, 1892.

effect, the illustration echoes several genre paintings with the "Fallen Woman" theme. If the illustration had been captioned "Abandoned," or "The Outcast," it would have been in keeping with such paintings as Rossetti's "Found," Redgrave's "The Outcast," or would have served as the rural version of Augustus Egg's "Past and Present No. 3," which depicts the "Fallen Woman" huddled against a wall under the Waterloo Bridge. But these genre paintings sometimes seem to condemn the figure of the prostitute; Helen Allingham's version is gentle and sensitive, as indeed Hardy's characterization is.

Reversing the only truly single figure scene (among the full size engravings) for Fanny Robin seems dramatically appropriate, since she is the loneliest of all the novel's characters, and this drawing effectively conveys that loneliness. It is interesting to note that her happier moments with Troy are omitted, indicating perhaps that the "Fallen Woman" could be presented through illustration, as long as suffering and not love or joy be presented. While only one of the full size illustrations depicts Fanny, Mrs. Allingham manages to make Fanny's story constantly present, as several of the vignette initials deal with the sub-plot. All of them, however, convey the suffering of Fanny as outcast.

The selection of illustrated scenes as a whole tends to de-emphasize the melodramatic realities of Hardy's text, and even in scenes where melodrama is unavoidable, Mrs. Allingham controls the situation, and actually stresses psychology rather then heightened, exaggerated dramatic moments of the text itself. In the scene (Plate 21) which depicts Troy leaning onto the coffin to kiss the lips of Fanny Robin, emphasis divides between the grieving Troy and a deeply disturbed Bathsheba. Troy has the central position in the engraving, and the sweeping lines of his kneeling figure, the grip of his hand on the coffin's edge, reveal his agony. But Troy's dark suit blends into the darkness of the coffin (an interesting omen), while Bathsheba's white dress, as well as her position at the edge of the frame, sets her apart from the scene she is unwillingly comprehending. Bathsheba's emotions, as well as Troy's, are suggested through hand and general body position. Troy's comprehending features are hidden from view, but the extent and depth of grief emerge through the positioning of his body, an economical way for the artist to convey emotion. The scene is one of Mrs. Allingham's best; she has effectively subordinated the potential melodrama that would come from emphasizing Fanny Robin and Child by focusing instead on the recognitions of the two living figures.

Only one scene among the series seems uncertain in its conception and faulty in its placement. Troy's "drowning" appears as only a distant spectacle in the single illustration that emphasizes nature rather than the human element. Troy's figure, in fact, is the least interesting item in the scene, as the human figure is dwarfed by the surrounding cliffs, but even here the panoramic landscape lacks interest because of its flat and wooden delineation. The actual choice of the scene, however, presents a puzzle. Troy's supposed drowning occurs in the previous installment (for October), and the reader is not aware at that time that a witness exists for the event. In the November number, the reader belatedly learns that a witness does exist, and that he has reported the drowning. Yet the fact of observation really adds nothing to the suspicions of his "death" that already exist, particularly in Bathsheba's own mind. This unnecessary complication of a witness is in the text itself, of course, but it is compounded by the placement of the illustration. The pictorial presentation of the scene is quite anti-climactic, since the reader knew of the drowning, but not of the witness, in the previous monthly installment. The illustration thus lacks dramatic meaning and does not possess the stature of the rest of Mrs. Allingham's drawings.

Bathsheba Everdene has a character complexity greater than the earlier Elfride Swancourt, but there is a capricious quality in Bathsheba that links her to that earlier heroine. Pasquier captured that quality in the early illustrations for *A Pair of Blue Eyes*. Caprice, however, is noticeably absent from Mrs. Allingham's depiction of Bathsheba. The early illustrations of *Far from the Madding Crowd* present her as a demure, sympathetic, mature woman—thus anticipating the textual development of her character. Even in the Bible and Key scene (Plate 6), so crucial to the confusion that develops from sending the valentine to Boldwood, Bathsheba seems steady, quiet and, surprisingly enough, too somber for the textual version of the scene. In these early illustrations, the Victorian audience did not see Bathsheba as she was created by Hardy in his text. The audience in this particular case lost a valuable pictorial insight into Bathsheba's psychology, into the impulsiveness that serves as explanation for later episodes. Regardless of the difference between early illustrations and text in the matter of Bathsheba's depiction, there is no evidence that Hardy criticized the drawings on this or any other basis. He was still a novice in the business of serial illustration, and accuracy of physical detail occupied his attention rather than the forceful rendering of character psychology.

Several of the later illustrations, however, are graphically faithful to Bathsheba's characterization as it emerges from Hardy's text, and offer insights that, in some cases, go beyond the text. Bathsheba is most often depicted in her relationship with the three men in her life. The one scene which focuses exclusively on Bathsheba appeared as the July engraving (Plate 23). Boldwood has just left Bathsheba, after confronting her with his accusation that she has been "dazzled by brass and scarlet," and his simple-minded hatred of Troy frightens Bathsheba. The illustration avoids the drama of a confrontation scene and shrewdly focuses, instead, on Bathsheba's reaction as Boldwood walks away. In her muddled attempt to understand what has happened, Bathsheba paradoxically understands Boldwood is "incomprehensible." Her obvious distress in this situation, her inability to cope with Boldwood when she knows that she is to blame for playfully encouraging him, emerges from this illustrated scene and thus prepares the audience to accept her attraction to the "strong" Sargeant Troy.

Other illustrations continue to clarify and at times even expand the textual interpretation of Bathsheba and the three male figures in her life. In the story's unfolding, the early focus on Oak shifts to the other male characters, Boldwood and Troy, as they take their turns being objects of Bathsheba Everdene's caprice, but they are almost always seen in their relationship with Bathsheba, and rarely alone. What emerges from these drawings is an explanation for Bathsheba's attraction to Troy. The three appearances of Oak in the full size engravings, for instance, emphasize his helplessness (as Bathsheba tries to revive him, Plate 3), his humility and abject financial position, as he asks Bathsheba for work (Plate 5), and his patient loneliness during the sheep-shearing supper (Plate 20). Interestingly enough, the text itself is full of Gabriel Oak's strength, determination, and courage, but the illustrations do not directly display this side of his personality. What does emerge, of course, is his perseverence, but this is not likely to appeal to Bathsheba at this stage of her development.

The illustrations depicting Boldwood convey his increasing madness, as his frustration over not getting Bathsheba's promise to marry him joins with a basic emotional instability to create an obsession for this woman whom he knows does not love him. The April illustration (Plate 24) reveals something of the awe he feels at speaking with Miss Everdene—a woman who likes him well enough to send a valentine. The stoop to his figure reveals his humility as he addresses Bathsheba, and his appearance here is in marked contrast to the August scene (Plate 25) where, with a vicious leer, he observes Bathsheba's meeting with Sargeant Troy. The final illustration of the series shows just how far he has gone in his madness. The frenzied facial expression joins with an expansiveness of gesture as he greets the muffled stranger (Troy). The scene's hospitality is overdrawn by the artist, but deliberately, and with good effect. The tragedy that follows in the text logically follows the uneasiness conveyed through the illustration. Boldwood's depiction in the Allingham drawings is well done, and pays considerable justice to one of Hardy's most interesting and complex male characters.

The first two illustrations depicting Sargeant Troy stress his military bearing and handsome appreance, and thus contrast him with previous suitors Oak and Boldwood. In the memorable sword-play scene, (Plate 26), Troy's posture suggests professional seriousness as well as personal confidence in his swordsmanship. (Bathsheba's face, naturally enough, reveals trepidation.) The scene itself, however, is disappointing, and does not convey the extravaganza of Hardy's textual description, perhaps because the scene's effectiveness depends on quickness and constant movement, on flashes of light created by the moving sword. The reader follows this movement in Hardy's text, but not in the illustration, primarily because of the flatness, that static quality of the engraving medium itself. The medium is superb at capturing the set piece, but continuous movement is more difficult to convey, and Mrs. Allingham has not succeeded in doing so in this scene.

Troy's appearance in two additional scenes has significance for his own characterization, but even more so for Bathsheba's. As noted, the July illustration depicts Bathsheba in an obviously distressed state after her forced interview with Boldwood. In the August drawing (Plate 25), Bathsheba appears once again against the woods as background, but this time she is in Troy's arms—a Troy who fills the visual void of the illustration as well as a very real psychological need of Bathsheba. Troy appears in the August scene as the image of all that Boldwood is not, in proud military bearing, in self-assurance, in ease of conversing with the opposite sex. Compared to the abject and frenzied Boldwood, Troy seems a center and source of stability. Troy's image becomes significant when the two illustrations depicting first Bathsheba's distress (Plate 23) and then comfort (Plate 25) are compared, but the image is of course very much present in the text itself. What the artist has done is to emphasize character qualities and to give a visual explanation for Bathsheba's attraction to Troy. With considerable astuteness, Mrs. Allingham conveys the idea that Bathsheba's attraction is much more than physical, though that is definitely present as well. In this sense, Bathsheba's capriciousness is much lessened, and the *Cornhill's* audience could see that Troy's playfulness and military bearing are what Bathsheba needs to counter Boldwood's frenzied impositions on her. Hardy's irony here is that Troy only *seems*, and it is Gabriel Oak who is the real source of stability. In the early illustrations depicting Oak, however, Mrs. Allingham conveys a humility (but not abject, as in Boldwood's case) that Bathsheba finds tiresome. The easy conquest of both Oak and Boldwood disappoints Bathsheba, since there is no adventure in winning before one has enjoyed the game. Troy's pride, which clearly emerges from the illustrations, appeals to Bathsheba, and displaces both the steady perseverence of Oak and the disturbing obsession of Boldwood. The July–August (Plates 23 & 25) contrast between Boldwood and Troy throws considerable light on Bathsheba's psychological state and her attraction to Troy, though the text itself conveys caprice as the main reason for her treatment of all three men.

Each of the full-size illustrations captures a specific moment from the text. The vignette initials, however, do not refer to a specific plot event but deal either with the setting for one or more events or, more significantly, with atmosphere and psychological states. Most of the initials feature the single figure, sometimes at work shearing sheep (Plate 4), working in the fields, or at domestic chores. Surprisingly few initials, however, deal with the rustic element, which is actually far more prominent in the novel than either the initials or full size engravings would seem to indicate. One of the most interesting initials features the Old Maltster (Plate 27), an example of one of Hardy's early and highly idiosyncratic rustics, staring at his tankard as he eats his meal. Other initials, with their stress on the details of nature, contribute to the pastoral atmosphere in a greater degree than do the full size engravings.

Fanny Robin appears in only one of the full size plates, but her presence is continually implied through the initials. The Casterbridge Union House, scene of Fanny's death, and her grave, where Troy is depicted as he plants flowers, both appear among the initials. Mrs. Allingham's use of the vignette initial to serve as subtle reminder of the sub-plot is most evident in the picture of Fanny, heavily muffled against the night air, travelling on the road in search of Sargeant Troy. This initial (for the March installment) counterpoints the full size engravings which immediately precede or follow it, since these illustrations feature Bathsheba at the height of her power over Oak and Boldood. Clearly, the counterpointing is in the text itself, but the artist's handling of the illustrations draws a subtle attention to the contrast between these two women and their respective situations.

The vignette initials also depict Oak, Bathsheba, and Troy in single figure scenes. In Hardy's text, Oak is prominent in the early part of the story, then becomes a background figure until, at the novel's end, he once again moves into the foreground. Yet the full size engravings do not convey his continuing presence, since he appears in only three of these, and they are all among the early illustrations. What the artist does, however, is remind the audience of Oak's steady presence through the initials. He appears in four of them, either shearing sheep, or pursuing Bathsheba during the night of her elopement with Troy, as pensively leaning over a gate or, finally, walking to the church on his way to marry Bathsheba. Used in this manner, the vignette initials effectively counterpoint the full size illustrations.

Other initials are important for their insights into psychological states. Troy's initial shows him planting flowers at Fanny's grave, and stresses a frenzy that ought to be seen as temporarily equivalent to Boldwood's emotional state in the novel's final sections. The initial featuring Bathsheba (for the November installment) has significance because it is her only depiction after she has learned of Troy's supposed death, a death she never really accepts. Her sadness and patience as she waits for her way to become clear emerge from the artist's side view, as she sits by the window, staring off into the distance. This particular type of scene, with its strong flavor of Patient Griselda, appears fairly often in post-1870 illustrations, and thus seems to have become a stock scene for the illustrator to use when no other suggestion came in mind. In Mrs. Allingham's hands, however, the drawing takes on importance. Referring to no specific moment in the plot itself, the vignette initial gives insight into Bathsheba's agony and, in its strong hint of her awaiting something, prepares the audience for Troy's re-appearance, or at least for the lack of surprise on Bathsheba's part.

The final initial depicts two people walking towards a distant church. With their backs to the viewer, huddled under umbrellas, some suspense exists as to their identity, or the reason for their apparent destination, and only after reading into the final installment does the audience realize that Bathsheba and Oak are wending their way in tranquil obscurity towards the church where they are to be married. In this last installment, however, the reader must move through Troy's reappearance, Boldwood's murder of Troy and his own imprisonment before the scene depicted in the initial comes true. The initial achieves suspense primarily through the hidden identities of the travellers, and so much happens during the course of the final installment that the initial can project the finale without actually disturbing the story's hold on its audience. Though this is a minor point among the illustrations as a whole, it is a sign of the thoughtfulness that lay behind the Allingham drawings.

The initials in Mrs. Allingham's hands thus become more than merely decorative, though this may seem to be the primary function of the early initials, and drawn most likely in obedience to Hardy's direction. But even here the initials make an important contribution to pastoral atmosphere with their finely detailed scenes of rustic life. Besides this pastoral quality and the emphasis on psychological states that occur in the later initials, the vignette initials link the set-pieces with the plot. Since they are most often not tied to a specific moment but are more generally related to the plot, the vignette initials give a sense of continuity to the twelve set-pieces depicted in the full size illustrations.

Though there may be one or two questions on the placement of the illustrations, they are minor points. A more serious question involves the characterization of the early Bathsheba. Mrs. Allingham's drawings do not do justice to Hardy's text in this one area, and it is a serious omission. Though Bathsheba's capriciousness is de-emphasized, her suffering clearly emerges from later drawings. The illustrations also stress Troy's physical attractions, and thus realistically explain Bathsheba's weakness for this shallow man—an explanation that is not so apparent through the text alone. And, in spite of Leslie Stephen's strictures on Hardy's handling of the Fanny Robin story, the pathos of her life and death quietly but clearly emerges through the engravings.

In general, the rural atmosphere does not have the same relative emphasis in the illustrations as it does in Hardy's text. Both full size illustrations and vignette initials contribute to the rural tone, but the initials carry the weight more than the larger drawings do. The Allingham illustrations are important for their careful rendering of nature's details, but nature here is definitely seen as background, more so than in the text itself. It is surprising, furthermore, to realize how very little of the pastoral beauty and how none of nature's ominous side actually appear in the illustrations.

Some of Hardy's best rural scenes, however, are highly melodramatic, and in the absence of such scenes as the destruction of Oak's flock, the threat to Boldwood's and Bathsheba's hayricks by fire or thunderstorm, the artist was not only avoiding melodrama but also eliminating one of the most notable features of Hardy's novel. The personalized struggle between Gabriel Oak and nature's elements does not emerge from the pictorial aspect of the serial text. Early reviewers of *Far from the Madding Crowd*, in fact, singled out these scenes from the text (together with Troy's swordplay and the coffin scene) as examples of extravaganza and sensationalism. So thought the *Westminster Review*, but *Athenaeum's* reviewer thought some of these scenes among Hardy's best because they were quite original, not copied from other, popular writers of the day.[15] Mrs. Allingham's illustrations, however, clearly do not fall into the category of sensationalism; if anything, she has de-emphasized this quality that is the graphic potential of the text by avoiding some scenes and controlling others, such as the coffin scene. Instead of choosing to stress melodramatic incidents of plot, the artist emphasizes Bathsheba's developing relationships with three male figures. The illustrations thus make a notable psychological contribution to the serial version of the novel, in spite of idealized facial detail found in several plates.

The full size illustrations, but not the vignette initials, were published when the novel appeared in book form and thus came to the attention of literary reviews. *The Academy's* critic noted the artist's "graceful illustrations,"[16] and *The Times'* reviewer, while mistakenly attributing some of the illustrations to George Du Maurier, noted that the story was "set off by a dozen admirable illustrations."[17] These early judgments must remain in force, though clearly the illustrations deserve more than passing mention. The Allingham engravings, with the notable exception of the early Bathsheba, faithfully capture the text, and do so with considerable spirit and expertise. In some cases, the illustrations give subtle clarity to developing plot lines, and certainly add to Hardy's characterization of the later Bathsheba. The illustrator's strong sense of composition makes several scenes into effective picture: Bathsheba and Boldwood framed in the window during the sheep-sheering celebration, Bathsheba gazing through the window as she waits for word of Troy, and, Fanny huddled against a wall, Bathsheba alone and then with Sargeant Troy in the woods, and, of course, the very effective coffin scene.

The strong lines in the drawings, together with excellent pastoral detail, create a pleasing visual experience. More than any other series of illustrations, these show the clear influence of the Millais school, where atmosphere, intricate detail, such as lines of human figure and costume repeating the lines or rhythms of nature, and graphic fidelity to the text define the methods and aim of the artist. But the pleasures in viewing such representational art, important though they are, are not the only effects of the Allingham drawings. The text shows a turmoil in the rural world caused by both man and nature, but the illustrations place the turmoil on the human figures, choosing to keep the rural world as a peaceful, contrasting background. By omitting Hardy's view of a changing, unpredictable nature, the illustrations shift the reading of his text: the cosmic dimension inherent in the text gives way, in the illustrations, to the human realities of Wessex.

The Return of the Native: A Classic-Romantic Tragedy

Hardy had originally intended a five part structure, in the manner of classical tragedy, for *The Return of the Native,* but then added the traditional Victorian marriage as finale. This shift in intention, as well as the novel's uneven characterization, affects the twelve illustrations provided by Arthur Hopkins. Yet the illustrations are not so easy to dismiss. The strengths they possess make them puzzling to anyone who attempts to evaluate their contribution to the text. The several strengths of individual plates, of Hopkins's handling of the novel's themes, of his characterization of Eustacia, ought to make the series a landmark among the Hardy illustrations. Yet the drawings are not among the strongest in the Hardy canon.

One of their great weaknesses is poor technical quality, due to the engraver's deficiency, as Hopkins noted in one of his letters to Hardy, but the weakness is also due to Hopkins's own deficiency in the handling of perspective and human anatomy. The human figures have no sense of life as they do in the Allingham drawings. With only two or three exceptions, too, the illustrations lack the strong, expressive lines that are called for by the very nature of this novel.

Yet there are several aspects of the Hopkins drawings that are noteworthy: a variety of characters is depicted, including the rustics, and occasionally there is clarification, as in the Mummers scene. Two of the drawings make important metaphorical statements, and several plates, when viewed as part of the series, convey issues that emerge more clearly in the illustrations than in the text by itself. Most interesting, though it is finally not enough to save the series, is Hopkins's use of light and darkness in an apparent attempt to reflect Hardy's pictorial technique and, quite possibly, to give a sense of the cosmic to the illustrations.

Eustacia Vye appears in five plates, as does Clym Yeobright. Other principal characters—Mrs. Yeobright, Tomasin, and Diggory Venn— each make single appearances. Only Wildeve among the principal figures is not prominently depicted.[18] The rustics appear in a total of six illustrations—a significant difference from their almost total absence in the full-size drawings for *Far from the Madding Crowd*. In the main, early illustrations focus on individual characters and establish relationships between character and environment—again a significant difference from the earlier novels, where character interrelationships were firmly established in early scenes. Later illustrations in *The Return of the Native* tend to depict dramatic moments, and are more concerned with complications of plot.

In Hopkins's first scene dealing with Eustacia (one disliked and criticized by Hardy), she is standing on the heath, looking more like a shepherdess, perhaps, than the woman Hardy links with Marie Antoinette or, in later editions, with Sappho or Mrs. Siddons (Plate 7). Eustacia has a dumpy appearance, unromantic and unsophisticated, which no doubt accounts for Hardy's disappointment in the illustration. (It should be noted, however, that Hardy himself describes Eustacia as "in person full-limbed and somewhat heavy. . . ." Hardy also describes Eustacia as being in partial disguise as she waits for Wildeve to make his appearance, and thus Hopkins was understandably handicapped in this early depiction of Eustacia.

While deficient in its presentation of Eustacia as Queen of the Night, as Hardy titles his chapter, the illustration is notable for its emblematic quality. The text mentions that a score of heath-croppers, small ponies that run wild in the Heath, fled at Eustacia's approach. In the text itself, this event occurs a short time after Eustacia has moved from the position depicted in the Hopkins drawing, and (again in the text) thematically stresses her eventual alienation from the world of Egdon Heath. Yet in the illustration, Hopkins includes the heath-croppers, placing them behind Eustacia, and limiting them to two. The tableau has sexual significance, pre-figuring the passion between Wildeve and Eustacia, since it is Wildeve Eustacia waits for on the heath. (Since there are two ponies, the scene suggests Eustacia's relationship with Clym, as well as with Wildeve.) With the wild brambles in front of Eustacia, and the horses behind, the drawing becomes a metaphoric statement of a trapped woman and, to a considerable extent, prefigures Eustacia's tragedy at the novel's end. The illustration, however, is not perfect in its statement; if it were not for the textual material accompanying the drawing, the understanding of Eustacia's alienation from the heath would be lost, since her dress and posture do not convey any sense of alienation in themselves. (Her loose costume, for instance, is actually more in tune with the heath than her later, Parisian costume is in the August drawing. The costume distinction works in the later drawing as it does not in the earlier one.) Still, with the image of Eustacia placed between the sexually suggestive ponies and the threatening brambles, the illustration has considerable significance because of its emblematic statement. On the other hand, it departs from Hopkins's own stated belief in graphic fidelity, since it is not faithful to the text in its inclusion of the ponies.

Hardy was definitely pleased with the later, August illustration (Plate 8), which depicts Eustacia looking on, undetected, while Clym sings as he works on the heath. Parasol in hand, Eustacia is clearly a woman of fashion, a point Hardy was intent on making in his text. The bitterness evident on her face conveys aggravation as she perceives that Clym can actually sing in the midst of his trial of near-blindness. Because it presents Eustacia as obviously out of place on the heath, contrasted with a husband who so clearly *belongs* at this point in his trials, the illustration creates some sympathy for Eustacia's plight, and thus faithfully reflects Hardy's own attitude toward this complex woman.

In the October illustration (Plate 28) Eustacia is most obviously depicted as the suffering, romantic heroine who had been compared earlier in the serial text with Lord Byron. As she moodily leans back against the sofa in her grandfather's house (after she has left Clym), the engraving establishes the depth of her ennui and depression, and thus serves as a fine statement of mood. In addition, it points up an ironic parallel not so clearly evident in the text itself. Young Charlie looks at her in a manner calculated to recall the way *she* had once idealized Clym Yeobright, when she had first heard of his return to the heath. The illustration thus calls attention to a textually submerged ironic parallel.

In the matter of facial detail, this drawing shows Hopkins at his best. Here and in his illustrations for other novels, he shows a predilection for the Pre-Raphaelite face—a mixture of the mystic and the sensuous. In Eustacia's case, at least, it is an effective mixture, for Hopkins emphasizes her moodiness and the sort of distraction one might expect from a character who is contemplating suicide. In his other illustrations for this series, Hopkins most often falls short of the Pre-Raphaelite ideal and creates, instead, the "pretty face," with a charming but vacuous expression. The result is that many of his women have a remarkably similar appearance. Eustacia actually shares in this similarity, but she is also given individualizing qualities through Hopkins's handling of her eyes and especially her posture.

One last scene dealing with Eustacia is worth noting, particularly when contrasted with another plate, that of Mrs. Yeobright on her death-bed (Plate 29). Eustacia's scene, too, is one of death (Plate 30), but differences are striking and, in fact, point up the confusion in the novel's motifs. Mrs. Yeobright's scene also depicts the Egdon natives gathered around her makeshift bed, and the scene is thus pleasingly staged. In Eustacia's death scene, Diggory Venn drags her body from the Weir. With her head thrown back, her body limp, Eustacia has style even in death—at least, according to Hopkins's handling of the scene. The melodrama of this episode, however, should be contrasted to the dramatic dignity of Mrs. Yeobright's posture in death, as if she were carved in stone. And while there is surely contrast in the life styles of these two women so prominent in Clym Yeobright's life, the classic pose of the one and the romanticized pose of the other do not really lead anywhere in terms of thematic realities—except that both women are "killed" by the heath. (Yet Eustacia's previous suicide wish clouds the issue.) The basic contrast between the two women is not supported by other illustrations or the text (since Mrs. Yeobright in her own proud way had been alienated from the ways of the heath.) One has the sense, though, that in these two drawings Hopkins was puzzling his way to some sort of important contrast, since the difference in death postures here is too stark to be mere coincidence. Each death posture, in fact, becomes an emblem of the personalities, even life styles, of these so very different women.

Clym Yeobright appears in four illustrations in the series, but in none of these is he the single figure, and he is given dominance in only one scene—an interesting situation since Hardy himself had designated Clym as first in order of importance among his characters in this work. In the May illustration (Plate 9), Clym is juxtaposed with the Egdon rustics, particularly Grandfer Cantle, and Clym has only slightly more dominance than the older man. The scene depicts the moment when, after Clym says to Grandfer Cantle that he hasn't changed much, Fairway remarks, "If there's a difference, Grandfer is younger." Clym's face had been described earlier in the scene as pensive, as revealing that "thought is a disease of the flesh." "As for his look, it was a natural cheerfulness striving against depression from without, and not quite succeeding." While the scene is interesting for its presentation of the Mummers in their costumes, thus capturing one of the Heath traditions with specific details of dress supplied by Hardy to his artist, its thematic significance lies in its contrast of Clym as a man of the future, harassed by modern thought, with

Grandfer Cantle, the man of the past. Cantle, explains Hardy, is an anachronism, but one who possesses the zest for life that escapes modern man, victim of the vice of unrest. Clym appears passive, quiet, even distant, in comparison with the strutting Grandfer Cantle under the mistletoe. The text actually uses a substantial amount of time in this chapter (The Two Stand Face to Face) and a later one (My Mind to Me a Kingdom Is) in establishing the contrast between Cantle and Clym Yeobright. The value of the illustration, in fact, lies not only its clarification of the Mummers tradition, but primarily in its succinct expression of this basic contrast between men of the future and men of the past.

Clym is one of a group in the well scene—where the Egdon natives are intent on raising the bucket from the depths of Captain Vye's well. The scene has melodrama in it, but is also important because it depicts a moment when the plot shifts into complications for Clym and Eustacia. The drawing thus brings into relief a dramatic moment which might easily have been passed over by the average reader. In the August illustration (Plate 8), Clym has an important place in the scene's composition, but still remains subordinate to the grand and imposing figure of Eustacia. What the scene reveals of Clym is his peace with the elements—a condition which, if contrasted to Eustacia's, means that his will not be the tragedy that comes with active warring against the heath. The scene's most important contribution to the series, however, is not particularly in its depiction of either Eustacia or Clym, but in the metaphoric statement it succinctly makes of man's relations with nature: three figures (the third is Fairway's) framed by trees, sky, and the stubborn undergrowth of Egdon. Their responses to the forces conveyed by the heath determine the futures of the three human figures. This particular scene, as well as the early scene of Eustacia on the heath, demonstrates that the representational illustration can indeed make important metaphorical statement.

In the remaining illustrations Thomasin Yeobright and Diggory Venn each appear in separate scenes, then appear together in the November illustration as they search for Wildeve in the darkness of night. Earlier, Thomasin appears against a background of domesticated nature, as she sorts apples in the loft, and her integration with this background contrasts with the illustrations showing Eustacia at odds with her environment. The domestic surroundings of Thomasin in this scene, and of Venn in the homey surroundings of his reddleman's van, counterpoint the tumultous passion of Eustacia, as well as the powerful influence of untamed nature that is Egdon Heath. Through lighting and composition these scenes dealing with Venn and Thomasin are reminiscent of Dutch realism.

One of the weakest scenes in the series occurs in the July installment (Plate 31), where Hopkins depicts Wildeve and Christian Cantle as they gamble for the money Cantle carries to give Thomasin and Clym as a present from Mrs. Yeobright. The scene is visually pleasing because of the positioning of the figures against the light, as well as for the actual event of throwing the dice, but Hopkins inexplicably leaves out the heath-croppers that Hardy mentions have crowded around as if to watch the human figures. The scene misses the most dramatic moment in the episode, since Hopkins depicts the situation just before Venn replaces Cantle, and the glowworms replace the candlelight. The problem of the glowworms might have been part of what Hardy meant when he apologetically referred to "outlandish" scenes Hopkins would be faced with illustrating. By omitting this unique situation, however, Hopkins lost much of the drama and spirit of Hardy's scene.

When viewed as a series, and in relationship to each other, the illustrations for *The Return of the Native* convey one of the novel's important themes—alienation, whether it be the individual separated from nature, or from a society intrinsically associated with nature. The first scene in the set of illustrations (Plate 32), for instance, presents the Egdon rustics on the occasion of the November fifth bonfire on Rainbarrow. Missing from this scene is the sense of panorama and high visual drama conveyed through the textual description of the Rainbarrow fire leaping into the sky, visible for miles around. The artist has chosen to omit the actual fire and depict, instead, its effects on the people gathered around it. The restricted focus of the scene has an advantage, however, since it emphasizes that the rustics are in tune with the Heath, as Eustacia is not, and as Clym wished to be. It is the first and last time that an entire group in harmony with their natural surroundings appears in the Hopkins drawings. The second illustration, as noted, presents Eustacia alone on the Heath; Clym will be depicted with the rustics on the night of the Mummers' play, but he will be shown as quite set apart from the rest of the group. The furze-cutting scene (Plate 8) completes the alienation motif by depicting Clym in harmony with nature, and with Eustacia more alienated (signified by her costuming) than she had been in her first appearance in the illustrations. The illustrations thus capture the novel's major thematic movement as they show increasing alienation/harmony for the major figures. Yet the single figure scenes of Thomas and Diggory Venn also show the isolated form—this time in harmony with environment. While this, too, is important to the basic issue, since Thomasin and Diggory are important contrasts to Eustacia and Clym, their inclusion in the series is confusing. The focus shifts too much here for the alienation/harmony motif, and the thrust of the other illustrations in this motif is dulled because of these domestic scenes.

One of the most striking effects in the Hopkins graphics involves the illustrator's use of light and darkness to convey atmosphere and meaning. Nine of the drawings are night scenes; seven of these have their light sources within the scene e.g., one of the human figures carries a lantern or candle which illuminates faces or actions. In the other scenes, the artist uses sunlight streaming into a dark stable loft, or the glow of a fire on the heath, to contrast effectively with the surrounding darkness. The main drama of the novel does actually occur at night, thus making such scenes graphically faithful to the text, but Hopkins is also careful to handle the light (in its direction and quality, for instance) in the manner described by Hardy, thus demonstrating his meticulous attention to the details of the text. Besides an inherent visual interest, the contrast between light and darkness increases the sense of drama and also organizes the scene's visual information. Because the light (or fire) sources also help to underscore the Promethean theme Hardy was so interested in conveying, the illustrator's handling of this kind of scene reveals his attempt to be faithful to the spirit as well as the facts of the text.

Illustrations for serial fiction do not usually present a scene which has only nature for its center of interest. Most often, the primary subject of serial illustration is the human element. In *The Return of the Native*, the custom holds true, since each view of Egdon Heath becomes only background for the human figures within it. None of the illustrations conveys the sense of barrenness, the horizontality of Egdon, of its "antique, seamed face," and surely none of the drawings captures or even makes any attempt to capture the dominant position Hardy gave to the heath in the novel's initial chapters. Admittedly, the awesomeness of Egdon would be impossible to capture adequately within the boundaries of the 4″ by 3″ line engraving used in *Belgravia*. (The much larger plates of *The Graphic*, however, might well have managed it.) In spite of the difficulties of illustrating the heath, Hopkins still tried to convey its sense. The heath does appear in the February and July engravings (Plates 7 & 31) as torturous, unkempt undergrowth, and in the August scene (Plate 8) as resistant to man's attempts at taming its growth. In the October drawing, (Plate 28) the view through Eustacia's window reveals the bare, horizontal panorama of Egdon, and in the November engraving, depicting Diggory and Thomasin in search of Wildeve, a chaotic nature is the background. Thus, Hopkins is aware of Egdon's importance in the scheme of Hardy's text, and he has attempted to give pictorial significance to Hardy's heath. None of these illustrated scenes, however, does real justice to Hardy's descriptions of Egdon's physical properties, nor to his belief in Egdon's cosmic significance.

Although many of the illustrations in the series have visual interest and thematic significance, much of importance in the novel is not illustrated. The strong, mutual attraction between Clym and Eustacia is not conveyed, for instance, and there is a curious absence of the relationships between other sets of characters, such as Venn and Thomasin (even though they do appear together in one scene), Clym and his mother, Wildeve and Eustacia. From beginning to end, the pictorial version stresses Eustacia more than other characters, and in her individual state rather than in her relationships with other characters. Her loneliness and suffering are stressed, while Clym's problems, at least equal in pain, especially after his mother's death, are not adequately conveyed through the novel's illustrations. Thus, though Hardy had placed Clym first in his hierarchy of character importance, the illustrations belie this arrangement. A considerable part of this stress on Eustacia is of course due to the text itself—Hardy was simply more interested in the figure of Eustacia Vye than he had ever been in Clym Yeobright. Even in his early instructions to his illustrator, Hardy was content to leave Clym's depiction to Hopkins's pen. The drawings thus reflect the situation of the text itself. Even so, Hopkins misses several opportunities to strengthen Clym's position (especially at the novel's end, where he sacrifices characterization to melodramatic events), and to emphasize the pain inherent in human relationships. The text does contain these materials, and proper illustration might have brought them into visual and dramatic relief.

Though several of his scenes are potentially exciting, Hopkins fails to capitalize on the text. In a novel that abounds in dramatic materials, it is hard to understand why Hopkins was not as successful as Pasquier was, for instance, in several of his plates for *A Pair of Blue Eyes*. Compared to Pasquier as well as to Helen Peterson Allingham, Hopkins is simply not as good an illustrator. His work lacks the vigor of strong lines which give direction to the full size engraving, as well as the memorable details of face and posture. The idealized facial features found in most of the plates depicting female characters detract from the uniqueness of situation as well as of personality. On the other hand, the moody Eustacia was a more difficult subject for the artist's pen than the less complex Elfride Swancourt or Bathsheba Everdene.

Though considerable unevenness exists in the Hopkins illustrations, the series as a whole must be commended for its recognition of the novel's basic movement of alienation-harmony. Many of Hopkins's details, furthermore, have metaphoric significance, as in the appearance of the health-croppers in one of the early plates. The contrast between light and darkness has additional significance beyond the handling of detail and visual drama. The prominence of the lighted lantern carried by man and surrounded by darkness, for instance, suggests that man is an intruder in the darkness of night, particularly in the encompassing darkness of Egdon. The handling of reflected light is one of the more pleasing images in the drawings and, of course, faithfully illustrates Hardy's own textual descriptions of light reflected in "Rembrandt's intensest manner." But even with these positive qualities, Hopkins's work is not among the best of the

Hardy illustrations. Uncertain focus and lack of skillful delineation are major deficiencies in the series, and the successful plates do not contribute enough in the way of character insight, explication of setting and detail, and even metaphoric statement to overcome major technical flaws and thematic confusion.

The Mayor of Casterbridge: Realism and Metaphor

The twenty illustrations that Robert Barnes contributed to *The Mayor of Casterbridge* are exceptionally well drawn, possess a strong focus, and create an atmosphere appropriate for Hardy's own powerful text. Especially noteworthy is Barnes's precision of detail, not only in the matter of background but even more so in the delineation of character relationships, and in the tracing of psychological change in the major characters. Barnes achieves all of this through highly individualized facial detail, backgrounds marked with the details of photographic realism, and human figures that have the recognizable gestures of genre painting. Yet Barnes is able to carry these figures beyond the conventions of genre painting; they seem ready to break into movement. This potential seems especially effective because the figures are set against backgrounds rich in detail. Photographic style is thus particularly influential in the *Casterbridge* illustrations. A judicious scene selection, furthermore, enables the series to stress the novel's basic rhythmic patterns. What is perhaps most interesting is the illustration's use of picture, sometimes reflecting Hardy's own techniques, but at other times complementing those techniques in a variety of ways.

As might be expected, the figures of Michael Henchard and Elizabeth-Jane dominate the illustrations, Elizabeth-Jane appearing in eleven plates, Henchard in nine. Of the remaining characters, Susan Henchard and Lucetta Le Sueur each appear in four scenes, while Farfrae, somewhat surprisingly, appears in eight. None of these characters appears alone, but always in pointed relationship with at least one other figure. Barnes thus achieves a good balance between the major characters, but still manages to have Michael Henchard in the dominant position.

Though Henchard does not receive the sort of emphasis carried by the single figure scene, his changing fortunes clearly emerge from the series of illustrations—a combination of focus and balance not achieved in the Hopkins illustrations for *The Return of the Native*.

Throughout the series of illustrations, either Barnes or *The Graphic's* editor demonstrates considerable care in the selection of scene. The opening illustration (Plate 33), for instance, has significance in terms of plot development and possibly also in character insight. Here Barnes depicts Michael and Susan Henchard, with their child, on the road in search of work. The family image, set against a pleasant rural background is, of course, essential to understanding the extent of the novel's tragedy, for never again will these three figures be in the same relationship. The youthfulness of Henchard and his wife, the wife's preoccupation with her child while her husband proudly asks directions from the farmer they meet on the road, capture the essence of each of these characters, for it is Michael's pride and Susan's immersion in her child, her avoidance of the external difficulties of finding their way, that do so much in forming the later events of their lives. In the positioning of the two major figures, Barnes suggests the burden of coping with the business of travel rests solely on Henchard, and this pictorial suggestion may help to mitigate the later action of wife-selling while he is under the influence of alcohol. Certainly the selection of this particular scene, placing the young family against a pleasing rural background, creates a far different effect than if the selling of Susan in the Furmity Woman's tent had been selected for illustration—yet the latter is by far the more significant scene in terms of the novel's logic, since all the later actions stem from this action of wife-selling. The Victorian audience, however, would have had this road scene with its family image shaping their first impression of Michael Henchard.

A rating of the novel's important characters often overlooks Susan Henchard, yet she appears in four of the first five illustrated scenes. Her character in the text itself is somewhat deceptive; Hardy presents her as meek, passive, but persevering. The illustrations in this case appear to shift this reading of character. When visible in the illustrations, Susan's face is bright and alive, especially in the scene (Plate 34) where she overhears the voice of her long absent husband. She is a curious mixture of passivity and strength, and the latter is conveyed in the scene with the Furmity Woman, when her look of easy confidence contrasts with the calculating leer on the Furmity Woman's face (Plate 35). Only in the scene depicting Susan's meeting with Henchard at night, in the shadows of Maumbury Ring, is Susan presented as the passive creature of Fate (Plate 36). The scene is a striking one because of its emotional quality, not only in Susan's case but also for Henchard's, as his posture reveals a mixture of strength and tenderness toward the woman he has deeply wronged. Aside from this plate (which has its own revelations), the early illustrations emphasize the strengths of Susan Henchard in her search for her daughter's security, and thus shift, if ever so slightly, the textual reading of Susan as passive, though persevering. Interestingly enough, the Barnes drawings present Lucetta Le Sueur in a favorable light—much more favorable than she appears in the 1912 edition of the text. The change, however, is due primarily to Hardy's own revisions between the serial and the 1912 text. The serial, for instance, explains Lucetta's relations with

Henchard have been solemnized by a secret marriage; the 1912 text refers to an intimacy, but no marriage, between the two. Thus, it is no surprise that Lucetta is not depicted as temptress in the Barnes drawings, as she might have been if the later text had been the basis for the illustrations.

In only one illustrated scene (Plate 37) is there a hint of shallowness or falseness in this woman (as she tells Elizabeth-Jane in cloaked language, of her love for Farfrae). For the most part, Barnes's depiction emphasizes Lucetta as a woman of fashion, hurt at Henchard's cutting her on the streets of Casterbridge (Plate 38), and as a woman in love, since the illustrations presenting both Lucetta and Farfree suggest she is truly in love with the Scotsman. Barnes's handling of facial detail becomes quite important for creating this suggestion, though the serial text, itself, does convey this interpretation. One of these later scenes (Plate 39) was cut altogether from the 1912 text, thus eliminating a highly favorable view of Lucetta's love for Farfrae. As the serial text explains, she has just returned from an interview with Henchard in which she played on his sympathies by making herself appear haggard through the skillful use of makeup. (The text stresses that her duplicity is due to her desperation—she is trying to get Henchard to return her incriminating letters before Farfrae might hear of them.) The fact that Barnes depicts the favorable domestic scene of her greeting by Farfrae, rather than the much more dramatic (and unfavorable) meeting with Henchard, helps to create a more positive reading of Lucetta's character.

In the scene depicting Lucetta's shock as she watches the skimmington-ride (Plate 40), the figures of the skimmington-ride itself are not shown in the drawing; instead, the focus is on the two observers. Barnes ably captures the drama of the event through the look on Lucetta's face, and through the concerned look on Elizabeth-Jane's face helps to create audience sympathy for Lucetta. Thus, the particular choices made in this scene, as well as in many other plates in the *Casterbridge* series, together with some essential differences in the serial text itself, result in a more favorable interpretation of Lucetta than emerges in later editions.

Illustrations depicting Elizabeth-Jane, the third woman counter-pointed with Henchard, focus on her support of Lucetta, her interest in Farfrae and, of course, her painful relationship with Henchard. This balance emphasizes that Elizabeth-Jane is betrayed in one way or another by all three: Farfrae, who all too quickly and casually turns his attentions to Lucetta; Lucetta, who has Elizabeth-Jane for a companion and then usurps her place in Farfrae's affections; and Henchard, who first unknowingly and then knowingly deceives her in the matter of her parentage. Such relationships are present in the text, but the illustrations stress them because of the specific choice of scene: Farfrae and Elizabeth-Jane dancing, Lucetta confiding in her, Henchard telling her he is her real father. Again, the spacing of these illustrations emphasizes Hardy's considerable attention to balanced structure, as these developments in Elizabeth-Jane's relationships with other characters are evenly spread throughout the story itself as well as in the series of illustrations.

Two scenes are particularly successful in capturing the pain of Elizabeth-Jane's life, as well as Henchard's, and a large part of the success is due to the way Barnes uses detail to convey emotion. In the final illustration for the series, for instance, where Henchard seeks to explain his actions, the position of Elizabeth-Jane's hands indicates that she has moved backwards to put more distance between Henchard and herself, thus emphasizing the fractured relationship between the two (Plate 41). In earlier drawings, the details of dress—from a somewhat dowdy daughter of Susan Henchard to the more respectable companion of Lucetta Le Sueur, and then to the fashionable wife of Donald Farfrae—are caught in the Barnes drawings. And when her face is not visible, or just partially visible, her posture provides the key to her thoughts and feelings, and reveals possibly as much of character as facial expression might have done. In the main, Elizabeth-Jane's presence in the illustrations is, as in the text itself, not dramatic, but in keeping with a woman who, as Hardy describes her, was surprised that she had found happiness after so many experiences which had seemed to teach her that life was to be painful.

Illustrations dealing with Donald Farfrae are faithful to Hardy's text: he is young, energetic, unchanging. His facial expression in the Barnes drawings reveals him to be congenial and confident. In the text his personality is further defined through his calm acceptance of Lucetta's death after he realizes what life with her would have been like had she lived. Farfrae possesses one of those "well-proportioned minds" Hardy had described in *The Return of the Native*, a reason why Farfrae is a mediocre character, regardless of his zeal and confidence. Yet Farfrae's presence in the Barnes drawings contributes something essential, for by having so many views of Farfrae with his laughter, ease, and domestic happiness, Barnes counterpoints the scenes presenting the burdened, suffering Michael Henchard. Both men have an almost equal number of appearances in the illustrations—a fact that does not seem justified in Farfrae's case. What Barnes successfully creates, however, is an alternating pattern of the light-hearted Farfrae with the burdened Henchard, a visual rhythm which parallels and inevitably stresses the rhythm in the text itself.

Illustrations dealing with Michael Henchard are the most powerful of the Barnes graphics. From the youthful hay trusser leading his family along the Wessex road, to the older man matured by guilt and suffering in the rest of the illustrations, Barnes conveys the ruggedness, the stubborn pride in his own strength that are the most prominent qualities of Michael

Henchard. The illustrations are well-balanced in that they capture a wide range of his emotions: his tenderness toward Susan; his deep concern for Elizabeth-Jane conveyed through his two-handed grasp of her hand, as well as through his bent figure (Plate 42); his balked pride at learning Elizabeth-Jane had lowered herself to serve, even temporarily, the customers at the King of Prussia Inn. These illustrations preceding Henchard's downfall reveal the tenderness of which he is capable, but also reveal the pride which will eventually lead to tragedy. In both cases, Barnes conveys emotion through Henchard's posture as well as through facial detail.

Two other scenes involving Henchard are particularly important for the insight they offer into the character of this complex man. In depicting the fight between Henchard and Farfrae (Plate 43). Barnes captures a bestial expression on Henchard's face as the defeated mayor seeks to punish Farfrae for taking Lucetta, his business, his house, his social standing. The drawing conveys Henchard's power and even his misguided honor by emphasizing his bound arm. This deliberate handicap on Henchard's part is surely an insult to Farfrae's own prowess and honor—thus the illustration emphasizes Henchard's invariable muddling of things, in spite of good intentions. This foreground delineation of Henchard's power, rage, frustration, and even miscalculation, combines with important details of corn, barn, and a glimpse of Casterbridge as background, and thus is a typical instance of Barnes's care in using the entire frame of his drawing to present important detail. The illustration is a powerful set-piece, yet Barnes is able to convey movement as well.

The final scene in the set (Plate 41) is as important for the characterization of Henchard as it is for Elizabeth-Jane. Through the upraised arm, Barnes shows that Henchard desires to calm Elizabeth-Jane as he explains his actions. The lines in his face clearly reveal his suffering, and ought to be contrasted with the youthful features in the first plate of the series to demonstrate how far Henchard has travelled in these twenty years. These details of posture and facial expression, as well as clothing, create in the viewer an awareness of Henchard's emotional life—from youthful self-confidence to tenderness, from haughtiness to anger and, finally, to despair over his own inability to set things right. The Barnes illustrations, in effect, reveal the best and the worst of Michael Henchard.

In giving these penetrating character insights, the Barnes illustrations do not neglect dramatic moments. Most of the scenes conveying the heightened dramatic moment, however, are carefully linked to character revelation or growth, and do not seem to be chosen for plot interest alone. Susan with her ear against the wall, hearing Henchard's voice after almost twenty years; Henchard telling Elizabeth-Jane she is his daughter (as he then believes); Henchard and Farfrae fighting; Lucetta and Elizabeth-Jane viewing the "skimmity-ride"—all these are intrinsically related to the sources of suffering, as well as having immediate, dramatic impact.

Barnes is not always successful, however, in this attempt to capture the dramatic moment. Two illustrations fail to convey much dramatic impact. The first depicts Lucetta as she turns around, expecting to see Henchard but finding Farfrae instead; the second portrays Farfrae coming to Lucetta's rescue after she and Elizabeth-Jane have been frightened by a bull. Each of these drawings lacks the power of the other dramatic incidents; the second scene, furthermore, is considerably anti-climactic, since the rescue is shown after the moment of its greatest need. Each of the other dramatic illustrations, however, reveals expectation, pain, hate, or fear, and the various emotions are superbly conveyed through Barnes's handling of facial expression. The use of gesture and the arrangement of the human figures often echo the conventions of genre painting. Yet the highly individualized facial detail gives originality to what might have become, in less skillful hands, a tired replay of the conventional. The Barnes drawings capture the dramatic moment with considerable success, and manage to link drama with psychological reality.

The spacing of the Henchard and Farfrae illustrations creates an alternating pattern, or rhythm, within the series. Another contribution to the novel's rhythm, though it overlaps with the Henchard-Farfrae pattern, is Barnes's use of domestic scenes. Four scenes deal with calmer and happier moments in the story—reminding the audience that there are many such moments. Three of these scenes take place, under convivial conditions, in sitting rooms; Lucetta telling Elizabeth-Jane of her love for Farfrae; Lucetta and Farfrae, after their marriage, sharing some happy moments (as indicated, the textual description of this particular scene was omitted in later editions, with the change in Lucetta's characterization); Elizabeth-Jane anxiously peering out the window, thinking of the exiled Henchard, but with the scene dominated by Farfrae and Newson enjoying a convivial chat (Plate 44). Here the audience becomes aware of those intermittent moments in *The Mayor of Casterbridge* when life seems full of promise, even after a time of great pain. The existence and positioning of these various moments of happiness demonstrate their importance to the full understanding of the novel. Their positioning against other scenes (admittedly dominant) which convey the sense of disaster that always seems to hang over these major figures creates an alternating visual pattern. This visual pattern does more than parallel the text; it provides insight into Hardy's method of creating the rhythm of this well-structured novel.

Unlike most of Hardy's other novels, *The Mayor of Casterbridge* has few landscapes in its text, though Maumbury Ring, as well as the road to and from Casterbridge, might qualify. Both are present in the series of illustrations, but are de-emphasized in favor of the human figures. The Barnes drawings quite properly stress the sitting room, Henchard's yard, a meeting on a bridge, since major events occur in these deceptively ordinary places. Casterbridge itself, however, is left to the reader's imagination. This so distinct Wessex town is not given any special place in the illustrations, nor is it really detailed in physical terms, especially when the visual Casterbridge is measured against Hardy's textual description. Yet the absence is not troubling because the *sense* of the town emerges from Barnes's excellent use of detail—a small corner of Henchard's yard, the interior of a barn, the furnishings of Lucetta's sitting room. This evocative use of detail occurs in Barnes's depiction of the major characters as well, in their clothing, posture, and particularly in their facial expressions.

Hardy's own great care in structuring certain scenes so that they create a visual impact is most definitely a significant part of the novel's illustrations. A careful textual reading reveals that many crucial scenes take place in or near doorways, or can be viewed by a select audience through or from windows. This technique of presenting scene "frames" the action. Many more of these scenes occur in the text than Barnes was able to include in the illustrations, but several of his drawings ably convey this visual structure contained within Hardy's text. These particular illustrations have an additional visual interest in that the character who is viewing through the frame is himself framed for the audience of the serial text. The Barnes drawings thus are able to convey an aesthetic concept that, while inherent in the text, is not easily or readily apparent to the reader's imagination. In certain scenes, too, (such as Susan's overhearing and recognizing Henchard's voice as she is framed by the bedposts) the stasis within the heightened moment is more clearly defined through the framing device. (In this particular scene, too, the bedposts are ironic and metaphoric comment on Susan's married life.)

Several other illustrations make important contributions to the details of the story's setting: Susan returning to Casterbridge Fair; Farfrae entertaining the townsfolk in the King of Prussia Inn (Plate 45), changed in later editions to the Three Mariners Inn; Farfrae and Elizabeth-Jane dancing. In all three scenes the rustics and Casterbridge folk in the background are handled with considerable individuality. Though the sense of group is important here, Barnes individualizes each of the figures, from distinctive facial details to dress, even to pipe, mugs, spectacles in the King of Prussia scene; to the posters and banners, interested onlookers, even to a rifle carried by one of the background figures in the Casterbridge Fair scene, where Susan encounters the Furmity Woman. The details of these scenes make it eminently clear that Barnes saw the story of the major characters set against a very vital and distinctive Casterbridge background. Again, a *sense* of the place emerges through these details, rather than through extensive physical delineation. As for the individualized treatment given to the rustic figures, Barnes achieves what neither Helen Allingham nor Arthur Hopkins was able to do in their handling of the rustics in group scenes. Through suggestive detail, Barnes conveys the calm stability in the lives of the novel's minor characters—distinctly at variance with the major figures' lives.

The realism of physical detail and the metaphor of its suggestion emerge from the Barnes illustrations in more specific ways than the basic framing technique used in scene presentation or in details of characterization. Several illustrations, for instance, depict the interior of a Casterbridge home—either Lucetta's or Henchard's (which later, after Henchard's fall, becomes Farfrae's home). All these interior settings contain one or more oil paintings as part of the normal furnishings. They possess no special iconographic significance in the *subject* depicted, since the actual subjects, whether portraits or street scenes, are either unimportant or not clear enough to be defined. They do have metaphoric meaning, however. The paintings themselves, together with their ornate and heavy frames, convey the respectability of Lucetta's and Henchard's homes—at variance with the pattern of their lives. For both characters, the search for social respectability is paramount, and the heavy, ornate paintings seem to stress the elusiveness of the goal, though at times in their stories, it seems that respectability and social standing have been achieved. The fragile nature of this external respectability is ironically underscored through the massive paintings, yet their continued presence in the illustrations emphasizes that the goal is still sought in the middle of the various disasters that befall Lucetta and Henchard.

When these paintings are viewed as part of Henchard's background, and when his figure is also part of the scene, the massiveness and rigidity of the framed painting echo the bulk of Henchard's body, as well as the rigidity of his personality. The framed painting, furthermore, repeats in miniature the framing technique used for several scenes and characters, as mentioned earlier. The framed painting thus repeats the visual image of doorway and window frames. The pattern completes itself through the bedpost frame and also through the square of the fireplace, present in several drawings. The massive squareness conveys the solidity of the Casterbridge world, as well as the reality of Michael Henchard. The framing devices also convey the metaphor of *entrapment*. As such, they are an important interpretation of Hardy's text. To the extent that they are not detailed in the text (as the picture frames are not), they are the illustrator's expansion of the text.

Several variations of this metaphor of entrapment occur in the illustrations. Considerable emphasis on the use of picture (aside from the oil paintings mentioned above) occurs within some scenes. The banners and posters in the Casterbridge Fair scene are a delightful means of conveying local color, and ironically emphasize the gaiety of the scene against the somberness of Susan Henchard's search. In other illustrations, the peacocks and other birds pictured on the screen in Lucetta and Farfrae's sitting room (Plate 39), or the stuffed birds or drawings of birds over the fireplace in the King of Prussia Inn (Plate 45) have important iconographic significance. Each of these bird images is caught within the confines of the screen, or frame and canvas (or even once living bodies as in the case of the stuffed birds). All these images echo the motif of entrapment, first presented in the text (and not illustrated) in the first visit to the Casterbridge Fair. When Henchard sells Susan to Newson, a bird flies within the Furmity Woman's tent, unable to escape its confinement. The entrapment image makes its final appearance in the text (again, not illustrated), at the novel's end, with Henchard's gift to Elizabeth-Jane of the caged goldfinch. These images are clearly metaphoric through the text itself; the pictures and other objects mentioned, however, are the illustrator's additions and serve to draw attention to the entrapment motif in general.

One "picture" within the illustrations has a very special iconographic significance that goes beyond the metaphoric contributions of those just mentioned. On the tapestry hanging in Lucetta's and Farfrae's sitting room is a serpentine design (Plate 39). This particular design echoes the entanglement in her own life, and even her deceptiveness, since the scene depicted occurs just after Lucetta has met Henchard in secret. Trying to play on his sympathies so that he will return her incriminating letters, she has used makeup to make herself look older and haggard with suffering. The serpentine design is an appropriate comment.

What Barnes has done through his strong lines and vivid rendering of detail is to infuse a satisfying combination of vigorous and austere strength into the scenes selected for illustration. His consistency in the handling of detail, and his economical and metaphorical use of the "business" within a scene (such as pictures, screens, and the various framing devices—not all of which are present in the text) make the engravings for *The Mayor of Casterbridge* the most distinctive among the Hardy illustrations. The powerful lines used by Barnes in the depiction of setting and character, furthermore, are particularly suited to the austere strength of the novel itself.

Not since *Far from the Madding Crowd* had the spirit of a Hardy novel been so consistently captured in its illustrations, but artist Robert Barnes succeeded in accomplishing just that. The sense of a developing central character, the alternating pattern of painful and joyful scenes, the pleasing and controlled shift of focus from one female character to another as they come into their importance for Michael Henchard's life, the favorable view of Lucetta—all these, of course, live within the serial text itself. What the Barnes illustrations do is to bring all these strengths of Hardy's text into relief. What is more, because of their special insights into character, the realistic and metaphoric uses of detail, and the selective stresses created through choice of scene which illuminate the novel's inherent rhythmic pattern, the Barnes illustrations become a visual expansion of Hardy's text.

Tess of the D'Urbervilles: The Individual and Society

Tess of the D'Urbervilles appeared in *The Graphic* in weekly installments, with twenty-five illustrations, including two in double page format. The size of *The Graphic* meant that the doublespread illustration was a very large engraving, a fact that was to enhance many of the *Tess* drawings. As explained earlier, *Tess* actually had four artists sharing the chores of illustration, a situation that created considerable diversity in the depiction of Tess and in the general style of drawing. Borough Johnson, for instance, tended to follow in the style of Hubert Herkomer, the principal artist for the illustrations. The work of Daniel Wehrschmidt and J. Syddall is quite unlike their collaborators' and much inferior. Yet the changes in Tess's depiction, as well as the mixture of styles within the rural scenes and between rural and domestic scenes, are truer to the novel's fundamentals than seem so at first glance.

Many abrupt shifts in mood occur as Hardy moves Tess from Talbothays' tranquility and lushness to Flintcomb-Ash's harshness and sterility, or from youthful innocence to a painfully acquired experience in the ways of men and the opinions of the world. The differences in style within the series of drawings may then be justified—yet the flaws in the conception of many of the *Tess* illustrations still remain. There is a vagueness in some of the drawings, and details are simply not given the same attention as they received in the work of Allingham for *Far from the Madding Crowd* or Barnes in *The Mayor of Casterbridge*. Sometimes suggestion works, as in several of the indoor scenes, but it is disastrous in the rural scenes. Here the detail of nature and its panoramic quality—so very evident in Hardy's text—are absent. Tess's characterization, too, lacks a coherent presentation.

Though the illustrations as a whole do not do justice to Hardy's insight into and use of nature, give little character insight, and are in some cases simply not well drawn, there are still many strengths in the series. Several of the individual plates are impressive in their depiction of important moments in the story. *Picture* becomes an important quality in many of the illustrations, since they convey a sense of completeness in design based on a formal arrangement of figures. Signals within these scenes convey information complete in itself.

In thematic terms, the drawings make an important contribution, demonstrating that considerable care went into scene selection. The illustrations, in fact, demonstrate that Hardy's sense of irony, his pictorial imagination, and plot manipulation are carefully interwoven. The *Tess* drawings are thus among the very few of the Hardy illustrations that do justice to his distinctively ironic vision.

Five of the drawings are quite impressive, and if the rest of the illustrations could measure up to these, the series would indeed be distinctive. The first drawing for the serial, for instance, is a double-page engraving which depicts Tess as she returns from the May Dance and steps into a house filled with children (Plate 14). The scene is dominated by a mother struggling with the family washing. While work is a prominent theme in the scene, so too is the sense of stability, of together-ness in the family grouping, and the engraving thus appears to be a calculated appeal to an audience looking for a "family" novel. The domestic scene with the young girl in white returning from an innocent dance must have reassured the Victorian audience that this was to be fit family reading. The engraving itself is superb, not only in its technical quality (that is, in the lines of the engraving, a perfection that seems to have been the rule for *The Graphic's* illustrations, and is quite separate from the artist's conception and general handling of the scene), but also in Herkomer's dramatic handling of large blocks of light and dark tones, as well as in Tess's facial expression.

The actual size of the double-page engraving contributes enormously to its dramatic impact, for the scene in its textual presentation is not particularly dramatic, nor even so important in its own right that it *had* to be chosen for illustration. The May Dance itself, for instance, might have been the more proper illustration for this first installment, since it foreshadows Tess's later relationship with Angel Clare. The selection of this first scene, however, is part of the domestic theme conveyed through the illustrations as a series. For itself and for its role in developing this theme, this first illustration is impressive.

Though the opening illustration to the serial publication of *Tess of the D'Urbervilles* would have appealed to an audience looking for a story fit for family reading, the second illustration would have warned the audience that the story was to have much pain in it (Plate 46). A tightly framed close-up of Tess dejectedly looking at the body of Prince, the family horse, and interpreting the event in cosmic terms, is significant for its detail, its subject matter, and its plot position. The event is extremely important because it marks the turning point in Tess's fortunes: the economic disaster of Prince's death causes Tess to seek work with the D'Urberville family and prepares the way for meeting Alec D'Urberville. We also see a different Tess from the happy youth of the first illustration.

In addition to this emphasis on a changing Tess and the fateful event itself, the drawing also serves to make immediate human reactions more credible. After Prince's horrible accident, for instance, Tess's younger brother Abraham philosophizes: "'Tis because we be on a blighted star, and not a sound one, isn't it, Tess?" Such reflections are common from Hardy's children (Johnny Nunsuch in *The Return of the Native*, and Father Time in *Jude the Obscure*), but if there were any doubt that a child could utter such thoughts, the Victorian audience would have been reassured because of the drawing's focus on the immediate and brutal physical cause. In this sense, the Wehrschmidt drawing of Prince's horrible death increases the credibility of Hardy's text.

An effective pastoral scene (and the only one among the generally disappointing nature scenes) is Herkomer's drawing for August 29, the Mead scene (Plate 15). Farmer Crick and his workers have been individualized, but more important than this is the mixture of hard work and camaraderie that emerges from the scene. The major, diagonal line of the Herkomer drawing is not only visually pleasing but also helps to give some perspective to the background, recreating something of the panoramic quality Hardy infuses into his textual descriptions of Wessex nature.

One of the most powerful illustrations in the entire series is Herkomer's drawing of Tess and Alec, as they work in the patch of ground tilled by the Durbeyfield family, just outside Marlott (Plate 41). Alec's madness and Tess's fear emerge with considerable starkness from this scene, and the two figures surrounded by the fires of couch-grass and cabbage-stalks are drawn with a sense of the scene's fine drama. Herkomer again demonstrates he knows how to blend blocks of light and darkness to create visual impact. The illustration catches a moment when human emotions are uncovered, a fearful moment which allows insight into both characters. The attraction-repulsion contrast, so dominant in this scene, points forward to the final scenes of Hardy's text, when Tess kills Alec at Sandbourne, even though the Victorian audience must have missed much of the agony in these later events, since Hardy deleted the section which indicates Alec and Tess are living together. But Tess's loss of self to Alec's powers does emerge in the later section of the text, even as *The Graphic* published it in bowdlerized form. The hideousness of those later events is increased because of the intense fear of this man so evident in Tess's face in Herkomer's drawing. The Marlott fire scene is frankly melodramatic because of its basic situation—yet the drawing has importance for character revelation, for plot preparation, and for emotional intensity because of Tess's later capitulation to this man she fears. Herkomer's drawing goes far beyond the *type* presentation of character that melodrama usually conveys.

One other scene deserves special consideration, and that is the drawing which depicts Angel Clare as he lies in his sickbed, after returning from Brazil (Plate 48). The drawing shows Clare as haggard and helpless, making him more human and possibly more acceptable to the Victorian audience, many of whom would already have sympathised with Angel in his earlier rejection of Tess either for her lack of "purity" or her failure to tell him of her past before she married him. Certainly the picture of an incapacitated Angel Clare underscores the reasons for delay in seeking out Tess after his return from South America. (Other plot changes in the serial text also explain his delay.) While Tess's tragedy can easily blind the reader and hinder a comprehension of the full dimensions of Angel's character, the Herkomer illustration draws attention to Angel's own great suffering, both of body and of spirit.

These five plates, then, make some subtle but important contributions to the way in which the Victorian reader would interpret the novel. As for the series as a whole, none of the other illustrations are impressive individually, but make another kind of contribution to the novel's interpretation. A significant feature of the illustrations is the number dealing with domestic scenes—some one-third of the plates are of this type. Besides the opening illustration depicting Tess returning from the May Dance, other scenes deal with episodes in the Crick farmhouse, and one presents Tess and Angel immediately after their wedding as they are congratulated by their friends. Still other scenes of this sort include the Clare household at Emminster, or the Durbeyfields on the road. The effect of these domestic scenes is to emphasize the human context—the family setting of home or work—that provides background for both Tess and Angel.

The illustrations depicting the Durbeyfield family are the most important of the domestic scenes, since they point up one of the novel's basic motifs, that of nineteenth century changes in what had been a relatively stable rural area. The domestic stability of the Durbeyfield family as shown in the first illustration contrasts starkly with a later, Wehrschmidt drawing (Plate 49) which depicts the fatherless family on the road, possessions piled high on their overburdened wagon. The destruction of the Durbeyfield way of life conveys the larger, changing scene in rural England. In effect, the contrast between the two illustrations reminds a reading audience that there is a very real and tragic background to the overwhelming personal tragedies of the major characters. It is not only Tess who wanders from place to place, but a family and a nation of nineteenth century families.

Several other illustrations contribute to a sense of stability by emphasizing the domestic element, particularly in the sense of group relationships, which will contrast later with scenes of Tess's and Angel's loneliness that appear either in the text (particularly in Tess's case) or in the illustrations, as happens with Angel. The two scenes depicting Angel with his family also emphasize the close ties he has with his parents, even though he believes he has rejected their traditions. This closeness needs to be remembered when Angel's later actions are judged, for the illustrations stress that Angel has never really forsaken tradition, as the depiction of family scenes reminds the serial audience. Once again, the illustrations point toward a sympathetic understanding of Angel Clare's situation and character. The dramatic handling of light, together with large blocks of rich shading, are distinctive marks of the Herkomer style, and in these particular scenes both Wehrschmidt and especially Borough Johnson demonstrate they can create drawings with the power Herkomer has. The technique creates drama in such scenes as Angel overhearing the conversation at Dairyman Crick's table between Tess and the other dairy workers (Plate 50), and Angel's appearance at his Emmister home to inform his parents of his love for Tess. The text itself does not really call for such intense renderings of scenes which (particularly in the Crick house) are not terribly dramatic or emotional in themselves. Details of background have been wisely sacrificed for the rich shadings which create dramatic, suggestive atmosphere.

The rural theme in both its pastoral and Darwinian aspects is clearly subordinate to the domestic scenes and especially to character relationships. In no illustration is the rural scene presented for its own sake; one or more human figures appears always in the foreground. In addition to the early scene depicting Prince's death (where there is some excellent background detail of Wessex nature), five other illustrations with nature as background occur in those installments which take the story up to the point when Tess leaves Talbothays, on the occasion of her marriage with Angel Clare. Each of these scenes, unlike that first scene of death in nature, stresses the pastoral side of the Wessex landscape.

Three of these pastoral scenes are the work of artist J. Sydall, whose work here is flat and uninteresting, with the exception of the September 5 illustration (Plate 51), when something of the lightness and beauty of Talbothays, as well as the emotional attraction between the two foreground figures of Tess and Angel, emerges from the drawing. There is a peacefulness here, mixed in a pleasing manner with a sense of human vitality, as the human forms caught in a moment of movement reveal their attraction for each other.

Another pastoral scene worth noting belongs to E. Borough Johnson, whose view of Tess lying on the grass conveys her anguish as she realizes she is not what Angel Clare thinks she is (Plate 52). Though the engraving is not noteworthy for its lines or even for his handling of Tess's reclining figure (since it seems mechanical and awkward), it stresses a loneliness and suffering even in the rural harmony of Talbothays and reminds the viewer that Tess's past is an important and continuing element in the story. As mood painting, the illustration is effective, and conveys a Pre-Raphaelite quality.

An additional three illustrations stress the anti-pastoral quality of Hardy's text, and relate to Tess's tragedy more specifically, yet fall short of being significant interpretations of that tragedy. In Syddall's view of Tess's encounter with the dying pheasants on the road to Flintcomb-Ash (Plate 53), Tess's clutching at her skirt seems to undercut the horror of her recognition. The text reveals that Tess is deeply disturbed when she realizes the birds are in their prolonged death agony. The movement of her hands may suggest her concern, but also may indicate her wish to avoid contact with the bloody, thrashing pheasants. This suggestion of squeamishness is out of character for a young woman used to farm life, and the suggestion also distorts the parallel relationship Hardy makes in the text between Tess and the pheasants as innocent victims of Nature's Law.

A later Syddall illustration presents Tess working at Flintcomb-Ash, watched by Alec, but the latter is so diminutive a figure as to be barely visible. The illustration is not particularly anti-pastoral in itself, but the textual description certainly conveys this sense. The illustration is thus misleading, and misses a good chance of penetrating character. Hardy's text, for instance, describes Tess's horror at realizing that she is never to be left in peace, even in the hell of Flintcomb-Ash, but neither the insight into character or the anti-pastoral reading of nature emerges from this particular drawing.

The rural scenes thus do not measure up to the demands of the text in the matter of grandeur or desolation, and they do not capture the panoramic quality of Hardy's descriptions, though several scenes contain views of a distant horizon, thus giving the audience some sense of the Hardy landscape. Fully one-third of the *Tess* illustrations give some attention to the rural scene, yet the viewer is never allowed to think that nature, whether pastoral or Darwinian in spirit, is to dominate the story, because each artist carefully infuses the human element into his drawing. Thus, the Mead scene (Plate 15) stresses the human vitality that has its setting—and nourishment—in nature; the riverbank scene (Plate 52) emphasizes human anguish even in a fruitful nature; the death of Prince (Plate 46) reveals the possibilities of pain in what seems to be a more neutral view of nature. In each of these rural scenes, another dimension is added to the information of the text itself. Still, the grandeur and desolation Hardy gives to his textual descriptions do not emerge from these illustrations. The characterization that does emerge from these plates is not impressive enough to make us forget that the illustrations do not do justice to Hardy's descriptions.

Several other scenes focus on character relationships. Drama results from the juxtaposition of characters within the scene, but several of the plates, whether through coincidence or deliberate choice, seem to relate to each other in pairs and, when this occurs, irony results because of counterpointed or reversed situation. Two of the early illustrations, for instance, present Alec and Tess meeting on the road in a pleasant situation (Plate 54). A playful quality emerges from the plate, since Tess appears rather coy, Alec dapper and teasing. The second plate (Plate 55), however, offsets this relationship by depicting a frightened Tess, drawing away from the outstretched arm of a now threatening Alec with a look of repulsion on her face. In another pair of reversal scenes, Tess is first shown opening the barn door to discover Alec holding forth as a preacher; the second drawing depicts Alec confronting Tess to blame her for leading him astray after his conversion. While not as powerful or as clearly ironic as the earlier reversal scenes, this set emphasizes first one, then the other, of the two characters holding the dominant position in confrontation.

A good balance between the appearances of Alec and Angel occurs in the series as a whole, and there is a set of ironic scenes dealing with the tragic relationship of Tess and Angel that is the best of the series in terms of ironic implications. In the first scene (Plate 56), Tess appears, candle in hand, at the head of the stairs, with Angel standing at the bottom of the staircase, pleading for her love. In the second illustration (Plate 57), Tess kneels before Angel, pleading forgiveness, in the manner of Victorian genre painting. The irony of this particular reversal is reinforced through the visual impact of the illustrations, as the positioning of character and the juxtaposition of light and darkness are carefully handled by artists Wehrschmidt and Johnson.

The appearance of these sets of reversal scenes among the *Tess* illustrations indicates that a great deal of foresight must have gone into the selection of scenes for the artist to illustrate, and that something more than dramatic impact or plot clarification was considered in the process of selection. Hardy's ironic vision of life must surely have been understood and appreciated by either *Graphic* editor Arthur Locker or by the artists themselves. The effect is important for the Victorian audience, as the reversal scenes remind them of the continually fatal attraction between the novel's characters, as well as the ironic twists in life's events.

Two other scenes emphasize the tragic relationship between Angel and Tess. Herkomer's illustration for October 17 presents Angel in the sleepwalking scene (Plate 58), when he places Tess on the stone slab (which becomes the abbot's coffin in the restored text). The illustration is disappointing, primarily because of Tess's placid features. She appears far too comfortable for someone in her position, and though the text stresses her acquiescence in whatever Angel might do to her ("He might drown her if he would; it would be better than parting to-morrow to lead severed lives") the artist has not been able to capture a credible facial expression. Angel's face, on the contrary, shows dissociation from reality, a condition that becomes more meaningful the longer the illustration is considered. The drawing is not particularly forceful, surprising since the textual scene is powerful in its grotesqueness.

Though it does not have a companion piece (showing reversal, of course) within the series of illustrations, the sleepwalking scene does have its reversal within the text itself. In Hardy's original manuscript (and later, in the restored version), Angel carries Tess and the other dairymaids, in turn, across the pond of water. Editor Locker asked Hardy to change that scene into one where Angel uses a wheelbarrow to transport the women across the water. Clearly, in the original manuscript, this Talbothays scene and the later sleep-walking scene are ironic reversals (in terms of Angel's consciousness and the object of his carrying Tess), but the irony was lost when the earlier scene was bowdlerized into a wheelbarrow instead of Angel's arms. Neither artist nor illustration had anything to do with that loss, however, since the decision was wholly Locker's. Fortunately the earlier, wheelbarrow scene was not selected for illustration. One suspects the Victorian audience was not quite so subservient to Mrs. Grundy as Arthur Locker believed, and the wheelbarrow scene would have appeared ludicrous even to *Graphic* readers.

The final illustration in the *Tess* series depicts Angel standing by a sleeping Tess, waiting for the constabulary to arrive at Stonehenge (Plate 59). In this Wehrschmidt drawing, the massive rocks of Stonehenge loom large in the background, creating mysterious reminders of time, nature, and sacrifice. The drawing also reminds the audience of earlier scenes in which the juxtaposition of Tess and Angel had stressed their relationship with each other. The situation now has shifted into Angel guarding Tess, standing by her to confront the constables and, through them, the world outside the ring of Stonehenge. This particular drawing stresses Angel's acceptance of Tess and, more than that, his loyalty as they become two against the world. In its basic visual appeal, however, the Stonehenge scene is most unsatisfactory. The engraving is poorly done, Angel's figure is nondescript and too unlike his image in earlier illustrations (even though he has changed from the Angel of the earlier story in an internal sense), and the grassy foreground of the scene receives too much emphasis, thus detracting from the illustration's major information. The impact of this particular scene comes from the text alone, and not from the illustration.

In spite of the problems deriving from bowdlerization and from having four artists illustrate the series, in spite of technical deficiencies and the failure to capture Hardy's nature, the *Tess* illustrations do make some surprising contributions in support of the text. Individual scenes such as

Tess and Alec confronting each other at Marlott, against a lurid background of fire (Plate 47), visually remind the reader of this novel's link with the tradition of the sensation novel. This particular drawing, furthermore, conveys Alec's madness and Tess's fear—psychological states important for understanding the impending tragedy. Several of the rural scenes at Talbothays, the drawing depicting Prince's death, and the very first scene of Tess's return from the May Day dance emphasize important moments within the plot, but also help the viewer to understand the preparations and dimensions of Tess's tragedy.

As might be expected from the bowdlerized text that Locker had demanded if *Tess* were to be published in *The Graphic*, the illustrations sometimes seem to have been selected for their suitability as family viewing. The murder of Alec, for instance, was not chosen for illustration, and the birth, baptism, and death of Sorrow could not be, since that entire episode in Tess's life had been removed from Hardy's text for the serial publication. In spite of the bowdlerized text and poor execution within some of the plates, however, many of the *Tess* illustrations make their mark because of their dramatic and psychological renderings of Hardy's text.

The sense of a completeness in design and, even more so, a set of signals within the illustration that conveys important information marks several of the *Tess* plates. *Picture* describes the Mead scene, with its easy camaraderie set against nature, and even the initial scene, as Tess returns home from the May Day celebration. Herkomer contrasts her young maiden innocence, on the right side of the engraving, with the older woman, surrounded by the experience of children, cradle, and washtub on the left side. The signals of genre painting are especially, but ironically, apparent in an engraving near the novel's conclusion: Alec holds Tess at arm's length, as he accuses her of causing him to fall from his previous, converted state. If the illustration is set in the context of the "fallen woman," or outcast theme, the fact of Alec's fall becomes a nicely ironic male-female inversion. (And since Alec's religious conversion is highly suspect anyway, there may be a double irony here.)

In addition to the pleasing sense of picture in several of the drawings, the series becomes noteworthy for the ironic vision it conveys through the sets of reversal scenes, for its balanced presentation of the novel's three major characters, and for its emphasis on the domestic theme. The *Tess* illustrations convey the understanding that the novel is more than the story of just one person or, as Hardy subtitled his work, a "Pure Woman Faithfully Presented." It is also the story of two men who find themselves attracted to this woman and who are destroyed by that fatal attraction. The *Tess* drawings trace these developing, fatal relationships between Tess, Alec, and Angel. The domestic motif, from initial Herkomer illustration of the Durbeyfield household to the other scenes of stable but sometimes painful family groupings, contrasts markedly with the last family scene of the Durbeyfields on the move through Southwestern England, a grouping now of uprooted, wandering souls repeating, in a larger way, the individualized tragedies of Tess, Alec, and Angel. By stressing the harmony and then the suffering of the community, as well as the more specific interrelationships of individual characters, the illustrations make the serial audience aware of the full dimensions of the novel's tragedy.

Jude the Obscure: A Modern Tragedy

William Hatherell's illustrations for *Jude the Obscure* demonstrate the continuing influence of photography on nineteenth century pictorial art. Earlier, the photographic influence revealed itself in the meticulous, realistic detail of *The Mayor of Casterbridge*, or in the use of photographs as a guide to Du Maurier's drawings. The increased gray scale apparent in the *Jude* illustrations, also evident in Paget's drawings for *The Well-Beloved*, is a more striking result of the photographic influence and the relatively new half-tone process used in reproducing the artist's work. Earlier illustration had to depend on the fine, engraved line, on the basic contrast between whites and blacks, and on texture and shadow created by delicate cross-hatching. In trying to create subtle effects of texture and shadow, the artist was thus quite dependent on the engraver's skill. In the latter part of the century, advances in reproductive processes could create these effects with far more predictable success, as well as create different effects. Photographic reduction was used in these last few years of the nineteenth century to create greater delicacy in the engraved line, and the half-tone process was able to create gradations of shadow, thus giving a water-color effect of gray tones to the illustrations.

But in addition to the technical innovations which made the *Jude* illustrations seem so different from those of *Far from the Madding Crowd*, for instance, is the radical difference in theme and atmosphere between the two novels. Thus, regardless of technical possibilities in the reproductive process, the pastoral quality of the earlier novel calls for the dominant white and blacks used by artist Helen Allingham, while the bleak atmosphere of *Jude* calls for the dominant gray tone. Of the twelve illustrations in the series, only four are indoor scenes, but all four are dimly lit, and each presents a rather grim situation. Seven of the remaining scenes are also marked by their gray atmosphere, though the drawing which depicts Sue and Phillotson immediately after their marriage is not as bleak as the other scenes (Plate 60).

The extended gray scale of the *Jude* illustrations clarifies distinctions between snow, twilight, fog and mist, and dimly-lit interiors, and is particularly effective in emphasizing the texture of clothing and the background of cottage interiors. Hatherell's handling of posture, facial, and background detail gives to his drawings a very rugged quality, and this quality, together with the effective use of the grey scale, emphasizes the grimness of the novel. Through emphasis on the novel's bleak atmosphere, together with scene selection, the Hatherell illustrations give to *Jude the Obscure* a grimness that reflects and sometimes even seems to go beyond the realities of the text.

The fact that Hatherell intended to convey Hardy's theme of "unfulfilled ambitions" through these gray tones becomes clear when the later illustrations are compared to the drawing for the opening installment (Plate 61), when young Jude comes upon the three women working in the barnyard. This first meeting with Arabella is a pleasant scene, marked by blocks of white and a few peaceful homesteads in the background, as Jude tentatively peers through the bushes. The scene has a refreshing quality, and is rather striking when seen in retrospect, for nature never again makes such a pleasant appearance in the *Jude* illustrations. The bright faces of Jude and the three women, Arabella included, mark this first plate as that time in Jude's life when the world held promise, and the grimness of the later plates becomes greater because of the contrast with this first illustration. The blocks of white and a much diminished gray scale in this scene indicate that Hatherell consciously used the gray tones to make his later illustrations convey the tragic, pessimistic atmosphere of *Jude the Obscure*. Thus, regardless of technical innovations, the artist was responsible for the tone within the *Jude* illustrations. Here Hatherell's skill is considerable.

There is other evidence of the photographic influence, as well. The formal juxtaposition of character that marked illustration for the earlier novels shifts to reflect photographic style of the 1880s and 1890s. Pointed relationships give way to more relaxed, informal groupings of characters, seen against casually arranged backgrounds. The normal, suggested and sometimes "out of focus" background thus contrasts with the earlier, staged backgrounds of the Rejlander style. (Du Maurier's use of costumed characters set against carefully arranged backgrounds as models for his illustrations shows the influence of this earlier style.) In their handling of detail and background, the Hatherell illustrations reflect the early theories of photographer Peter Emerson. "Fuzziness" was an important quality of the "natural" scene, but "it must not be carried to the length of *destroying the structure* of any object, otherwise it becomes noticeable, and by attracting the eye detracts from the harmony, and is then just as harmful as excessive sharpness would be. . . ." The outlines of objects are not "hard," "but everything is seen against something else, and its outlines fade gently into that something else, often so subtly that you cannot quite distinguish where one ends and the other begins."[19] This out-of-focus technique, of course, is related to the impressionistic style of painting and was used by Hardy in his own handling of description, particularly in The *Woodlanders*.

Scenes which reveal this different handling of foreground figures and background settings occur relatively often in the series of twelve illustrations. Sue and Father Time looking for lodgings, Jude and others gathered around the fireside, Jude reciting the Creed in a local tavern, Jude standing outside Sue's window, Sue tearing her nightgown—these are not the formal scenes present in some of the drawings for *The Return of the Native* or *Tess of the D'Urbervilles*, but are relaxed, almost candid views which often use "out of focus" techniques. On the other hand, the illustration depicting Sue lying on the pavement is a throw-back to the genre painting of the earlier Victorian era. Seen against that context, the fact that Sue is lying there as a result of her terror at "legal," conjugal relations with her husband Phillotson is an ironic handling of the "fallen woman," or outcast theme.

The landscape scene appears very rarely in the text of *Jude the Obscure*, and not at all in the illustrations. Nature as background occurs in the first illustration, as well as in the second plate, when Arabella runs out into the snow, confronting passers-by with her accusation of how Jude has mistreated her (Plate 62). Here, however, nature's bleakness is emphasized. Again, the final plate of the series, "Jude at the Milestone," stresses nature's bleakness, as Jude clutches his thin coat around him, trying to keep out the cold rain (Plate 16).

While it is not surprising to see so few nature scenes in *Jude*, since the text does not call for them in the way that *Tess of the D'Urbervilles* did, what is unusual about the general setting for the twelve illustrated scenes is the absence of the Christminster setting. Nowhere does the artist convey that dominant image in Jude's life. There is no Christminster in the distance, as it appeared to the youth who yearned to attain the knowledge symbolized in its beckoning spires, nor is there the dark, richly textured buildings of the individual colleges as Jude first views them when he is thirty years old. Each of these moments is crucial to Jude Fawley's development, but neither receives pictorial treatment. One Christminster street scene appears, but it might as well have been any street in any English village or town. By omitting a view of Christminster's colleges, even as dim or vague background, the Hatherell illustrations lose an opportunity to reinforce the novel's central conflict——the Ideal and the Real, so clearly joined by Hardy in the dominant images of the Christminster colleges, as well as in the contrast between the "town and gown" aspects of Christminster.

The omission reveals much about how this novel was interpreted by artist and serial audience. The illustrations omit Christminster but strongly emphasize the individual characters, an emphasis that differs from earlier novels, where human relationships were stressed. This distinction leads to some puzzling conclusions about the rationale behind the Hatherell illustrations.

Arabella appears in only two scenes, and the first one, as noted earlier, presents her in a pleasant light. Her public display of aggravation over Jude's preoccupation with books and the fiasco of the pig-killing is the subject of her only other appearance (Plate 62) among the illustrated scenes. The vague figure in the scene's background is Jude, and the relative emphasis given to the two figures seems to suggest Jude's helplessness in their relationship.

As might be expected, the illustrations focus on Sue and Jude, but primarily as individuals, and not in their relationship with each other. (Yet Arabella is presented only in her relationship with Jude, never alone. Admittedly, the text provides extremely few opportunities for a single figure illustration for Arabella.) Still, Hatherell seems to have been exceptionally careful to avoid depicting Jude and Sue alone with each other. Only when Jude is sick and confined to his bed does Sue visit him without a companion or chaperone. Otherwise, Sue and Jude appear with either Phillotson, the Widow Edlin, or Father Time in the same scene. In the text, Hardy had to delete parts of the plot which make it clear that Sue and Jude are living together. The serial version, for instance, explains that Jude has separate living quarters across the street from Sue's. By not stressing the Jude-Sue relationship in the double figure scene, however, the illustrations go beyond the textual attempt to play down their physical intimacy. There are several scenes (in the text) where Jude and Sue appear together in conversation, and without overt sexual suggestion, that might have been chosen for illustration. By not stressing their relationship, however, the artist misses a chance to give pictorial insight into the intensity between these two characters who love each other with a perversity that leads them into great pain.

At the risk of being unfair to editor and artist, pointing out some of the other omissions among the Hatherell drawings helps to explain the weaknesses in the plates for *Jude the Obscure*. None of the happier scenes in the Jude-Sue relationship, for instance, are depicted: their first meeting at the cross which marks the Martyrdoms, where each is so tentative toward the other; a half-drowned Sue staying in Jude's quarters to dry her clothes, instead of returning to the Melchester Training School; Sue watching Jude at work restoring the tablets of the Ten Commandments in the small church outside Aldbrickham; Jude, Sue, and Father Time having an outing at the Agricultural Exhibition. Nowhere in the illustrations is the fact of Jude's occupation made known, yet the novel's text emphatically reveals the satisfaction he receives from working with stone, either in simple masonry work or in the more complex task, his specialty, of Gothic restoration.

As a whole, the illustrations show no relief from the gloom and pain of relationships gone wrong (Jude and Arabella, Sue and Phillotson, Sue and Jude.) Yet there are several happier moments in the text. Both Hardy and the editor had already revealed their concern over the story line, a concern which had led to the bowdlerization of the original text. Why the drawings for the serialization were allowed to depict only the unhappy moments, and thus make a visual addition to the pessimism of the text, is quite puzzling. The lighter scenes could just as well have been illustrated in order to placate the audience and, in fact, actually be true to a part of the novel, especially in those early moments in the Jude-Sue relationship, in the symbolic attraction of Christminster, as well as Jude's satisfaction at working with his hands. Yet none of these appears in the series of illustrations to relieve the gloom of the novel's later, tragic scenes.

The novel itself does not have the moments of high drama that Hardy wrote into his earlier works. There are no scenes of an Elfride standing on the church parapet, no bonfires as in *Tess*, no "skimmity ride" to depict. *Jude's* most dramatic scene, the death of young Father Time, would obviously not be illustrated, as its gruesome subject would surely have been too much for the Victorian audience. Even in its textual presentation, it remains too stark and melodramatic for a twentieth century audience. The initial illustration (Arabella throwing the pig's bladder at Jude), and a later scene (Sue lying on the ground after she has jumped out the window (Plate 63), do convey some degree of drama, though in both cases, the drawing just misses the actual dramatic moment. Two other scenes—Arabella in the snow (Plate 62), and Sue tearing her nightgown as she prepares to return to Phillotson (Plate 64)—more properly qualify as dramatic scenes. In general, however, the illustrations stress the static scene: Jude and Sue lamenting their fate as they sit before the fire—in company with Father Time and Widow Edlin (Plate 65); Sue visiting a sick Jude as he lies in bed; Jude reciting the Creed in a Christminster tavern. The importance of these relatively peaceful moments, however, is their contribution to the very intense psychological drama of *Jude*. In the scene depicting Sue and Phillotson immediately after their marriage, for instance, Sue has turned away from Phillotson to give a painful and yearning look toward Jude (Plate 60). The illustration is static in a physical sense, yet conveys the dilemma of Sue's situation, and makes her later return to Phillotson that much more painful and incredible.

The quiet, static scene predominates, but Hatherell creates drama even in these by emphasizing faces and hands. Hardy's textual descriptions, of course, had consistently given an impressionistic attention to the faces of his characters from *A Pair of Blue Eyes* to *Jude the Obscure*, and the Hatherell illustrations do justice to Hardy's belief in the importance of suggestive facial detail.[20] The strong face of Arabella, the finer features of Sue, are effectively drawn. Jude's face is often in shadow, and only in two scenes (Jude by the fireside and then the final drawing, the Milestone scene), is his face prominent. His suffering is apparent in both scenes, however, and the later one also emphasizes his physical debility. Hatherell's depiction of Jude at the Milestone, as Hardy himself realized, is superb (Plate 16). With considerable economy, the drawing captures Jude's suffering, loneliness, illness, and nature's indifference, if not hostility. As in the text, the Milestone itself is an ironic note, since it was from this point that a young Jude had started his journey to what he saw as the promise of Christminster. The irony would have been reinforced in the pictorial treatment if that earlier scene had also been included among the illustrations.

With the exception of these two views of Jude, Hatherell gives greater prominence to Sue's face, from her demure "prettiness" evident in the drawing of her meeting with Phillotson in his role as Jude's former schoolteacher, to a look of puffiness in the wedding scene, which suggests she has been crying, then, later, to a look of depression, as she and Father Time search for lodgings and, finally, to an expression suggesting hysteria, as she tears her nightgown. The Hatherell illustrations clearly spend much more time in delineating the character and suffering of Sue Bridehead than of Jude Fawley, though none of the drawings of Sue can match the power of the Milestone scene.

Young Father Time appears in two scenes (Plates 65 & 66) and, if there is any doubt that he is Jude's child, it must be dispelled in the illustrated, serial version. Hatherell shows the father-son relationship through the shape of their heads. Father Time is presented as a strange-looking, gnome-like figure, and is effectively drawn, though he must have been a challenge to the artist's pencil as he has been to the novel's readers. The other children do not appear in the illustrations. In the serial version, there is only one child, besides Father Time, and Hardy had to change the text to indicate this child is an orphan, adopted by Jude and Sue. In the restored manuscript, Hardy makes clear the two nameless children are Jude and Sue's, and that Sue is pregnant with a third child. Clearly, the illustrator as well as the author were making concessions to Mrs. Grundy, since emphasizing the children, whatever their number, would inevitably cast suspicion on the nature of Jude and Sue's relationship.

Though Hatherell conveys a sense of the bleak surroundings of Jude's life and the agony of Sue Bridehead with considerable expertise and insight, there is too much missing from the drawings. Christminster itself, if only as dim background, is a disturbing omission from the series. Less serious, but certainly having ramifications for the impression the serial left on the reader's imagination, is that the illustrations do not convey the intimacy in the Jude-Sue relationship. Yet, through those omissions Hatherell makes his series of drawings focus clearly on the loneliness and pain in the world of Jude Fawley and Sue Bridehead. In their emphasis on suffering, in the predominance of the gray tonal scale, the illustrations convey the grim spirit of the text and, in fact, actually increase the pessimistic tone of Hardy's serial. Though the Hatherell series omits much which would explain and, in some cases, even mitigate the pain and suffering that most necessarily be conveyed through many of the major scenes selected for illustration, they convey the grimness of Jude Fawley's world with considerable power and thus shape the serial text in a very special way for its Victorian audience.

The Minor Novels

Among Hardy's minor novels, *A Pair of Blue Eyes* had been successful in several of its illustrations, and at that early stage in Hardy's serialized works demonstrated the potential even a minor novel could offer through illustration. None of the drawings for the other minor novels measure up to the potential held out by the Pasquier illustrations, though it is useful to understand the failures as well as the limited strengths of these other illustrated works.

George Du Maurier's engravings for *The Hand of Ethelberta* do not reflect very well on Hardy's intent to create a "society" novel, nor on Du Maurier's reputation as a "society" illustrator. There are relatively few illustrations of the several dinner scenes or social gatherings which form a large part of the story. Instead Du Maurier's illustrations stress the landscape that Hardy used as background for Ethelberta's search for a foothold in high society. More than half the eleven full page engravings place considerable emphasis on nature as background. Eleven vignette initials, however, stress the human figure.

As might be expected, several plates present Ethelberta in a family or group relationship—either in a double figure scene with her sister Picotee (Plate 67), or in a grouping with her many brothers and sisters (Plate 68). Each of the supporting characters also appears in the series. The earnest and loyal brothers Sol and Dan are depicted as they arrive in France to complete their "education" under Ethelberta's tutelage; Neigh and Ladywell appear in one of the vignette initials, and Christopher Julian appears in several scenes. Two of the best initials capture the presence and pride of Mr. Chickerel (Ethelberta's father) and her brother Joey as they appear in servant livery. Lord Mountclere makes his first appearance in one of the vignette initials, which actually becomes a prophecy of his very interesting future dominance. In a later, full size engraving, he examines some of Julian's music (Plate 69). Here Du Maurier has captured the crafty look on Mountclere's face as he begins to perceive the relationship between Julian and Ethelberta. Other vignette initials echo the presence of nature through scenes from France or of Knollsee. The effect of the several family groupings does convey one of the novel's basic issues—Ethelberta's strong sense of solidarity with her family.

Du Maurier is at his best in capturing the regal bearing of Ethelberta, as he had caught the pride of the self-made man through the figures of Ethelberta's father and younger brother. One sees that this is the family trait, whether in "service" or "society." Ethelberta on her way to visit Corvsgate Castle, the only single figure illustration of the series, is quite effective. Her look of bravery mixed with uncertainty as she regally sits on a donkey captures character and situation admirably well. Yet both the text and the illustrations do not make as much as they could of the extreme loneliness of this young heroine as she attempts to find a place for herself in what is essentially an indifferent world. To some extent, the final illustration does capture this loneliness. Though it presents three figures, two of them remain in the background, and the focus falls on the lonely but proud figure of Ethelberta riding in the basket carriage (Plate 70). Her bittersweet victory over Mountclere has cost personal happiness, but she has successfully completed her mission of providing for her family as well as herself. Thus, there is nobility in Ethelberta's bearing in some of the drawings, but in general, as *Athenaeum's* reviewer pointed out, Du Maurier's Ethelberta is "the familiar lady of Punch."[21] *Athenaeum* noted that the illustrations were in "Du Maurier's well-known style, and therefore pretty enough." This faint praise was then followed by admiration for the artist's handling of Lord Mountclere (Plate 69), and then criticism of another scene, where Ethelberta and Picotee "are walking on the edge of a stormy sea on a November night with no protection but short jackets."[22] The reviewer suggested that the illustrator pay more attention to the text in order to avoid such absurdities. George Saintsbury, reviewer for *The Academy*, was even more critical: "The illustrations which accompany the book are not, as a rule, worthy of it, and some of them are decidedly slovenly."[23]

Du Maurier's scenes, in the main, do not excel in composition or perspective as those of Pasquier's do, nor do they carefully render detail, as do the drawings of Helen Allingham. The aristocratic and upper middle class drawing room was Du Maurier's specialty, and theoretically *The Hand of Ethelberta* should have provided the right material for his pen. For whatever reason, Du Maurier left his natural forté. The effect is one of uncertainty. On the other hand, the special gift Du Maurier had for capturing the life of high society, though not sufficiently strong to save the entire series, is still very much present in the engravings. The Du Maurier women, for instance, have an elegance in their bearing and a stylish manner of dress that considerably strengthens Hardy's description of "society." In addition, Du Maurier delineates facial expression very well. Fear, determination, craftiness, haughtiness and even innocence peer out of the Du Maurier faces, whether upper or lower class, and demonstrate the artist's powers of giving life to his pen and ink drawings. (His skill as artist may be measured from the very few lines needed to create character.) In his contribution of "style," and in the delineation of faces, the Du Maurier illustrations do, in fact, strengthen Hardy's novel for its Victorian serial audience.

Thirty-two drawings by John Collier, five of them full page plates, were published with the 1880 serial text of *The Trumpet Major*, Hardy's fictional portrayal of the Napoleonic threat to the Dorset coast. The novel uses an historical background carefully researched by Hardy (see Chapter III), as it presents heroine Anne Garland and her two suitors, brothers John and Bob Loveday. Misunderstandings between these three, the treachery of Festus Derriman, together with the Napoleonic references, constitute a varied but weak plot.

Several illustrations are sketches of single characters, a somewhat unusual occurrence among the Hardy illustrations. Also unusual is the landscape drawing, and this too appears among the Collier drawings, as in the opening scene depicting Loveday Mill. A later sketch of the ship *Victory* provides a decorative element to the series, reminding the audience of the British navy's romantic grandeur in the Trafalgar days, but also demonstrating a lack of design or focus in the Collier series. The variety of subject matter and distinct differences in the style of drawing are disturbing and indicate this lack of focus.

The first visual presentation of the novel's heroine attempts to establish character, and to some extent succeeds. With its view of Anne Garland anxiously looking out the casement window, the scene captures a mood and depth of character not often apparent in this young woman, and does provide an initial focus for the novel's movement, since Anne will move out into the life she is now passively contemplating. A later illustration (for Chapter 18), however, is the finest of the series (Plate 71). Anne gazes into the mirror, "apparently lost in thought." The pose and situation of Miss Garland suggests the famous nineteenth century painting, Millais's *Mariana*, painted some twenty years earlier and based on Tennyson's poem of the same name. Collier's admiration for Millais, as well as the time he spent studying under him, emerges through the similarity between the two women. The basic situation was supplied by Hardy in his text, but Collier has added a rather interesting Pre-Raphaelite touch not present in Hardy's description. Hardy's addition of John Loveday's coming upon the scene and being struck by Anne's pose is not included by the artist, and the omission reveals a basic difference between the dramatic conceptualization of Hardy the novelist and the static, "mood-painting" of Collier the artist. Though the plate is technically well-executed, and Anne's presentation is provocative as she ponders her fate and her womanhood in the mirror before her, the scene ironically serves to emphasize the unsatisfactory quality of the other illustrations. Miss Garland emerges from the story as a serious but uninteresting young woman who has difficulties in knowing her own mind as she shifts her love from Bob Loveday to brother John and back again. The illustrations reflect this uncertainty because of their uneven quality and lack of purpose, but it is not a thematic advantage.

Two other scenes should be mentioned because of their dramatic quality: Derriman burying the casket containing his fortune, and Anne running away from Derryman's nephew. Both scenes are somewhat flat, though the first has a Dickensian flavor, due to the expression on Derriman's face. Another scene, depicting Anne looking out over the water (Plate 72), is effective because of the panoramic view (the view is implied here more than actually presented in any kind of visual detail) and also for the wistful quality conveyed through the features and posture of Miss Garland. Interestingly enough, this same scene was considered by *Academy* reviewer George Saintsbury to be one of the finest in Hardy's text:

But there is one scene which is, we think, the very best thing that Mr. Hardy has done—the scene where Anne watches her lover's ship sail down Channel from the heights of Portland. For carefully subdued pathos and artful management of "surroundings" we hardly know anything better.[24]

Unfortunately, *The Trumpet Major* has too few of this sort of contolled scene, according to the reviewer.

The Mill kitchen (Plate 10) mentioned in Collier's letter seems almost caricature, as features and bodies of Miller Loveday's friends have little relation to reality in their distortion. Such handling contrasts radically with those scenes which present Anne Garland, for instance, and disturb the tone set by the majority of the engravings. The final plate depicting John Loveday wistfully saying farewell (Plate 73), seems particularly sentimental, but is in tune with Hardy's handling of this curious young man as he goes off to die on the battlefields of Spain. Finally, illustrations which present landscapes, either as foreground or background, are flat and uninteresting—perfunctory and not individualized. The novel's actual setting, of course, is quite a distinct part of England, and its generalized quality as presented in the Collier illustrations is particularly surprising, in view of Hardy's concern for detail and his love of the Dorset coast. As noted earlier, however, landscape was not the forté of magazine serial illustration, and none of the Hardy illustrators is able to do justice to Hardy's descriptions of nature or his fine sense of nature's drama.

The weakness of the Collier illustrations demonstrates how dependent the artist was on the text he had to illustrate. Like Du Maurier in *The Hand of Ethelberta* drawings, Collier had a weak novel to begin with, and found it difficult to make his engravings go beyond what the text had to offer. The details of dress—fashionable and military—stand out in these illustrations, yet that very fact may explain the deficiency of the drawings. Both artist and novelist seem to have been distracted from the heart and spirit of the novel by the fact of its historical background. In the eagerness for accurate detail, a distinctly wooden quality overwhelms whatever life might have emerged from the basic story. It is apparent from the effort and care that Hardy put into the preparation of this novel that he wanted his story to come alive, that he wanted to convey his fascination for the Napoleonic tales he had heard in his childhood through the medium of his fiction. Individual scenes giving special insight into character or situation are far too few in the series, and clarification of historical setting remains the chief contribution of the Collier illustrations.

Though Du Maurier has been criticized for the decline in his technical prowess in the later years of his career,[25] the drawings he created for *A Laodicean* refute that opinion. Technically, the illustrations are quite good, and easily surpass the quality of the *Hand of Ethelberta* drawings. Delicacy of line is quite noticeable, a result of the engraver's skill, but also a result of Du Maurier's practice of having his drawings photographically reduced in order to enhance the perfection of line. Faces are distinctive, as are the figures of the central characters—they can be recognized from one engraving to another, an individuality that is not so apparent, for instance, in the earlier, Collier drawings for *The Trumpet Major*, and in several of the plates for *The Return of the Native*.

Careful attention to detail, and the habit of filling the frame of his drawing, instead of using large expanses of blank space, show that Du Maurier had been influenced by the growing field of photography—an influence particularly appropriate for *A Laodicean*, since part of the plot turns on Dare's use of a photograph to create misunderstanding between Somerset and Paula. In terms of composition, not since the Allingham engravings for *Far from the Madding Crowd* had the illustrations for a Hardy novel given such close attention to the arrangement of figures—a fact which makes viewing this set of drawings a pleasant, though certainly not powerful experience.

Only three plates contain just two figures, not surprising in view of Du

Maurier's being bothered (and, in turn, bothering Hardy) about having to illustrate an installment that had too many scenes limited to just two figures. Obviously Du Maurier felt more at ease in drawing group scenes. Nine of the total thirteen illustrations have more than three figures depicted in them, and there are no single figure illustrations.

Although Du Maurier complained to Hardy about the number of figures in the scenes suitable for illustration, and lamented the absence of dramatic incidents in Part II of the installments, the facts of the matter are that when an installment of the story *did* have a dramatic incident, Du Maurier chose a non-dramatic, static situation for his illustration. Paula's perfunctory introduction of her uncle to Somerset, for instance, was chosen over the scene among the players in their amateur production of *Love's Labour's Lost*, where De Stancy pretends to be kissing a surprised Paula. And in installment three itself, the fear of being caught by the train, with Somerset pulling Paula out of harm's way, would have been a powerful scene, but it is discarded in favor of one showing Paula and Somerset calmly climbing the hill after their escape (Plate 13). Here Du Maurier revealed he was aware of the choice, as his correspondence with Hardy indicates.

Three scenes in the series deal with nature, and they are quite faithful to the text, for this is the tamer nature of Somersetshire (or Outer Wessex, as Hardy called it), and the coastal resort area of France, not the majestic, austere Cornwall, or the primitive, powerful world of Dorset (Wessex proper). The deft handling of detail in the third illustration demonstrates Du Maurier's control over the fine line, and the later scenes in France (Plate 74) are pleasant, unobtrusive background for confrontations between the various characters.

One of the strongest features of the series is the sheer power of Captain De Stancy's presence, his impressive military and aristocratic bearing. Du Maurier is being graphically faithful to Hardy's description of De Stancy, even to his stolidness, yet this sort of character was long one of the Du Maurier staples. His *Punch* drawings of the "handsome, broad-shouldered men and elegant ladies of classic beauty . . . mightily pleased the middle classes who loved to think English society was like that," explains one art historian.[26] The figures of De Stancy and Paula Power, impressive and stylish, belong to this type Du Maurier had so often drawn for *Punch*, yet they have a striking individuality, as well (Plate 75).

In the case of Paula Powers, this elegance of characterization is not present in the drawing for the first installment, depicting Paula waiting to be baptized in the Non-conformist chapel (Plate 11). The wooden quality in this scene, possibly caused by Hardy's instructions, is completely absent from a later scene (Plate 76), where Paula in all her elegance is set against a London background. (Interestingly enough, however, the wooden, "fixed" nature of the figures in the first scene is quite appropriate to the rigidity inherent in the baptism situation, as the text surely indicates.) In the fashionable London scene, Du Maurier's use of detail is masterful. His use of models to aid him in illustrating a scene, his meticulous attention to the details of costume, mean that his illustrations for serial fiction, as well as his *Punch* cartoons, are accurate and historically valuable pictures of contemporary costume and manners. That this was a prime function of magazine illustration in Du Maurier's view, as explained earlier, accounts for this concern for accuracy.

Although there are several scenes which convey the sense of *A Laodicean's* fashionable world, there are many problems in this series of engravings. Perfunctory group scenes dominate the series. The chase in France, from church to church, might have provided interesting visual material, as well as emphasized Paula's agony as she searches for Somerset. The dramatic material is in the text, but Du Maurier makes nothing of it. For a novel that so clearly depends on De Stancy Castle for much of its interest, as well as its structural and thematic focus, it is surprising that no view of the castle appears among the illustrations. The castle ruins, or a scene of the tower where Somerset was accidentally imprisoned, would have been visually effective, and also could relate to the modernism theme in Hardy's story—for surely the symbol of the train counterpoints the antiquity of De Stancy castle, and the castle, in turn, parallels the massive physical presence of De Stancy himself—but only the latter is conveyed through the illustrations.

The burning De Stancy Castle, as another example, would have provided fine drama and a fitting final illustrated scene. Instead, Du Maurier depicts Somerset and Paula meeting on the Etretat beach, in a scene of reconciliation that is considerably vitiated in both illustration and text because of the presence of other people, including a likeness of Du Maurier himself, together with his dog, in the right hand corner of the plate.

The famous paintings, on which much of the action turns, appear in two drawings (Plates 12 and 75), and for that Du Maurier must be commended because the illustrations thus keep the novel's central conflict (of aristocratic privilege and the past, versus modern industry and self-help) alive in the reader-viewer's mind.

But the primary effect of the Du Maurier illustrations is conviviality because of the group scenes, and triviality because of the absence of many of the more powerful scenes. The novel has a happy ending, to be sure, but there are moments of drama and pain for Paula, Somerset, and De Stancy, and these moments are not conveyed through the illustrations. Du Maurier's earlier reservations about illustrating a story that might not suit his style had come true in the *Laodicean* drawings. His illustrations for this novel, in fact, are not often recognized by his biographers or by art historians, suggesting that others, as well as Du Maurier himself, preferred to forget the experience.

The flaw in the *Laodicean* illustrations, quite simply, is that they have not been selected for appropriateness to the text, but for what the illustrator could do best: group scenes and the static "conversational" scene. Style, characterization, and some metaphorical statement are strengths, but they appear in only a few of the illustrations. Hardy's novel deserved better from an artist with the skills of Du Maurier, and, judging from the interest Hardy had shown in preparing the illustrations for the first few plates, much of the static quality in the later illustrations might conceivably have been eliminated if Hardy had not become ill, and had been able to discuss the later plates with his artist.

The Paget drawings for *The Pursuit of the Well-Beloved* are considered to be "pleasant drawings with some of the quality of water-colour."[27] The artist's proportioning of figure to landscape and juxtaposing of one human figure with another are especially well done, and give to this set of illustrations considerable strength in composition.

Paget includes several scenes depicting the Isle of Slingers as background—a place whose stone quarries, close blood relationships, and special customs of betrothal play an important part in the novel's plot. As noted earlier, most of the Hardy illustrators saw graphic fidelity to the text as their aim, but that fidelity most often did not include the landscape—at least, not in the way Hardy had emphasized it in his text. Paget, however, gives the peninsular, rocky landscape an emphasis proportionate to Hardy's handling of it in the text itself (Plate 77).

Though Paget's drawings are significant because he gives such an important position to landscape, his special talent is really the indoor scene. He fills the frames of these interior scenes with details marking the time of the novel as clearly Victorian. The decorative screens, bentwood chairs, costuming, and other such details tie the novel to a particular time, more so than any other illustrated Hardy novel, even those of Du Maurier or Collier which had given so much attention to costuming, but much less to the details of physical setting.

The Paget drawings are also noteworthy for their many single figure scenes. None of the Avice Caros can properly convey the Ideal that Pearston saw in each of them, but Paget's drawings of Pearston, particularly the five in which he appears as a single figure, effectively convey his loneliness and suffering and, in fact, help to give credibility to a story whose plot line is so hard to accept. The single figure scene, as noted earlier, is another type of illustration that is not used very often among the Hardy illustrations, nor in many other illustrations for serial fiction, since editors preferred to have group scenes, filling the engravings with human figures. Paget demonstrates, however, that he is not afraid to let the single figure carry the weight of the drawing. There are times, in fact, when the single figure scene is crucial to the pictorial treatment of the story. One such scene shows Pearston, twenty years after he has jilted the first Avice, arriving at her grave, just in time to witness her burial (Plate 78). The scene is crucial to the plot, since it is here that Pearston meets the daughter (Avice II) of the dead woman, but it is also important for Pearston's psychological presentation, since the scene marks the first time he gives way to remorse and loneliness.

Paget's handling of detail lends credibility to an otherwise fantastic plot. Two scenes taking place in Pearston's studio, for instance, give strong emphasis to his life as artist—a life not really stressed very much in the text, and simply referred to as important (Plates 79 & 80). Paget's drawings of Pearston's sculpture concretizes an important part of the story line—the inspiration, the Ideal, that Pearston seeks in woman he transfers into his own art. The scene which depicts Avice (II) dusting the sculpture (Plate 79) stresses Pearston's art as well as the ironic situation of the human Ideal in such close and uncomprehending juxtaposition with the artistic copy. Together with other women who momentarily embody the Ideal, the *human* Avice is the reason why Pearston has become a successful artist, as he seeks to capture the fleeting Ideal he thinks he sees in human form into the static perfection of his sculpture. For an audience that might not have been familiar with the world of sculpture or the artist's studio, the two scenes offer clarification and important detail that might not be visualized in the reader's imagination. The scenes are more important, however, for the metaphorical, ironic juxtaposition of Real and Ideal. The irony that lies within the text is sharpened through its visual treatment in these illustrations.

Hardy's novel did not offer the most promising material for illustration, and though Swinburne, Proust, and D. H. Lawrence thought the novel had merit, most readers today would agree with A. J. Guerard's conclusion that Hardy's story "is not the worst book ever published by a major writer. But it is certainly one of the most trivial."[28] Yet, for such a weak work, the Paget illustrations do more than justice. Although the illustrations in one sense actually counter Hardy's theme of the evanescence of the Ideal, since the drawings by their very nature emphasize substance rather than the Ideal, the drawings do contribute something important to the story by clarifying setting (the Isle of Slingers) and the artistic milieu of Jocelyn Pearston.

The illustrations also help to create an ironic view toward the material, a view that Hardy was not able to create through text alone. As Guerard points out, "An incisive rather than merely tender irony might even have made palatable the succession of Avice Caros. Unfortunately Hardy looked on Jocelyn Pearston's immaturity as an artist's necessary defect; looked on it with professional sympathy. As a result the irony . . . dwells on the mere fact of his repeated disappointments."[29] What Hardy seems to have wanted to do was to point out the deficiency of Pearston, point out that he was blind to reality, and self-centered as well. The Ideal, Hardy suggests, can never be captured, and while the pursuit is necessary to the artist, the blindness to reality can destroy the man. Pearston is mistaken to think he can ever reach and hold the Ideal, even though he is driven to continue his search. To think that he can find the Ideal in a living person is, in fact, a blindness to his own ideals and *raison d'être* as artist.

None of this is realized by Pearston, and in the text itself Hardy does not handle the ironic implications of this blindness very well. The illustrations, however, stress the concrete terms, including the attractive bearing and features of the three Avice Caros. Pearston is also only passively aware of the beauty and grandeur of his Isle of Slingers, and thus misses the poetic beauty of both nature and humanity. By focusing on the beauty of nature and woman, by presenting beauty in concrete and realizable terms, the Paget drawings clarify an ironic vision inherent but not clearly defined in the text itself.

V

Conclusion

The Hardy illustrations demonstrate both the advantages of the representational style as well as certain of its weaknesses. Though perfunctory illustration sometimes occurs, though scene selection is not always judicious and technical execution not always as good as it could have been, illustration adds a vital dimension to Hardy's novels.

For the audience that had difficulty in visualizing what they read, illustration was a distinct aid. But by the 1860s and later, the Victorian audience had become more sophisticated in their understanding of the semiotics of representational art through their increasing experience with magazine illustration, genre painting, and photography. Thus, for a very significant part of that later audience, picture published with serial fiction possessed a whole series of signals that not only could give visual pleasure but also convey information on social, psychological, and moral states. These signals re-inforced the text but could also emphasize aspects that might not have been emphasized in the text alone. By stressing certain scenes, character relationships, posture and mannerisms of characters, the illustrated text was able to control at least some audience response.

Hardy's pictorial imagination gave his illustrators considerable material to work with, such as lighting effects, framing techniques, double figure scenes of characters in confrontation, eavesdropping scenes with the voyeur or "doubling" effect, and a great deal of pastoral, even historical, detail. Many of these materials become part of the *picture* created in the illustrations. Often, however, representational illustration goes beyond the pictorial effects that are spelled out by Hardy and creates its own picture, still based on the text, but this time on pictorialism sometimes textually inherent and sometimes external, or partially so, to the actual text. The illustrator creates picture out of recognizable situations, such as the "Fallen Woman" theme, domestic, or confrontation scenes from genre painting. Representational illustration thus had its own schema, drawn from *picture* as it existed in the other visual arts media. In reading the serial fiction of Hardy, who had his own unique pictorial expression, the Victorian audience had before them a highly enriched visual experience.

In the history of art, representationalism has been considered an insult to the artistic imagination—or so the Gillray, Rowlandson, and Gainsborough school would have it. Opposed to this view is the Constable and Wordsworthian school: to these artists, the representing of reality through art is a supreme challenge.[1] To a considerable extent, these attitudes lie behind nineteenth century magazine illustration. The post-1860 illustrator found his challenge in re-creating reality as found within the text and reflecting the Victorian world, but he was also able to "stylize" that reality by relating it to the pictorialism of his time.

The artist's basic responsibility to the text emerges from his choice of scene, accuracy of detail, and the combination of scene selection and detail that creates atmosphere in the illustrations. The precise detail presented in the drawings for *A Pair of Blue Eyes, Far from the Madding Crowd,* and *The Mayor of Casterbridge* makes those sets of engravings most successful in conveying the spirit of the novels.

The meticulous detail evident in these illustrations exists not only for the sake of vividness and accuracy but for the larger sense of person and place. The precision of the details gives a delicacy and richness to the image that is not apparent in the text alone. The charms of Elfride Swancourt, for instance, are enhanced in several of Pasquier's drawings for *A Pair of Blue Eyes.* The light, pastoral quality as well as the clear-cut characterization of the major figures in *Far from the Madding Crowd* makes Helen Allingham's meticulous drawings a valuable addition to the text, especially when one realizes how subtly and thematically she combines the vignette initials with the full size engravings to convey character psychology and crucial moments of dramatic action. In the case of Bathsheba's relationship to the three men in her life, furthermore, considerable insight is offered through the illustrations. In Robert Barnes's drawings for *The Mayor of Casterbridge,* the sense of person, place, and event is conveyed in a way that not only emphasizes the strength of Hardy's text, but also expands the text through stressing the relationship of structure and human emotion—the basic rhythm of the novel. In the use of detail, the illustrations for these novels, particularly in the case of *Far from the Madding Crowd* and *The Mayor of Casterbridge,* demonstrate the finest of what *picture* in post-1860 illustration could do for the strong novel.

It was in this area of detail that Hardy had most collaboration with his illustrators. He offered advice, sent sketches of costumes and sometimes of situation (or composition), and even occasionally met with his artists, most notably Helen Paterson Allingham and George Du Maurier. In the aid he gave to his artists, Hardy was primarily concerned with details relating to local color. The special problem of the rural novel being read by an urban audience was slightly more complex in Hardy's case, since *Far from the Madding Crowd* and *The Return of the Native* contained traditions endemic to Dorset, and thus his advice to his illustrators was particularly useful. Quite clearly, the illustration of costume for a piece of period fiction, as in *The Trumpet Major*, was extremely useful for the Victorian audience as it sought to follow Hardy's linguistic re-creation of the Napoleonic era.

Yet the contributions Hardy made to John Collier's illustrations for *The Trumpet Major* were certainly disproportionate to the results, since an overwhelming number of the drawings are undistinguished. The inherent textual weakness of some of Hardy's novels, notably *The Hand of Ethelberta*, *The Trumpet Major*, *A Laodicean*, and *The Pursuit of the Well-Beloved*, is a considerable problem for the illustrator. Emphasis on minute and accurate detail does not in itself create a strong illustration, but the strong illustration can be created when the detail works to convey insight into character and the place which surrounds character, or the crucial moment of the novel's action. The novel must already possess these elements of character, place, and action, however, for the mimetic illustration to capture and convey. It is highly possible to create a weak illustration to accompany a strong novel, but highly unlikely to create strong illustrations when there is no correspondence in the text. The post-1860 belief in the mimetic illustration (in its responsibility to represent the text) meant that the illustrator bound his achievement with the strength and worth of the story he was commissioned to illustrate.

Thus, the Du Maurier illustrations for *The Hand of Ethelberta* and *A Laodicean*, the Collier drawings for *The Trumpet Major*, and the Paget illustrations for *The Pursuit of the Well-Beloved* have almost insurmountable obstacles to overcome in the weaknesses of their texts, and the drawings for the most part do not overcome those weaknesses. But the Pasquier illustrations, though they accompany *A Pair of Blue Eyes* which is surely not one of Hardy's strongest novels, do manage in many plates to capture the spirit of the text, and thus give to the audience visual pleasure in the image of a capricious Elfride Swancourt. Yet Pasquier's strong drawings are for those very scenes that are among the strongest in Hardy's text. While the illustrator for a weak text may occasionally strike upon a memorable scene and convey it admirably through the line engraving, he finds his greatest problem in achieving consistency in the series as a whole. At this point, the weakness of the text reveals itself as a supreme hindrance to his best efforts. It should be noted, however, that in the weakest of Hardy's novels, the illustrations still make some contribution and may sometimes even strengthen the text. The line drawing can give pleasure in and of itself; drawings such as those of Du Maurier (with his elegant female figures) and Paget (with his view of the Isle of Slingers as background) and Collier (with his period costume) make their graphic contributions even to a weak text.

One of Hardy's greatest powers as a novelist lies in his creation of the architectural image and the landscape. In the former category are the colleges of Christminster and the De Stancy castle, even Stonehenge, which combines architecture with landscape. Among the various Hardy landscapes are Talbothays and Flintcomb-Ash in *Tess of the D'Urbervilles*, Egdon Heath in *The Return of the Native*, even the more general rural vista in *Far from the Madding Crowd*. The man-made edifice of stone and the panoramic vistas in nature become central symbols in Hardy's fiction, and give considerable perspective to his human figures, but the architectural and the natural vista are not often pictured through illustration. At times, as in *A Laodicean's* De Stancy castle, or in the Christminster colleges in *Jude the Obscure*, these images seem to be avoided deliberately. Certainly the architectural and the natural have been deemed less important than the creation of local color, the handling of interior detail and, most prominently, the human figure. In these choices, however, the illustrator has opted for a graphic reality that represents the Victorian world rather than the full dimension of Hardy's text. Yet, in the text, the larger sense of *place* is of great importance, not only because Wessex has its own peculiarities, but because the cosmic dimension so often grows *out of place*, such as in the various landscapes of *Tess of the D'Urbervilles*. This absence of the cosmic element in the illustrations creates a basic tension between the human emphasis in the illustration and the cosmic dimension of the text.

Though the illustrators were not able to convey the sense of something beyond the immediate background for novels like *The Return of the Native* and *Tess of the D'Urbervilles*, where the cosmic dimension was so important for the fullest understanding of Hardy's world, the sensitive and talented artist such as Helen Paterson Allingham, Robert Barnes, and William Hatherell was able to convey the spirit of the human dimension in Hardy's world. The strong but graceful lines of the Allingham images, the strong and austere lines of Barnes's drawings, and the grey tones in Hatherell's drawings for *Jude the Obscure* admirably convey the spirit of these novels.

The most significant contribution that illustration made to the post-1860 novel—to Trollope's work as well as Hardy's—was its emphasis on the human dimension, from the isolation and suffering of the individual to the various kinds of relationships that can occur between human beings. In the depiction of the human qualities in Hardy's novels, his illustrators were exceedingly successful, and it is a success that offers considerable insight into Hardy's world.

In Hardy's text, the cosmic dimension often occurs in the single figure scene, where the reader becomes aware of man's loneliness in nature, for instance. The illustrations, however, generally avoid the single figure scene. The result is a diminished sense of individual isolation, particularly as it might relate to cosmic causes. Yet the suffering and loneliness of an individual character do emerge from many of the double figure scenes, and here the emphasis is on human causation. The comparative absence of the single figure scene also conveys the understanding that there are no "star" figures in the illustrations for Hardy's novels—Bathsheba shares scenes with Oak, Boldwood, Troy; Tess with Alec and Angel; Michael Henchard with Susan, Lucetta, and Elizabeth Jane. The tendency to widen the focus of the drawings so that major characters share scenes with the central figure, and so that a healthy proportion of scenes deal with minor characters (sometimes in groups) means that the audience becomes sensitive to the roles each plays in the novel's action, aware too that there is a real and vital *community* in Hardy's novels, however tragic the relationships between the members of the community might become. The suffering of the individual, in fact, becomes intensified because of this sense of community.

Group scenes were the preferred subject matter for the illustrators of many Victorian serials, since they offered variety and a chance for a "full" engraving, thus giving the audience as much visual material as possible. While the Hardy illustrators included several group scenes, such scenes are not in the majority. Instead, there is a marked predilection for the double figure scene. These scenes bring a special dramatic and psychological strength to the Hardy illustrations. But when group scenes are chosen, they are less successful in areas other than simple (though still important) local color. Undoubtedly, the influence of Trollope's illustrated serials operated here, but for Trollope's or Henry James's world, of course, the group or parlour conversation scene was often the crucial moment of the plot, or of character revelation. Not so in Hardy's world, and when these scenes appear, they generally add little to plot development or characterization. One exception occurs in *Tess of the D'Urbervilles*, when the group scene with its depiction of domestic harmony and then discord becomes a central motif of the illustrations. The story of Tess as an individual is so powerful that it almost overwhelms the family or group motif in the text itself, but the illustrations re-adjust these two aspects of the text by de-emphasizing Tess as individual and stressing her place in and against the community. In this case, the group scenes do make an important contribution to the text.

Then, too, careful scene selection may stress and sometimes even clarify Hardy's ironic vision for his reading audience, as in the "reversal" scenes in *A Pair of Blue Eyes*, several sets of these scenes in *Tess of the D'Urbervilles*, and ironically juxtaposed material within a scene, as in some of the plates for *The Pursuit of the Well-Beloved*. Metaphoric statement conveyed through a scene's details, such as the pictures, portraits, or other framing devices in *A Laodicean* and especially in *The Mayor of Casterbridge*, the alienation theme conveyed through the light-darkness contrast, as well as through the group-individual situations in the engravings for *The Return of the Native*—all these are ways in which the representational illustrations for Hardy's novels convey the idiosyncratic terms of his texts. Often these materials or devices clarify, sometimes they very capably support, and occasionally they enhance or "open" up the text for the reading audience, as in devices of irony and "framing."

The illustrated scene can give much valuable support to the novel in its focus on character and character relationships, in its stress on the psychology as well as the physical reality of the individual. In the astute handling of character and character relationships, as they join with the well chosen physical details of setting, the novel's basic rhythm can emerge as it does in *The Mayor of Casterbridge*. Through judicious scene selection in *The Mayor of Casterbridge*, *Far from the Madding Crowd*, and *Tess of the D'Urbervilles*—a selection that emphasizes the alternating emotions of joy and sorrow—the illustrations convey a rhythm that is not confined to plot development or character or symbol, but is that of life itself.

The cosmic dimension, finally, may well be the least important aspect of this Victorian novelist—at least to the readers of the illustrated serial editions of his works. His contemporary audience saw his works, not primarily in the cosmic terms that so many modern readers like to stress, but in recognizable, human terms. The illustrations rarely negate and most often emphasize Hardy's great gifts in the creation of character and in the perception he had of the relationships between men and women.

Representational illustration offers a distinct visual pleasure to its audience as it mirrors the text through the form and content of *picture*. Often, however, representational illustration can do much more than mirror the text, important though this will always remain. In the case of the Hardy illustrations, representational graphic art demonstrates it can also extend the life of fiction.

Notes

Preface

1. A brief survey by Norman Page still remains the only published material on the matter of the Hardy illustrations. See "Thomas Hardy's Forgotten Illustrators," *Bulletin of the New York Public Library*, 77 (Summer, 1974), 454–64.

Chapter I

1. For more information on Dutch Realism and Victorian fiction, see Mario Praz, *The Hero in Eclipse in Victorian Fiction* (London, 1956).

2. Malcolm Salaman, *British Book Illustration Yesterday and Today* (London, 1923), p. 19.

3. Hardy reveals his interest in the visual arts in his thinly disguised autobiography, first published in two volumes: Florence Emily Hardy, *The Early Life of Thomas Hardy, 1840–1891* (London, 1928), and *The Later Years of Thomas Hardy, 1892–1928* (London, 1930). Reprinted in one volume as *The Life of Thomas Hardy, 1840–1928* (Hamden, Conn., 1970). For an explanation of how much Hardy's second wife "authored" the text and how much Hardy himself wrote or dictated, see Robert Gittings, *Young Thomas Hardy* (Boston, 1975), pp. 1–6.

4. See *The Literary Notes of Thomas Hardy*, Ed. by Lennart A. Bjork (Goteborg, Sweden, 1974).

5. "The Profitable Reading of Fiction," in *Thomas Hardy's Personal Writings*, ed. by Harold Orel (Lawrence, Kansas: University of Kansas Press, 1966), p. 120.

6. For a discussion of Hardy as anti-realist, see Albert J. Guerard, *Thomas Hardy* (Cambridge, Mass., 1949). For Hardy as illusionist, see Penelope Vigar, *The Novels of Thomas Hardy* (London: Athlone Press, 1974).

7. See, for instance, Ian Gregor, *The Great Web: The Form of Hardy's Major Fiction* (London, 1974); J. Hillis Miller, *Thomas Hardy: Distance and Desire* (Cambridge, Mass., 1970).

8. (Chicago: University of Chicago Press, 1958), pp. xxi–xxii.

9. "Thomas Hardy's Rhetoric of Painting," *REL*, VI(Oct., 1965), 62–73.

10. Review of *A Pair of Blue Eyes*, *Saturday Review*, 36(August 2, 1873), 158.

11. Vigar, pp. 14, 15.

12. See, for instance: Richard C. Carpenter, "Thomas Hardy and the Old Masters," *BUSE*, V(Spring, 1961), 18–28; Alistair Smart, "Pictorial Imagery in the Novels of Thomas Hardy," *RES*, XII(1961), 262-80; Norman Page, "Hardy's Pictorial Art in *The Mayor of Casterbridge*," *EA*, 25 (Oct-Dec, 1972), 486–92, and *Thomas Hardy* (London: Routledge, Kegan & Paul, 1976); F. B. Pinion, *Thomas Hardy: Art and Thought* (Totowa, New Jersey: Rowman & Littlefield, 1977).

13. *Hardy of Wessex*, 2nd Edition. (New York: Columbia University Press, 1965), pp. 38–39, 297.

14. Bjork, #382, p. 39.

15. *Life*, p. 76.

16. Smart, p. 279.

17. Chapter II. All quotations are from the Wessex Edition, and will hereafter be noted immediately following the passage quoted.

18. Norman Page believes, however, that pictorialism is used more in the major than minor novels, and thus strongly implies it is a cause for the dramatic impact of such novels as *The Major of Casterbridge* and *Tess of the D'Urbervilles*. "That the pictorial element is so much more evident in the major than in the minor novels may well be an index of the extent to which the former embody a much fuller involvement of Hardy's imaginative (image-making) powers." *Thomas Hardy*, p. 89.

19. *Moments of Vision* (Cambridge, Mass: Harvard University Press, 1974), p. 4.

20. P. 63.

21. *Ibid.*, pp. 71–72.

22. See J. Hillis Miller's *Thomas Hardy: Distance and Desire* for a more extensive treatment of narrative effects in Hardy's novels.

Chapter II

1. Stevens, " 'Woodcuts dropped into the Text': The Illustrations in *The Old Curiosity Shop* and *Barnaby Rudge*," *SB*, XX (1967), 113–34; Steig, "*Martin Chuzzlewit's* Progress by Dickens and Phiz," *DSA*, II (1972), 119–48, and *Dickens and "Phiz*," (Bloomington, Indiana: Indiana University Press, 1978); Harvey, *Victorian Novelists and Their Illustrators* (New York: New York University Press, 1971); Q. D. Leavis, "The Dickens Illustrations: Their Function," in F. R. and Q. D. Leavis, *Dickens the Novelist* (Harmondsworth: Penguin Books Ltd., 1972).

2. White, *English Illustration. 'The Sixties'. 1855–70.* (London: Westminster, Constable & Co., 1903); Reid, *Illustrators of the Sixties* (London: Faber & Co., 1928).

3. But see N. John Hall, "Millais' Illustrations for Trollope," *Library Chronicle*, XLII (Spring, 1977), 23–45.

4. *The English Novel in the Magazines: 1740–1815* (Chicago: Northwestern University Press, 1962), p. 12.

5. *Ibid.*

6. The relationship between crime illustration and audience can be seen in the case of *The Weekly Chronicle*. Established in 1836, it had made its reputation by publishing sensational woodcuts depicting great crimes. The famous Greenacre murder provides an example, since *The Weekly Chronicle* published engravings showing "the heart of the murdered woman as preserved in spirits in Paddington Workhouse," "the room where the horrible mutilation was committed," and "the osier-bed in Cold Harbour Lane where the legs were found." The *Chronicle's* circulation figures rose phenomenally during and immediately after it published these illustrations. C. N. Williamson," Illustrated Journalism in England: Its Development," *The Magazine of Art* (1890), p. 298.

7. Harvey, pp. 2–3.

8. *Ibid.*, pp. 3–4. In *English Caricaturists and Graphic Humourists of the Nineteenth Century* (London, 1893), Graham Everitt claims: "The etched illustration of [Dickens's] day formed a most important—in some cases . . . by far the most important—portion of the work itself. . . . The novel issued in monthly numbers depended on two sources of attraction—the skill of the novelist and the skill of his artistic coadjutor." See pp. 348–49.

9. Harvey, p. 84.

10. Salaman, p. 4.

11. (London, 1962), p. 10.

12. "The Illustrating of Books from the Serious Artist's Point of View," *Magazine of Art* (1890), pp. 349–50, 374.

13. (London, 1901), p. 15. But critics and practising artists of course disagreed as to what constituted the aims and definition of good illustration. M. C. Salaman contended the illustrator's work "shall not merely interpret for us the literary idea, or the mental image suggested by it, but that it shall do this with decorative effect—that it shall take its place upon the page with charm, dignity, and beauty." *Modern Book Illustrators and Their Works*, ed. by C. Geoffrey Holme and Ernest G. Halton (London: The Studio, 1914), pp. 1–2. According to Joseph Pennell, however, "there is a distinction between drawings which, while they ornament the text, are specially intended for its elucidation, and those which, though they may illustrate the text, are intended primarily to ornament the page according to conventional rules." *Pen Drawing and Pen Draughtsmen* (London, 1897), pp. 385–86.

14. Blackburn, pp. 34–5.

15. "English Book Illustration, 1800–1900," in *New Paths in Book Collecting*, ed. John Carter (London, 1934), p. 172.

16. Alvar Ellegard, "The Readership of the Periodical Press in Mid-Victorian Britain," *Victorian Periodicals Newsletter* (September, 1971), p. 17.

17. *Ibid.*, pp. 20–22.

18. Du Maurier, p. 350.

19. *An Autobiography* (Berkeley: University of California Press, 1947), pp. 230–31.

20. Du Maurier, p. 371. This view is roundly disputed by artist-critic Joseph Pennell: "The most awful misfortune that may occur to an illustrator is to be compelled to use the photographs or sketches made by an author; here almost certain disaster awaits the artist. The author who cannot draw, but will sketch, is terrible; the author who can photograph is impossible. Both are sure they could make the illustrations if they had the time, and the artist who is compelled to illustrate them could write the story or do the description, he knows, if he but took the trouble. At least, that is the view they hold of each other. The result is almost certain failure." "The Illustration of Books," in *The Art Journal* (1895), p. 309.

21. Du Maurier, p. 371.

22. (London: Faber & Co., 1935), p. 253.

23. *The Making of a Great Magazine* (New York, 1890), p. 22.

24. Blackburn, p. 189.

25. *The Reminiscences of Edmund Evans, Wood Engraver and Colour Printer 1826–1905* (London, 1969), p. vii.

26. "The Illustration of Books," *The Art Journal* (1895), pp. 137–38.

27. *Modern Illustration* (London, 1895), p. 84.

Chapter III

Most of the Hardy correspondence is located in the Dorset County Museum (DCM). Parts of several letters can be found in Richard Purdy's indispensable work, *Thomas Hardy. A Bibliographic Study* (London: Clarendon Press, 1968). First pub. 1954. Hardy's own letters can be found in Richard Purdy and Michael Millgate, *The Collected Letters of Thomas Hardy*. Vol. 1: 1840–1892. (Oxford: Clarendon Press, 1978), *(CL)*.

1. *Random Recollections of an Old Publisher* (London, 1900), p. 323.

2. *Life*, p. 91.

3. *Ibid.*

4. Weber, p. 85.

5. *Life*, p. 90.

6. Purdy believes, however, that Hardy provided the sketches "for some if not all" of the Pasquier illustration. P. 10.

7. *Life*, p. 96.

8. Letter from Leslie Stephen, Oct. 6, 1873, DCM.

9. Letter from Hardy to Smith-Elder and Co., *CL*, p. 25.

10. *CL*, p. 25.

11. *Life*, p. 97. Hardy's recollection of the sequence of events is faulty. A letter to him from *Cornhill Magazine*, dated Dec. 2, 1873, states: "We have the pleasure to acknowledge your acceptance of our terms for your new story, entitled 'Far from the Madding Crowd,' the first portion of which we propose shall appear in the next number of the 'Cornhill Magazine,' with an illustration." (Dorset County Museum). Thus, the date of publication, as well as the fact of illustration, was known by Hardy in advance.

12. *Life*, p. 97.

13. Stewart Dick, *Cottage Homes of England* (London, 1909), p. 279.

14. *Notes of the Academy*, 1875. Cited in C. E. Clement and L. Hutton, *Artists of the Nineteenth Century and Their Works* (London, 1879), pp. 9–10.

15. Ruskin later revealed his basic dislike of the wood engraving as an art form. See *The Art of England*. Lectures in Oxford in 1883–85 (London, 1898), pp. 122–23.

Speaking of Mrs. Allingham's exhibits at the Water-Colour Society, Ruskin commented, in a patronizing manner, that the artist was mistaken in drawing miniatures, single heads, "instead of fulfilling her true gift, and doing what . . . the Lord made her for—in representing the gesture, characters, and humour of charming children in country landscapes. Mrs. Allingham does very well in illustrating rustic life." Pp. 117–18.

16. Purdy, p. 337.

17. *Life*, p. 100. Hardy wrote Miss Paterson on May 7, 1874 sending her some "particulars" of the story and offering to send sketches, "though I am afraid my drawings will be a somewhat melancholy performance beside yours." *CL*, p. 30.

18. Carl Weber notes that the illustration clarifies the textual description, as Hardy does not give details of the custom in the story itself. Weber believes, however, that the artist was using her own knowledge of the Bible and Key custom: "She obviously knew how the key is tied inside the Bible and is then supported on the wedding-ring fingers of the two women." P. 92.

19. *Ibid.*, pp. 91–2.

20. *The Times*, (Jan. 25, 1875), p. 4.

21. *Scribner's Monthly*, (March, 1875), 637.

22. *Harper's New Monthly* 50 (1875), 598.

23. *Saturday Review* 39(1875), 57–8.

24. Letter to Edmund Gosse, July, 1906. Purdy, p. 220.

25. Robert Gittings, in *Young Thomas Hardy*, pp. 2, 4–5, further postulates that Hardy was bothered by his own humble family origins. "So, perhaps from an inborn necessity to write the teasing problem somehow out of his system, was evolved the most uneven and contradictory of all Hardy's novels, *The Hand of Ethelberta*." In "his typically devious way, [Hardy] chose . . . to project his own dilemma into that of a woman."

26. *Descriptive Catalogue of the Grolier Club*, Item #61. Colby College Monograph #9 (Waterville, Maine, 1940).

27. Hardy was later to explain that it was his custom to send sketches to guide the illustrator, and he left the impression that he had sent sketches for all his novels. In this matter, his memory may have been faulty, as there is no evidence such sketches were sent to Du Maurier to guide the illustrations for *The Hand of Ethelberta*.

28. Letter from Du Maurier to Hardy, date uncertain, DCM. The manuscript carries the pencilled date 1880, with a question mark. This ideal state of collaboration was realized

in Du Maurier's own case when his three novels (*Peter Ibbetson*, 1892; *Trilby*, 1894; *The Martian*, 1897) were published with illustrations from his own hand.

29. Letter to Chatto and Windus, Aug. 28, 1877, *CL*, p. 51.

30. Letter to George Smith, April, 1887, *CL*, p. 48.

31. Cited in F. W. Maitland, *The Life and Letters of Leslie Stephen* (London: Duckworth & Co., 1906), pp. 276–77. F. B. Pinion explains that Hardy had earlier sent the manuscript to John Blackwood, of *Blackwood's Magazine*, but that Blackwood "could not accept it for serialization in 1877." See "The Composition of 'The Return of the Native'," *TLS* (August 21, 1970), 931.

32. *Life*, p. 117.

33. Tinsley, p. 62.

34. In the same year that Arthur Hopkins illustrated Hardy's novel, Gerard Manley Hopkins commented: "My brother's pictures . . . are careless and do not aim high. . . . But . . . he has somehow in painting his pictures, though nothing that the pictures express, a high and quite religious aim." This is also how Arthur himself had explained his work. *The Journals and Papers of Gerard Manley Hopkins*, Humphrey House, ed. (London, Oxford University Press, 1959), p. 304.

35. *Ibid.*, p. 269.

36. *Ibid.*, p. 304.

37. Reid, p. 269.

38. (Berkeley, Calif: University of California Press 1960).

39. Paterson explains that revisions of the text for later editions "did much to repair the original damage." Yet, "in having operated as a basic condition of the act of composition, the editorial censorship must have inflicted damage that no amount of readjustment or reorganization could possibly have corrected." P. 164.

40. Stephen had urged that Hardy change the Ur-version; *Belgravia* was seeing a different manuscript, and the magazine's requirements involved the addition of the sixth book to the text and "the suppression of the Wildeve-Eustacia relationship." Paterson, p. 163.

41. As Paterson concludes, "Her transfiguration from satanic antagonist to romantic protagonist suggests, then, that what began as a bowdlerization developed spontaneously into a free and creative revaluation, the effect of which was to reverse the fundamental values of the novel." pp. 29–30.

42. Letter to Thomas Hardy, Feb. 5, 1878, DCM.

43. *Ibid.*

44. "We have no evidence as to when it was commenced or finished, but the first 7 chapters were written by 28 August 1877 and the first 2 books by 8 November. . . ." Purdy, p. 27. Purdy believes the novel "must have been concluded at Upper Tooting where the Hardys took a house in March 1878."

45. Letter to Arthur Hopkins, February 8, 1878, *CL*, pp. 52–3.

46. Letter to Thomas Hardy, February 19, 1878, DCM.

47. Letter to Arthur Hopkins, August 3, 1878, *CL*, p. 59.

48. Letter to Thomas Hardy, February 19, 1878

49. Letter to Arthur Hopkins, February 20, 1878, *CL*, pp. 54–5.

50. *Ibid.*

51. Letter to Thomas Hardy, February 19, 1878, DCM.

52. Letter of Feb. 8, 1878, *CL*, p. 53.

53. Letter to Thomas Hardy, February 19, 1878, DCM.

54. Letter to Smith, Elder and Co., Oct. 1, 1878, *CL*, p. 61.

55. (Dorset County Museum).

56. Letter to Thomas Hardy, August 29, 1879, DCM.

57. Walter Herries Pollock, "The Art of the Hon. John Collier," *Art Annual* (1914), pp. 1–24.

58. Letter to Thomas Hardy, August 29, 1879, DCM.

59. Letter to Thomas Hardy, November 20, 1879, DCM,

60. Hardy's British Museum Notebook is transcribed in Richard H. Taylor's *The Personal Notebooks of Thomas Hardy* (New York: Columbia University Press, 1979).

61. *Ibid.*

62. *Life*, p. 145.

63. Letter to *Harper's*, April 16, 1880, *CL*, p. 72.

64. Letter to Hardy, May 24, 1880, DCM.

65. Letter to Hardy, June 5, 1880, DCM.

66. Letter to Hardy, June 7, 1880, DCM.

67. Letter to Hardy, June 9, 1880, DCM.

68. Letter to *Harper's*, June 11, 1880, *CL*, pp. 74–5.

69. E. McClung Fleming, *R. R. Bowker* (Norman, Oklahoma: University of Oklahoma Press, 1952), pp. 155–56.

70. *Ibid.*

71. *Ibid.*

72. Quoted in Leonée Ormond, *George Du Maurier* (London, 1969), p. 368.

73. 1880, DCM.

74. *Ibid.*

75. Quoted in Ormond, p. 368. I have substituted "tunnel" for Ormond's transcription "tumuli," as neither illustration nor text make any reference to "tumuli." The scene referred to, however, involves Paula and Somerset's escape from a railroad tunnel.

76. Ormond, p. 368.

77. "The Illustrating of Books, from the Serious Artist's Point of View," *Magazine of Art* (1890), p. 353.

78. *Life*, p. 179.

79. June 25, 1890, DCM.

80. Pp. 256–57.

81. *Ibid.*, p. 257.

82. Purdy, pp. 72–3.

83. *Life*, p. 222.

84. Weber, p. 177.

85. *My School and My Gospel* (London, 1908), pp. 75–80.

86. *Descriptive Catalogue of the Grolier Club*, Item #118.

87. "Hubert Herkomer," in F. G. Dumas, *Illustrated Biographies of Modern Artists* (London, 1882), p. 69.

88. *Modern Illustration* (London, 1895), p. 101.

89. See Purdy, pp. 93–94, for further information, especially for his outline of the serial version.

90. *I Remember* (New York, 1934), p. 164.

91. See Purdy, pp. 87–91, and Part III of this study for further information on textual changes.

92. "W. Hatherell and His Work," *The Art of the Illustrator* (London, 1918), p. 6.

93. *Ibid.*

94. Letter to Hatherell, Nov. 10, 1895, (M. L. Parrish Collection, Princeton University Library).

95. Cited in Charles Morgan, *The House of Macmillan* (New York: Macmillan Co., 1944), p. 159.

Chapter IV

1. *Art and Illusion: A Study in the Psychology of Pictorial Representation* (Princeton, N.J.: Princeton University Press), p. 21.

2. See Part II, and Du Maurier's "The Illustrating of Books from the Serious Artist's Point of View," *Magazine of Art* (1890), pp. 349–74.

3. "The Dickens Illustrations: Their Function," in F. R. and Q. D. Leavis, *Dickens the Novelist* (Harmondsworth, England: Penguin Books, 1972), p. 434–5.

4. *Ibid.*, p. 469.

5. Even Millais receives criticism. See N. John Hall, "Millais' Illustrations for Trollope," *Library Chronicle*, XLII (Spring, 1977), 23–45.

6. See "Psychology and the Riddle of Style" in Gombrich, pp. 3–30.

7. See Wm. M. Ivins, Jr., *Prints and Visual Communication* (Cambridge, Mass: M.I.T.Press, 1953). Ivins devotes considerable space to explaining the "catastrophic revolution" and "enlargement of vision" caused by photography.

8. "The Fiction of Realism: *Sketches by Boz, Oliver Twist*, and Cruikshank's Illustrations," *Dickens Centennial Essays*, ed. Ada Nisbet and Blake Nevius (Berkeley: University of California Press, 1971), pp. 129–30.

9. "Illustration and the Mind's Eye," in *Victorian Novelists and Their Illustrators*, pp. 160–81.

10. As cited in Leavis, p. 434.

11. As Alan Thomas explains, the Victorians were accustomed to reading "large meanings into small, everyday acts and were encouraged to do so." See *The Expanding Eye* (London: Croom Helm, 1978), p. 125.

12. Purdy, p. 10.

13. Carroll A. Wilson, *Descriptive Catalogue of the Grolier Club*, Item #30.

14. As Weber has commented, the illustration gives a clearer understanding of the Bible and Key custom than Hardy's text does. See p. 92.

15. *Westminster Review* 47 (Jan.-April, 1875) 265–67; *Athenaeum* (Dec. 5, 1874), p. 747.

16. A. Lang, *Academy* 7 (Jan. 2, 1875), p. 4.

17. *The Times*, (Jan. 25, 1875), p. 4.

18. Wildeve's almost total omission from the illustrations seems due to Victorian propriety—an attempt to de-emphasize the intimacy between Wildeve and Eustacia.

19. As quoted in Beaumont Newhall, *The History of Photography*, 4th ed. (New York: Museum of Modern Art, 1978), p. 98.

20. Hardy's impressionistic use of facial detail is a central part of his technique and relates closely to his philosophic stance. See my article on "The Evolutionary Aspect of Hardy's Modern Men," *Revue Belge de Philologie et D'histoire* 56 (1978), 641–49.

21. *Athenaeum*, (April 15, 1876), p. 523.

22. *Ibid.*

23. *Academy*, 9 (May 13, 1876), 453–54.

24. *Ibid.*, 18 (Dec. 11, 1880), 420.

25. See T. Martin Wood, *Du Maurier: The Satirist of the Victorians* (London, 1913), p. 83, and Forrest Reid, p. 176.

26. David Low, "British Cartoonists," in W. J. Turner, ed., *Aspects of British Art* (London, 1947), p. 237.

27. James Thorpe, *English Illustration: The Nineties* (London, 1935), p. 36.

28. *Thomas Hardy* (New York: New Directions, 1964), p. 68.

29. *Ibid.*, p. 67.

Chapter V

1. Gombrich, pp. 388f.

Bibliography

Altick, Richard D. *The English Common Reader*. Chicago: University of Chicago Press, 1963.

Baldry, A. L. *Hubert von Herkomer*. London: George Bell & Sons, 1904.

Balston, Thomas. "English Book Illustration, 1800–1900." *New Paths in Book Collecting*. Edited by John Carter. London, 1954.

Barkley, H. "Nineteenth Century Illustrators and Others." *Penrose Annual*, 53 (1959), 36–42.

Beatty, C. J. P. *The Architectural Notebook of Thomas Hardy*. Dorset: Dorset Natural History and Archaeological Society, 1966.

Bjork, Lennart A., ed. *The Literary Notes of Thomas Hardy*. Goteborg, Sweden: Acta Universatatis Gothoburgensis, 1974.

Blackburn, Henry. *The Art of Illustration*. London, 1901.

Bland, David. *A History of Book Illustration*. Berkeley: University of California Press, 1969.

Bradshaw, Percy. "William Hatherell and His Work. *The Art of the Illustrator*. London, 1918.

Brooks, Jean. *Thomas Hardy. The Poetic Structure*. London: Elek Books, Ltd., 1971.

Carpenter, Richard C. "Thomas Hardy and the Old Masters." *Boston University Studies in English*, V, 18–28.

Carr, J. Comyns. "Hubert Herkomer." *Illustrated Biographies of Modern Artists*. Edited by F. G. Dumas. London, 1882.

Carter, John. *New Paths in Book Collecting*. London, 1954.

Cecil, Lord David. *Hardy the Novelist*. Indianapolis: Bobbs-Merrill Co., 1946.

Charteris, Evan. *Life and Letters of Sir Edmund Gosse*. London, 1931.

Chase, Mary Ellen. *Thomas Hardy from Serial to Novel*. Minneapolis: University of Minnesota Press, 1927.

Clement, C. E. and Hutton, L. *Artists of the Nineteenth Century and Their Works*. 2 Vols. London, 1879. Rev. ed., New York, 1884.

Courtney, W. L. "Hubert Herkomer. His Life and Work." *Art Annual* (1892), pp. 17–23.

Crane, Walter. *Of the Decorative Illustration of Books Old and New*. London, 1896.

Cruse, Amy. *The Victorians and Their Books*. London: George Allen & Unwin, Ltd., 1935.

Dick, Stewart, *Cottage Homes of England*. Drawings by Helen Allingham. London: Edward Arnold, 1909.

Du Maurier, Daphne. *Life of Du Maurier*. London, 1937.

Du Maurier, George. "The Illustrating of Books, from the Serious Artist's Point of View." *Magazine of Art* (1890), 349ff.

Ellegard, Alvar. "The Readership of the Periodical Press in Mid-Victorian Britain. *Victorian Periodicals Newsletter* (September, 1971), pp. 3–22.

Evans, Edmund. *The Reminiscences of Edmund Evans, Wood Engraver and Colour Printer, 1826–1905*. London, 1969.

Everitt, Graham. *English Caricaturists and Graphic Humourists of the Nineteenth Century*. London, 1893.

"*Far from the Madding Crowd*." Anon. Review. *Athenaeum* (Dec. 5, 1874), p. 747.

——. *Harper's Magazine*, 50 (March, 1875), 598.

——. *Saturday Review* (London), 39 (Jan. 9, 1875), 57–8.

——. *Scribner's Monthly*, 9 (March, 1875), 637.

——. *Times*, (Jan. 25, 1875), p. 4.

——. *Westminster Review*, 45 (Jan., 1875), 265–67.

Fernando, Lloyd. "Thomas Hardy's Rhetoric of Painting." *REL*, 6 (1965), 62–73.

Fleming, E. McClung. *R. R. Bowker*. Norman, Oklahoma: University of Oklahoma Press, 1952.

Fletcher, Geoffrey. *Popular Art in England*. London: Harrap, 1962.

Giovanninni, G. "Method in the Study of Literature in Relation to the Other Arts" *JAAC*, VIII (1950), 185–95.

Gittings, Robert. *Young Thomas Hardy*. Boston: Atlantic-Little, Brown, 1975.

——. *Thomas Hardy's Later Years*. Boston: Little, Brown and Co., 1978.

Gombrich, Ernest H. *Art and Illusion*. A Study in the Psychology of Pictorial Representation. Princeton, New Jersey: Princeton University Press, 1969.

Graham, W. *English Literary Periodicals*. New York, 1930.

Graphic Portfolio. London, 1876.

Gray, Basil, *The English Print*. London, 1937.

Gregor, Ian. *The Great Web: The Form of Hardy's Major Fiction*. London: Faber & Faber, 1974.

Guerard, Albert J. *Thomas Hardy*. New York: New Directions, 1964.

Hagstrum, Jean H. *The Sister Arts*. The Tradition of Literary Pictorialism and English Poetry from Dryden to Gray. Chicago: University of Chicago Press, 1958.

Hall, N. John. "Millais' Illustrations for Trollope." *Library Chronicle*, XLII (Spring, 1977), 23–45.

"*The Hand of Ethelberta*." Anon. Review. *Athenaeum* (April, 1876), p. 523.

Hardy, Florence Emily. *The Early Life of Thomas Hardy, 1840–1891*. London, 1928. *The Later Years of Thomas Hardy, 1892–1928*. London, 1930. Reprinted in one volume. *The Life of Thomas Hardy, 1840–1928*. Hamden, Conn.: Archon Books, 1970.

Hardy, Thomas. *Far from the Madding Crowd. Cornhill Magazine*, (Jan.-Dec., 1874).

——. *The Hand of Ethelberta. Cornhill Magazine*, (July, 1875–May, 1876).

——. *Jude the Obscure*. Published serially as *The Simpletons* (first installment), then as *Hearts Insurgent. Harper's New Monthly Magazine*, (Dec. 1894–Nov., 1895).

——. *A Laodicean. Harper's New Monthly Magazine*, (Dec. 1880–Dec., 1881).

——. *The Mayor of Casterbridge. The Graphic*, (Jan. 2–May 15, 1886).

——. *A Pair of Blue Eyes. Tinsley's Magazine*, (Sept., 1872–July, 1873).

——. *The Return of the Native. Belgravia*, (Jan.–Dec., 1878).

——. *Tess of the D'Urbervilles. The Graphic*, (July 4–Dec. 26, 1891).

——. *The Trumpet Major. Good Words*, (Jan.–Dec., 1880).

——. *The Pursuit of the Well-Beloved. Illustrated London News*, (Oct. 1–Dec. 17, 1892).

Harper, J. Henry. *The House of Harper*. New York, 1912.

——. *I Remember*. New York, 1934.

Harvey, John. "The Novel and the Cartoon. *Cambridge Quarterly*, (Autumn/Winter, 1969–70), pp. 419–29.

——. *Victorian Novelists and Their Illustrators*. New York: New York University Press, 1971.

Henley, William E. *A Century of Artists*. Glasgow, 1889.

Herkomer, Sir Hubert von. *My School and My Gospel*. London: Constable & Co., 1908.

Hind, Arthur M. *A History of Engraving and Etching*. New York: Dover Publications, 1963.

Hodson, James Shirley. *Guide to Art Illustration*. London, 1884.

House, Humphrey, ed. *The Journals and Papers of Gerard Manley Hopkins*. London: Oxford University Press, 1959.

"Illustrated Periodical Literature." *The Bookseller*, (Nov. 30, 1861), pp. 681–83.

Ivins, William M., Jr. *Prints and Visual Communication*. Cambridge, Mass: The M.I.T. Press, 1953.

Jackson, Arlene M. "The Evolutionary Aspect of Hardy's Modern Men." *Revue Belge de Philologie et D'Histoire*, 56 (1978), 641–49.

Jackson, Mason. *The Pictorial Press*. London: Hurst & Blackett, 1885.

James, Philip Brutton. *English Book Illustration, 1800–1900*. London, 1947.

Kaufman, Robert F. *The Relationship Between Illustration and Text in the Novels of Dickens, Thackeray, Trollope and Hardy*. Unpublished Dissertation, New York University, 1974.

Lang, A. Review of *Far from the Madding Crowd*. *Academy*, 7 (Jan. 2, 1875), 9–10.

Leavis, F. R. and Q. D. *Dickens the Novelist*. Harmondsworth, England: Penguin Books Ltd., 1972.

Lewis, C. T. C. *The Story of Picture Printing in England in the Nineteenth Century*. London, 1928.

Lister, Raymond. *Victorian Narrative Paintings*. London: Museum Press, Ltd., 1966.

Lodge, David. "Thomas Hardy and Cinematographic Form." *Novel*, 7 (1974), pp. 246–54.

Low, David. "British Cartoonists." *Aspects of British Art*, ed. W. J. Turner. London, 1947.

Maas, Jeremy. *Victorian Painters*. London: Cresset Press, 1969.

Maitland, Frederick W. *Life and Letters of Leslie Stephen*. London, 1906.

The Making of a Great Magazine [Harpers]. New York, 1890.

Mayo, Robert. *The English Novel in the Magazines, 1740–1815*. Chicago: Northwestern University Press, 1962.

Miller, J. Hillis. "The Fiction of Realism: *Sketches by Boz, Oliver Twist*, and Cruikshank's Illustrations." *Dickens Centennial Essays*. Ed. Ada Nisbet and Blake Nevius. Berkeley: University of California Press, 1971.

————. *Thomas Hardy: Distance and Desire*. Cambridge, Mass: Belknap Press, 1970.

Mills, John Saxon. *Life and Letters of Sir Hubert Herkomer*. London, 1923.

Morgan, Charles. *The House of Macmillan*. New York: Macmillan Co., 1944.

Newhall, Beaumont. *The History of Photography*. New York: Museum of Modern Art, 1978.

Orel, Harold, ed. *Thomas Hardy's Personal Writings*. Lawrence, Kansas: University Press of Kansas, 1966.

Ormond, Leonée. *George Du Maurier*. London: Routledge and Kegan Paul, 1969.

Page, Norman. "Hardy's Pictorial Art in *The Mayor of Casterbridge*," *EA*, 25 (Oct–Dec., 1972), 486–92.

————. *Thomas Hardy*. London: Routledge, Kegan & Paul, 1976.

————. "Thomas Hardy's Forgotten Illustrators," *Bulletin of the New York Public Library*, 77 (Summer, 1974), 454–64.

"A Pair of Blue Eyes." Anon. Review. *Athenaeum*, (June 28, 1873), p. 820.

————. *Saturday Review*, 36 (Aug. 2, 1873), 158.

————. *Spectator*, 46 (June 28, 1873), 831–32.

Paterson, John. *The Making of the Return of the Native*. Berkeley: University of California Press, 1960.

Pennell, Joseph. "English Book Illustration, 1860–70." *Journal of the Royal Society of Arts* (April 3, 1896), pp. 455–65.

————. "The Illustration of Books." *Art Journal* (1895), pp. 138 +.

————. *Modern Illustration*. London, 1895.

————. *Pen Drawing and Pen Draughtsmen*. London, 1897.

Pinion, F. B. "The Composition of 'The Return of the Native.' *TLS* (August 21, 1970), 931.

————. *A Hardy Companion*. New York: St. Martins Press, 1968.

————. *Thomas Hardy: Art and Thought*. Totowa, New Jersey: Rowman and Littlefield, 1977.

Pollard, Graham. "Serial Fiction." *New Paths in Book Collecting*. Ed. John Carter. London, 1934.

Pollock, Walter Herries. "The Art of the Hon. John Collier." *Art Annual* (1914), pp. 1–24.

Praz, Mario. *The Hero in Eclipse in Victorian Fiction.* Tr. Angus Davidson. London: Oxford University Press, 1956.

———. *Mnemosyne.* The Parallel Between Literature and the Visual Arts. Princeton, New Jersey: Princeton University Press, 1967.

Purdy, Richard, and Millgate, Michael. *The Collected Letters of Thomas Hardy. 1840–1892.* Vol. 1. Oxford: Clarendon Press, 1978.

Purdy, Richard Little. *Thomas Hardy.* A Bibliographical Study. Oxford: Clarendon Press, 1968.

Quilter, Harry. *Preferences in Art, Life and Literature.* London, 1892.

Ray, Gordon N. *The Illustrator and the Book in England from 1790–1914.* New York: Pierpont Morgan Library, 1976.

Reid, Forrest. *Illustrators of the Sixties.* London: Faber & Co., 1928.

Reynolds, Graham. *Victorian Painting.* London: Studio Vista, 1966.

Ruskin, John. *Art of England.* London, 1884.

Saintsbury, George. Review of *The Hand of Ethelberta.* Academy, 9 (May 13, 1876), 453–54.

Salaman, Malcolm C. *British Book Illustration Yesterday and Today.* London, 1923.

———. *Modern Book Illustrators and Their Works.* Ed. C. Geoffrey Holme and Ernest G. Halton. London: The Studio, 1914.

Schapiro, Meyer. *Words and Pictures:* On the Literal and the Symbolic in the Illustration of a Text. The Hague: Mouton Press, 1973.

Scott, James F. "Spectacle and Symbol in Thomas Hardy's Fiction." *PQ,* 44 (Oct., 1965), 527–544.

Shorter, C. K. "Illustrated Journalism: Its Past and Future." *Contemporary Review* (April, 1899), pp. 481+.

Singer, Hans Wolfgang. *Etching, Engraving, and Other Methods.* London, 1897.

Sitwell, Sacheverell. *Narrative Pictures.* A Survey of English Genre and Its Painters. New York: Scribner's Sons, 1938.

Sketchley, Rose E. *English Book Illustration of Today.* London, 1903.

Smart, Alistair. "Pictorial Imagery in the Novels of Thomas Hardy." *RES,* XII (1961), 262–280.

Steig, Michael. *Dickens and "Phiz."* Bloomington, Indiana: Indiana University Press, 1978.

———. "*Martin Chuzzlewit's* Progress by Dickens and Phiz." *DSA,* II (1972), 119–48.

Stevens, Joan. " 'Woodcuts dropped into the Text': The Illustrations in *The Old Curiosity Shop* and *Barnaby Rudge.*" *Studies in Bibliography,* XX (1967), 113–34.

Sullivan, E. J. *The Art of Illustration.* London, 1921.

Taylor, Richard H. *The Personal Notebooks of Thomas Hardy.* New York: Columbia University Press, 1979.

Thomas, Alan. *The Expanding Eye.* Photography and the Nineteenth Century Mind. London: Croom Helm, 1978.

Thorpe, James. *English Illustration: The Nineties.* London: Faber & Co., 1935.

Tinsley, William. *Random Recollections of an Old Publisher.* London, 1900.

Trollope, Anthony. *An Autobiography.* Berkeley: University of California Press, 1947.

Vigar, Penelope. *The Novels of Thomas Hardy.* London: Athlone Press, 1974.

Weber, Carl J. *Hardy of Wessex.* 2nd Edition. New York: Columbia University Press, 1965.

Wedmore, Frederick. *Etching in England.* London, 1895.

———. *Studies in English Art.* London, 1880.

Weitenkampf, Frank. *The Illustrated Book.* London, 1938.

White, Gleeson. *English Illustration 'The Sixties': 1855–70.* London: Westminster, Constable & Co., 1903.

Williamson, C. N. "Illustrated Journalism in England: Its Development." *Magazine of Art* (1890), pp. 297+.

Wilson, Carroll. *Descriptive Catalogue of the Grolier Club Centenary Exhibition of the Works of Thomas Hardy*. Waterville, Maine: Colby College Monograph #9, 1940.

Wood, T. Martin. *Du Maurier: The Satirist of the Victorians*. London, 1913.

Wright, T. *A History of Caricature and Grotesque in Literature and Art*. London, 1865.

Zietlow, Paul. *Moments of Vision*. Cambridge, Mass: Harvard University Press, 1974.

Index